Socialist Thought in Modern India

To

MY FATHER

SOCIALIST THOUGHT
IN
MODERN INDIA

RAI AKHILENDRA PRASAD

M.A., Ph.D.

Head, Department of Political Science,
Rajendra College, CHAPRA

•

With a Foreword by
Dr. A. APPADORAI

Meenakshi Prakashan
MEERUT ● **DELHI**

MEENAKSHI PRAKASHAN
Begum Bridge, MEERUT.
4, Ansari Road, Daryaganj, DELHI.

PRINTED IN INDIA
at Meenakshi Mudranalaya, Meerut

FOREWORD

There has been for some considerable time a felt need in India, and elsewhere, for a meaningful survey of socialist thought in India ; not only has socialism been accepted officially in India as the goal of social policy, but the literature published in India in social sciences and the newspapers contain much about the objectives and methods of socialism. The citizen in a democracy needs competent guidance from scholars to enable him to understand the concepts like socialism which guide public policy. Dr. Rai Akhilendra Prasad has made a useful, pioneering attempt to supply the felt need and I commend his scholarly effort to the scholar as well as the ordinary citizen.

The task is by no means easy. All over the world socialism has the reputation of being like a hat that loses its shape when worn by several people. The bewildering variety of meanings given to the concept in Indian writings makes one wonder if serious thinking has been given to it or if any consensus on socialism as a way of life can ever be reached. Jawaharlal Nehru thought that a vague, confused socialism was already part of the atmosphere of India when he returned from Europe in December 1927 and that mostly they thought along utopian lines; such confusion still exists among ordinary people about what socialism connotes.

Dr. Prasad has dealt with the socialistic ideas of the principal Indian thinkers on socialism such as Jawaharlal Nehru, Acharya Narendra Deva and Rammanohar Lohia (and several others) ; he has studied them in the context of their lives and times. In his view, the major contribution of socialist thought has been to attempt a synthesis of Marxism and Gandhian methods in realising the socialist order ; the individual is an end in himself ; the State is certainly to occupy a place of power and yet a decentralized socio-political order should be established and democratic and non-violent means must be adopted, as the equation of means and ends demands that the means must be democratic and peaceful.

Dr. Prasad's study is useful not only as a pioneer survey ; his study raises a number of issues which demand further study by students of political science. Socialist theory, as Dr. Lohia mentioned, instead of borrowing its basic aims from capitalism and communism, should strike out an autonomous direction, that of political and economic decentralization. How can such decentralization be reconciled with the increasing sphere of the centralised State in developing societies like India ? There has been a persistent strain of thought in Indian socialist theory, (*e.g.* J. P. Narain) that the limitation of wants by the individual, instead of the indefinite, unlimited multiplication of wants, is essential to achieve a just social order ; what are the constructive implications of this analysis ? Recent socialist theory, even in the West, is inclined to lay less and less stress on nationalization as the key to socialism ; it has been argued for instance by the Nobel Laureate J. Tinbergen that the essence of socialism is the institutionalization of solidarity among human beings and a recognition that in the last resort the community is responsible for the well-being of its members. What are the implications of this view for social organization ? What is the relative role of (*a*) State, (*b*) Cooperative, and (*c*) Private enterprise in a socialist society ? Rajgopalachari, a vehement critic of State socialism, argued that State socialism results in self-alienation, that the entire ideology of socialism is based on a huge fallacy that creative energy can be isolated from personal interest and that what the State should do is to watch, control and regulate production and distribution in order to prevent exploitation ; by entering business it will be depriving itself of its governmental function. Does experience of nationalisation in India substantiate or refute these arguments ? Socialism demands economic equality, economic security and economic freedom ; is all-comprehensive State regulation more relevant for the achievement of these objectives than State ownership and management of the means of production ?

In the final analysis, every society must work out for itself the elements of a just social order, for those elements must be consistent with the genius and traditions of its people, the moral and technical competence of the personnel available, the incentives available to keep production at the optimum level and the willingness and the capacity of the citizens to adjust their interests as individuals to the larger good of society. Constructive thinking on these and other issues will be an invaluable contribution to socialist theory in India ; Dr. Prasad has provided a useful survey which should provide a stimulus to such constructive thinking.

—A. APPADORAI

Jawaharlal Nehru University,
New Delhi.

PREFACE

The present work is primarily a study of Indian socialism between 1930 and 1964—the Nehru era in Indian politics. However, it has been tried to make it as up to date as possible. In this study the three principal tasks that have been undertaken are (1) to highlight the indigenous roots of Indian Socialism, (2) to present a socialistic account of the life and times of the principal, non-communist, socialist thinkers of India—Jawaharlal Nehru, Narendra Deva, Sampurnanand, Jayaprakash Narayan, Rammanohar Lohia and Asoka Mehta, and (3) to bring to light a connected thinking of the socialist thinkers and socialist parties of India on major theoretical issues, such as, materialism and spiritualism, the place of individual and state, the methodology of socialist transformation of society, and the concept of democratic socialism in India.

The expression 'Socialist Thought' in the title has been preferred in the customary fashion of designating the ideas of individual thinkers as 'thought'. However, there is no dearth of such critics who hold that there is nothing like socialist thought in India, for that matter, they even deny that there is anything like socialism. It is, however, suggested that polemics like these should not hinder a researcher in surveying a field of study very little explored till now. Indeed, there have come out recently some creditable works on Indian Socialist Movement, but the theoretical aspect of it has occupied very little attention. It was to fill this gap, in a limited way, that this study is being presented.

Shri Jayaprakash Narayan was kind enough to permit me to look into some of his private papers; the late Dr. Rammanohar Lohia found time to discuss the whole theme with me; Shri Asoka Mehta, found convenient to answer some of my important queries. I am beholden to all of them.

I am greateful to Dr. A. Appadorai, for lending a Foreword to this work ; and to Dr. V. P. Varma, Dr. Bimal Prasad, Dr. L. P. Sinha, and Dr. Manoranjan Jha for constant help and encouragement.

I also thank my wife who prepared the bibliography with meticulous care.

R. A. Prasad

CONTENTS

INTRODUCTION

PROBABLY NO IDEOLOGY in Political Science remains as vexed today as Socialism ; and in a way, even more vexed than what it was during the period of its origin. It requires a considerably intense survey of the historical, sociological and politico-economic processes through which modern socialism has evolved to shape itself into the various facets of contemporary socialism. The possible method to make it explicable is to avoid any set definition of it ; for naturally there must be several definitions, even as we have several definitions of State down from Aristotle to Marx and Gandhi.

One may wonder as to what all these difficulties are about ; socialism is what Marx described it to be. Marx is the father of modern socialism and all other connotations are nothing but derivations and departures from it. This approach is often indicated not only among laymen but also among a few experts of the field.[1] We consider this, however, as the first major hurdle in the way of understanding contemporary socialism.

Even as a new ideology, socialism, a nineteenth century product, has run a long process of evolution in its making, and what the orthodox might call its un-making ! Contemporary socialism has spanned not so much the chronological number of years ; what it has spanned through is peculiar national, topical and local varieties presented in every nation or state even in a single decade of history. And here what has mattered is not any absolute concept of socialism,

[1] In November 1968, the Nehru Memorial Museum and Library, New Delhi organised a Seminar on 'Socialism in India' in which over thirty Indian scholars were invited for participation. The present writer, being one of the participants, carried the impression that even such gatherings are inclined to avoid any theoretical discussion about 'what socialism is'. The above Seminar began without any such discussion. Obviously, this attitude ignores the complex aspect of the evolutionary ideology like socialism.

but the aspirations of peoples who have made socialism a tool to achieve a somewhat programme-bound objective. Hence socialism is not a single theory, complete in itself to suit each and every country, nor a theory eternally valid for all stages of societies from the past to the future. Socialism has relevance only in the context of a given society, its problems and aspirations at a given stage in history. It is rather a theory continuously related to the present.

But, it does not mean that socialism as an ideology has no unique characteristics of its own, just as democracy, individualism and capitalism, in all their changing forms, have still their distinctive features.

Modern socialism is a doctrine chiefly concerned with eradicating *inequality* in a capitalist and technology-oriented civilization. As such, all theories concerning removal of inequality in the ancient and medieval period, or even during the French Revolution period, technically, are not socialism, whatever they be. In spite of the brilliance of Platonic Communism or Thomas Moore's Utopia or Manu's socialistic order of Varnashrama Dharma, those were not socialism of our meaning. Such pursuits as from 'Moses to Lenin' or 'Manu to Gandhi' have generally been considered a 'confusion' of thought. And, indeed, it is, if the context and connotations attached with the word 'socialism' and 'communism' are not kept in mind. Even the word 'socialism', in its first appearance in Italian print around 1803 and 'communism', around 1830s in France,[2] have altogether unconnected meaning with that of socialism of our concept. Naturally, the expression or ideology of socialism during the Greek or Medieval period, or what Bhagavan Das describes as 'Ancient Scientific Socialism'[3] of India must have been poles apart from the modern ideology of socialism. And yet if some one pursues the 'socialist traditions' from 'Moses to Lenin'[4] or 'Manu to Gandhi'[5] that by itself should not be denigrated as a 'confusion'; for, a thought has necessarily much deeper roots than what it appears to be on the surface. What is necessary, however, is to keep in mind the subtle differences in the concept of that ideology or expression

[2] G. D. H. Cole, *Socialist Thought* I, pp. 1, 7.

[3] Bhagavan Das, *Ancient vs Modern Scientific Socialism*, 1934.

[4] Alexander Gray, *The Socialist Tradition*, 1946.

[5] Bhagavan Das, *op. cit.*, and Kamala Gadre, *Indian Way to Socialism*, 1966.

in each context. We do begin our concept of state with the Greek word *Polis* but we cannot call our state today a *Polis*. Similar is the case with the ancient and medieval use of the term socialism and our concept of modern socialism.

Now, coming down to modern socialism, as has been indicated earlier, it is somewhat a product of the late eighteenth century and early nineteenth centuries. Further, it is also connected with the growth of capitalism and technology-oriented civilization. In this framework socialism was best expounded and scientifically explained by Karl Marx and that is why we call him the father of modern scientific socialism. Even *Marxian* socialism does not comprehend the total ideology of modern socialism.[6] Modern socialism appeared both prior to Marx as well as posterior to Marx. Whatever was professed before Marx, in the name of socialism, has been called *Utopian* socialism and whatever was considered after Marx has often been dubbed as *Revisionary* socialism. Thus, at least, even modern socialism wears a three-faced-mask, bearing Utopianism, Marxism and Revisionism. Let nothing be said here of different shades of thought under modern socialism, taking forms of different 'schools' of thought that characterise contemporary socialism.

The first socialists, who took notice of the evils of capitalism, especially inequality, and suggested ways to eradicate such evils were Owen in England and Fourier and Saint-Simon (and later Louis Blanc also) in France. Let nothing be said of Rousseau, Mably, Morelly, Babeuf, Godwin, and others. But, in due recognition, it may be mentioned that Rousseau's *Discourses on Inequality* smacked the meat of the matter which later the socialists were to grab.[7] And that way, even closer anticipation of Marx is to be found in the English writers such as Charles Hall, William Thompson, Thomas Hodgskin, J. F. Bray and John Gray, whom we usually describe as 'Pre-Marxians'. Bray's *Labour's Wrongs and Labour's Remedy* and Gray's *Lecture on Human Happiness* were indeed the themes very close to Marx. Even Marxian concepts of labour theory of value

[6] C. A. R. Crosland, *The Future of Socialism*, pp. 20–21; also the full chapter on *The Meaning of Socialism*, pp. 97–116. Also, Julius Braunthal, 'Marxism and Socialism Today', *Janata* IX (16), 9 May, 1953, pp. 3–4. Also see 'Is the end of Scientific Marxism in sight?', *Janata*, XX (35), September 19, 1965, p. 15.

[7] G. D. H. Cole, *op. cit.*, p. 15; A. Gray, *op. cit.*, pp. 78–85.

4

and surplus value are found in the writings of Turgot and Ricardo. Thus a host of writers go into that stream which has often been characterised as Utopianism or Utopian Socialism. These thinkers emphasised the evils of capitalism and underlined the need to replace it by workers' ownership, or control of industries, or cooperative associations, or state-controlled trade unions and in such other ways.[8]

Marxism as a concept is an improvement upon the utopian socialism, principally, in two ways. Firstly, it provided the law of the development of human history and secondly, it exposed the law of motion governing the capitalist mode of production and the bourgeois society in such a way as to make it clear why the conflict between labour and capital is inevitable. And, we may add, Marx also set out a path for violent overthrow or revolution for the inevitable decay of capitalism, or, in other words, for the transformation of capitalism into socialism (this, however, is subjected to the controversy whether Marx advocated violence outright, and if so, to what degree and under what circumstances). In short, he clearly laid down the method how socialism can be brought about and put forward the concept of class-war which was totally absent in the visions of the early utopian socialists. It is this radical posture of Marxism, based on the dialectical process of historical evolution, that has added the prestige to it as 'scientific socialism'. More than any body else, Marx made it a faith that socialism is bound to come just as day follows the night.

Revisionism, is yet another off-shoot under modern socialism itself. It comprises again a host of thinkers such as Bernstein, Rosa Luxemberg, Trotsky, Bukharian, and many such, down to M. N. Roy and Marshall Tito. The revisionists are undisputedly socialists, and yet on what Marx meant and did not mean, on the prognosis of capitalist society, the degree of violent struggle required, on the inevitability of class struggle, on the 'withering away' of the state and many such implications of Marxism, they held different positions or altered positions than that of Marx. They showed the points where Marx had gone 'wrong' and tried to prop it up over their own ideological pillars, with probably the similar fate as that of Mill's revisionism of Benthamite doctrine of utility, and causing its

---

[8] J. Bandopadhyaya, 'Socialism : A review', *Janata*, Special Number on Socialism Today, No. 1 and 2, Republic day 1964, p. 11.

slow demolition, intended or unintended !

The ideological progress following these can conveniently be categorised under contemporary socialism, bringing it much nearer to our times and aspirations, than even modern socialism—that is, Utopianism, Marxism and Revisionism, even though many such off-shoots are as old as Bernstein or even older. These have invariably taken regional colourings with typical characteristics, such as Syndicalism of France, Fabianism and Guild Socialism of Great Britain, Bolshevism of Soviet Russia, and recently Democratic socialism of the British Labour Party. In our own country in the post-Independence period we have the concept of democratic socialism and fusion of Marxism and Gandhism, leaning heavily towards what one might call 'Gandhian socialism'. Added to all these, we often hear of 'Yugoslavian road to socialism', 'Burmese road to socialism' and, even 'Algerian road to socialism' and such other expressions. These necessarily connote trends of thought wherein there is typical dilution of socialist thought, making it appear complex, almost unrecognisable, in form as well as features. Recently, variations of Marxism by itself have created various facets of Neo-Marxism, such as, Sovietism, Maoism, Titoism, and in India, we might mention, even Naxalism.[9]

What has brought the concept of socialism to the point of utter complexity in terms of definitions and descriptions are these perforative evolutions ; and yet, such 'complexities' are not inherent in the doctrine, but are the product of the staleness of pursuit. If somebody still pursues the coherency of Marxism in any of the off-shoots of contemporary socialism, he is bound to be disappointed. If the doctrines of class-war and proletariat dictatorship are still pressed to their logical conclusion, the future world might negate the very concept of such socialism. If socialism in India today has come to be stuck up in the efforts towards land-ceiling and urban property-ceiling, one just cannot help ; for, in a given context, these are considered the first major steps forward towards socialism in India. In a way it has the same relevance as the 'Beard Movement' of Russia had once with the history of freedom movement in general. Any one who desires to seek socialism, especially contemporary socialism,

---

[9] Joseph S. Roucek, *Contemporary Political Ideologies*, pp. 31–88, and, G. R. Irani, *Bengal, The Communist Challenge*, 1968, p. 167.

beyond the issues and programmes advocated at a given stage to eradicate poverty, inequality, and imbalance in the distribution of the means of production and output, is probably seeking socialism in a stale dogma and not in a genuine radical movement, which it is today. The true meaning of the contemporary socialism lies in the moral values and aspirations to which people are committed.[10]

It has often been said that socialism inheres not so much in objectives as much as in the method. Even individualism, which, it is said, socialism negates, has probably the same objectives. Contemporary capitalism, as Stratchy points out, has much to its credit today what socialism envisaged during the late and early twenties. Even soviet authors recognise today the relevance of the liberal doctrines with socialist ideas.

What is permanent in socialism is not this or that form, this or that dogma, this or that programme, nor this or that method, but a consistent relationship with emotive impulses in men which lead them to seek *equality* in society. That is why socialism is a product of human nature. Socialism also, like democracy, is deeply ingrained in the emotive factors that characterise all human beings. Even since the dawn of the modern age and the decay of the medieval era, modern political thought strives to lay greater and greater emphasis on individual and correspondingly less and less emphasis on Church and theological state. The Renaissance and Reformation symbolise the undaunted spirit of man and the giant strides of human intelligence and science. In the process the beconing lights that enchanted man were the ideals of *liberty* and *equality*. These have been the two basic aspirations, almost inseparable, peeping through almost the entire ideological and pragmatic upheavals that have taken place in human history in the shape of events like the Glorious Revolution of 1688 or the French Revolulion of 1789. Such upheavals have consistently been taking place in a row, down to our own decades.

In the beginning *liberty* was conceived to inhere only in a democratic state and hence the movement primarily took a political turn in the form of rebellion against the state, denial of the sovereignty of the King and proclamation of natural rights and liberty of the individual. The political mechanism that was evolved to suit the purpose was to clamour for separation of powers within a

[10] Crosland, *op. cit.*, p. 101.

government and demand for a written and rigid constitution with an independent judiciary as its watchdog. Parliamentary democracy and Presidential democracy together succeeded, with the framing of the American Constitution in 1787 and the passage of the Reform Act of 1832 in achieving political liberty, if not wholly, atleast, largely.

But, the desire to have equality deluded man. What was presumed in the beginning (to an extent what is being presumed even today) that dawn of democracy itself will bring liberty as well as equality proved untrue. The desire for liberty was partially satiated but the urge for equality remained completely unfulfilled.

Hence the ideological as well as pragmatic movements were diverted towards seeking greater and greater equality, especially economic equality. Socialism is the product of this diversion ; the process of such a turn in modern history marks the beginning of what we generally call Utopian socialism. The origin of inequality, is as old a subject as Aristotle, or even older, but in modern political thought Rousseau's *Discourses on Inequality*, already referred to, is probably the beginning. So long the dimensions of inequality were confined to natural inequality, say arising out of incapacity, ill health, poor intelligence, and such other factors, man could believe lessons like 'some are born to rule and some are born to be ruled' or that 'inequality is natural'. The obvious inequality that characterised an agricultural civilisation and even a feudal civilisation as that of the pre-French Revolution period set reaction against it among the reformers and radical thinkers alike. Yet the reaction was within limits *i.e.,* within the range of possibility to achieve equality through democracy.

But the pinch of inequality that man felt in course of time, especially at the dawn of capitalist civilisation under the impact of technological and industrial advancement was unparalleled at any stage of human history. And, it is primarily this sort of inequality that is sought to be eradicated under modern socialism. Hence socialism as an ideology is inseparably connected with modern capitalism and industrial civilisation.[11] This relationship has been understood by Marx and other socialists in an unfailing measure. And hence this is a permanent feature of all socialism, at all stages whether Utopian, Marxian, contemporary or whatever be its label.

Contemporary socialism, in different countries, have followed

[11] Robert Freedman, *Marxist Social Thought.*

the emotive pursuit of equality, especially economic equality. In the process, intellectually all socialists, for a time, short or long, remained under the spell of Marxism ; and Marxism, indeed, permeates in small doses in almost all shades of contemporary socialist thought. But the calculated intellectualism has given way, to bear out Graham Wallas's thesis, to emotive impulses which do stride over calculated intellectualism. And it is these emotive impulses of peoples, in all parts of the world today, that are responsible for lending colour to different shades of contemporary socialism.

Contemporary socialism has also very much to do with the values that people attach to their civilisation and way of life. It has travelled from the 'bread and butter' to the 'incentive to goodness'. *The Twentieth Century Socialism* of the British socialists or Jay Douglas's *Socialism in the New Society* establish new task for socialism. In our own country Jayaprakash Narayan pointed out that 'mere economic development is not a measure of socialism and what I wish to emphasize is the danger of that development.' He defined a socialist society 'as one in which the individual is prepared *voluntarily* to subordinate his own interests to the larger interests of the society.' This could be possible, he opined, only when the Gandhian method of 'internal change in man' is made a tool for our tasks. Even though, Gandhiji was keen enough to realise that socialism is deeply connected with human nature and human psychology his approach was quite different from that of Graham Wallas. The varying values and aspirations are bound to shape themselves in varying forms and facets of contemporary socialism, and this should neither be dubbed as 'heresy' or 'revisionism' nor as 'development' or 'correctives'. Values determine contemporary socialism, pure and simple.

Apparently, what appears to characterise contemporary socialism, even more than values are the forms or methodology of achieving the tasks the socialists set before themselves under relevant circumstances. And it is probably here that socialism is more colourful. Whether 'violent transformation from capitalism to socialism' or 'peaceful transition from capitalism to socialism' is possible and desirable or not constitutes a dilemma that explains literally a considerable bulk of socialist literature.[12] Violent destruc-

---

[12] Victor M. Fic, *Peaceful Transition to Communism in India,* p. 415.

tion, ceaseless class-war, saboteuring violence, acid-bomb cult, sporadic violence, guerrilla warfare, open shooting, what and what not among these assure greater rapidity in bringing forth socialistic objectives has been a matter of debate ever since it appeared to man that violence alone could do the trick. And Marx set the ball rolling. Equally fancifully, the 'dreamers' and the 'visionaries' have sought the sophisticated methods of gradualness, parliamentary processes, propaganda media, persuasion, moral appeals, reforms and corrective methods, planning, and a variety of other subtle democratic methods to bring about the socialistic results. Contemporary socialism, whether of Soviet, German, French, British Chinese or Indian origin has been characterised by the kind of method it adopted for fulfilment of the objectives and programmes, it set before itself. Hence contemporary socialism appears to inhere more in the method than in the objectives. And this is probably true of socialism at all stages of its evolution.

Subjectively also contemporary socialism has come to enlarge itself much more from what it had been during the Marxian days. What the socialists were generally concerned with was the toiling class of labourers, especially labourers of the factories. Peasants occupied their concern much later, probably, only when they realised that the reality of the situation demanded as much attention to the labourers in the farms and fields as any other. That came to espouse the cause of the peasants also. However, Lenin character-ised peasants as less 'revolutionary' and hence less reliable class as a tool for socialist movement.[13] Naturally peasants formed only the secondary subject for the socialists.

Gradually, however, this distinction wore itself out and the socia-lists came to preoccupy themselves with the toiling classes as a whole. Many other classes such as the third and fourth grade employees of the offices, teachers of the schools and even the upper strata, such as the middle classes, were still much farther from the socialist's concern. These gradually began to clamour for recognition, so much so that very little distinction prevailed between skilled and unskilled labourer, educated and uneducated labouring classes. Socialists realised gradually that intellectuals, especially, teachers and students of the universities could not be ignored, and hence they too

[13] John H. Hallowell, *Main Currents in Modern Political Thought,* p. 491.

were sympathised by the socialists. Especially, in countries where socialists were to compete in electoral constituencies, enlarging the scope of 'labouring class' became a compulsive necessity. Hence contemporary socialism does not exclude even the white-collar, the high-ups in society, including big zamindars and even capitalists. Contemporary socialism does not preclude the clerks, assistants, teachers, doctors, and such others from being included in the 'class' which once was a term for only the factory labourers. This change in the scope of socialism is little highlighted, yet it is unique under contemporary socialism. Socialists, under contemporary socialism, are broadly concerned with almost all sections of the people, except of course the anti-socialists and hardened hoarders ; equally it covers almost all aspects of life, economic, political and ethical of course with exception here also, not the mystical and superstitious aspect of life. Thus contemporary socialism has shifted its growing concern from classes to masses.

What is significant, more than anything else, is the humility of socialism as a doctrine today. It has negated, unless not ortho-doxically asserted without conformity to facts, any *a priori* relation-ship with any philosophy or dogma, such as Marxism or Anarchism or Fabianism in recent times. Contemporary socialism, even when tried to be fitted in the categories of recent radical off-shoots like 'Maoism' or 'Naxalism' shall be all the more a square in the hole. The sooner it is realised that socialism is not *a priori* philo-sophy, the better it is for understanding contemporary socialism. Marxism, with all its brilliance and ingenuity, will be irrelevant for the future of contemporary socialism. The established notion of socialism has come to fluidify itself in a series of programmes, indeed progressive programmes, in socialist countries with varying contents so much so, that in our country the language issue takes precedence over the issue of holding the price line of the commodities, Racial equality on a universal scale yields precedence to national interests between two countries. The socialist programmes deter-mine more the character of contemporary socialism than dogmas and theories ; and it is a worldwide phenomenon, initiated right from the beginning not by the revisionists like Bernstein but by Marxists like Lenin.[14]

[14] It was Lenin who first realised the need to modify Marxism to the

In our own country contemporary socialism, propounded by the same bunch of one time Marxists, Nehru, J. P., and Lohia, if not Deva also, has been weaned away from Marxism towards Gandhism, to the great distaste of those who consider Gandhism to be a dogma. But the more we realise that the contemporary experiences are taking us back, for good or bad, in the reverse gear and are revolting against the cult of reason and negating all attempts at human perfection, the nearer we shall be to the truth and realities. In the words of Hallowell, 'We will realize that the task of achieving a just social order is an ever-continuing one and that justice is a goal to be striven after rather than finally obtained.'[15] Braunthal also regards democratic socialism as an international movement 'which does not demand a rigid uniformity of approach. Whether socialists build their faith on Marxist or other methods of analysing society, whether they are inspired by religious or humanitarian principles, they all strive for the same goal —a system of social justice, better living, freedom and world peace.'[16] Contemporary socialism is also an 'ever-continuing' search, and hence an evolving ideology.

It is only in the above setting that Indian Socialism may appear to stand on its own. The major distinguishing features of Indian socialism, as will appear in the pages of this work, may be set as follows :

1. Socialist thinkers in India have realised, and expounded the intimate relationship of socialism and the innate nature of man and his craving for equality. They have approached socialism, not only as a problem of improvement in the environment but also as a problem of reform in the human nature ; not only as corrective form without, but also from within.

2. Indian socialists, unlike their western counterparts, have consistently maintained that, man is basically a spiritual entity, of course not in religious sense but only in philosophical sense. They have never regarded man as just a biological product. That explains greater leaning of Indian socialism towards spiritualism than of the western socialism generally, and Marxism particularly.

practical task of building socialism and initiated the New Economic Policy in 1921.
    [15] Hallowell, *op. cit.*, p. 292.
    [16] Braunthal, *op. cit.*, p. 4.

3. The Indian socialists have consistently put faith in the machinery of the state, and even those who advocated decentralisation of functions of state, or emphasised the communitarian way of life, avoided reaching, even remotely, the periphery of the concept of the 'withering away' of the state.

4. In the sphere of the method and means, probably Indian socialism has attracted the focus. Whether it is the Gandhian method of non-violent satyagraha, or its many latest variations, none of the socialists in India, generally, have suggested the method of bloody revolution and outright violence.

5. In the evolution of the concept of democratic socialism, the Indian socialist thinkers have not less to contribute. It is to the credit of Jawaharlal Nehru and Asoka Mehta, and many others, that they conceived and experimented planning under parliamentary framework. Those who believed in the fundamental antagonism between planning and democracy have a new dimension of possibilities under Indian socialist thought and practice.

I
BACKGROUND

WITH THE EMERGENCE of socialist ideas particularly around the early thirties, a heated controversy arose with regard to the question whether the socio-economic and other conditions were suitable for the growth of socialism in India or not. Jayaprakash Narayan, one of the first organisers, and the chief theoretician of the Congress Socialist Party, made this a theme of his early writings and speeches. Whatever scanty socialist literature of the late twenties and thirties is available today, more or less takes for granted that Indian conditions were conducive to the growth of socialism; with equal emphasis, however, Mahatma Gandhi and Bhagavan Das, to mention only a few, contended that they were uncongenial and unsuited to the 'foreign' ideology like socialism. Bhagavan Das went to the extent of suggesting that the old order of *Chaturvarna* as propounded in the *Manusmriti* as well as the principles underlying the *Varnashrama Dharma* and the joint family system provide a better basis for Indian socialism to thrive than the one advocated by the socialists. This kind of socialism, however, was different from what the socialists were advocating then.

Unfortunately, the question of suitability or otherwise of Indian conditions did not appear to have been considered dispassionately and much heat was generated in this process. It was little realised then that it was, in fact, largely a matter of opinion and of a few *a priori* convictions. Had that not been the case, J. P. would have devoted full attention to the 'what' before pleading the 'why' of socialism. Likewise, Bhagavan Das would have analysed why certain socio-economic situations cropped up in Indian society before asserting that such conditions were incompatible with the growth of modern socialism. While the first task involved ideological precision, the latter embraced complex historical and sociological investigations.

Unfortunately, as neither of the tasks was undertaken fully in that period, they ended only in asserting one's point of view and magnifying the controversy. Needless to say that it is beyond the scope of this study to get entangled into this controversy, and far less, to pronounce any judgement upon it. Yet, we can realise how unsubstantive will be the study of Indian socialism without an academic and objective understanding of the socio-economic and political conditions of Indian life around that time which have great bearing on the germination of socialist ideas in this country.

SOCIAL CONTEXT

On the basis of some recent sociological studies of the rural life in India, it may be pointed out that the traditional faith in the idyllic conditions of the old village order, its peaceful and contented living, its independent existence, its democratic institutions like the traditional village panchayat, its self-sufficiency in needs and economy, etc., have not been wholly corroborated nor have some of them been proved to be correct and wholesome.

On the contrary, evidence of factionalism on the basis of kinship rivalries, familial supremacy and caste lines has even traditionally been traced as the factual reality of the Indian village life.[1] Its backwardness, insecurity through invasions and brigandage, discontentment, retarded and primitive economy and poor standard of living have been increasingly brought to light.

With the growth of scientific knowledge, technological advancement, improvement in the means of communication—such as the railways, roads, radio and propaganda machinery—and with the spread of education the old pattern of the village order gradually changed. Particularly, after the First World War the change began to be more perceptible. The villages now came in greater contact with their outer surroundings. The findings of the sociologists, historians and political reformers at once tended to disprove the traditional belief that the caste and joint family systems had religious sanction. The fortification that these systems were supposed to provide to the traditionally closed village pattern and its social order slowly came to be exploded. The increasing

[1] Baljit Singh, *Next step in Village India*, Bombay, Asia Publishing House, 1961, pp. 1–15, 108.

realisation of this, paved the way for the introduction of newer ideals and aspirations. The changes and elasticity thus created provided the social context under which the germination of progressive ideologies like socialism could be possible. The consciousness generated also lead to the rise of the middle class. Most of the pioneers of Indian Socialism, under our reference, belong to this class.

ECONOMIC CONTEXT

India was not as poor as it became after the advent of the East India Company's rule in India. The British rule and their policy led the country to gradual poverty. Indian indigenous industries were made to decline so that the British industries could flourish and find easy market in India. The peasants were heavily burdened with excessive land-tax. The land revenue policy of the Government of introducing the Zamindari system under the Permanent Settlement and of the Raiyatwari and Mahalwari systems, together, in effect, served one big purpose from the point of view of British imperial interests. It created an intermediary class of landlords within the country whose interests came to be inter-linked with the continuance of the British rule in India. This led to the rise of class-antagonism between the zamindars and the peasantry.

Another class of money-lenders also grew parallel to that of the zamindars, and together they became the classes which dominated the village scene and exploited the poor landless peasants. There was seething discontent among the peasants. This led to a series of class-riots in the villages, and the class antagonism once started was not to go. This often led to conflicts with the zamindars as well as the Government of the day.

The misery of the peasantry and the artisans grew with the pressure on land because of progressive decline in the indigenous industries and unemployment among its artisans. There was a trend towards increasing fragmentation of land into small holdings, which was uneconomic. Peasants' indebtedness grew, and the rigidity of its recovery made them feel the pinch of it. The Government did little to remove their ignorance, illiteracy, conservatism and backwardness. The artisan classes were equal sufferers with the peasants, if not more.

During the period, before the First World War, India was reduced to a typical colonial country. There was the rise of Company's capitalist monopoly in different enterprises in India. Particularly, it started with the investment of British capital, in the construction of Indian Railways on assured minimum profit on investment. No consideration was given to the need of giving priority to the means of irrigation which in the context of recurring famines should have attracted precedence over other things.

The spread of education in India led to the rise of the middle classes which were in need of support and sustenance through employment, failing any agricultural and industrial scope. In addition to the peasants and the workers, this class was now a third and an additional one, which was not only economically discontented but also conscious, to an extent of its rights and privileges. These classes manifested growing discontentment with their economic lot and became conscious of the need to press for the amelioration of their conditions. This economic discontentment, poverty, and to an extent, consciousness of their plight, provided a favourable economic background which, on all accounts is the *sine qua non* of the germination of socialist ideas.

POLITICAL CONTEXT

The political conditions in India, during the thirties were no less conducive for the growth of radical ideas. The policy of omission and commission of the Government of India, and the growing realisation that India was increasingly exploited for meeting the needs of Britain's imperialistic wars and other factors, made the people demand self-rule. The partition of Bengal, against all opposition in the country radicalised the Indian political scene continually thereafter ; the half-hearted reforms through the Morley-Minto Reforms did not prove adequate. The radical leaders, particularly, the trio—Lal-Bal-Pal, gave a call for vigorous and patriotically inspired Swadeshi Movement and even the moderates within the Congress supported the move. There was a religious mooring in the political climate and politics was raised to the height of religiously inspired cause.

The government's policy for higher education, supplemented by the efforts of private business class and political leaders, augmented a phase of educational growth in India, in which a class of unemployed university-educated youth sprang up in the country. This class was easily amenable to radical and progressive ideologies like socialism.

The Swadeshi Movement, around this time, reflected a sort of economic nationalism, which was also an additional factor in radicalising the Indian politics.

The coming of the First World War, under the already radicalised political temper of the country, forced the government to make lofty and hasty promises in order to woo the sympathy of India. The political hope in India for a responsible government was raised to a high level, only to be dashed to the ground, even before the War was over. Instead, the infamous and unpopular Rowllat Bills were hastened through, even in the wake of a country-wide protest ; and then was inflicted that grievous blow, in the form of 'Jallianwala Bagh Massacre', which turned the tide of politics.

The War itself was regarded as a big step towards the growth of socialism in the world. In India, the short industrial boom following the War, led to the rise of a small organised class of labour. This marked the formation of the AITUC in 1920. On the international plane this coincided with the period of the formation of the Third International in Moscow in 1919 and the ILO in 1920. The discontent of the organised labour was reflected in the increasing number of strikes since 1921.

There was growing discontent among the peasants also. Ever since the Champaran indigo planters' struggle, there was a consciousness in the country about the plight of the peasantry. The agrarian movement in U.P. was led by Jawaharlal Nehru himself.

About this time the news of the success of the Bolshevik Revolution in Russia, under the leadership of Lenin, gradually reached India. Its anti-colonial ideology inspired the Indian leaders, who sympathised with Lenin in his efforts.

Since 1920 the impact of British Socialist ideology was marked on the Indian National Congress. The Labour Party's representatives came often to be present at its annual sessions regularly. The scholars going to England for higher studies, particularly to the London School of Economics under Harold J. Laski, returned to India during the twenties and thirties with marked socialist leanings.

Thus, politically and educationally India was becoming conscious of her duty to cast off slavery. It was against this background that the first Non-Cooperation Movement was led by Gandhiji. The urge for greater freedom prompted the need for adopting radical ideologies, and socialism was one such.

It may be mentioned here that the decade 1922-32, from the point of view of the growth of socialist thought and movement in India, was of great importance. M. N. Roy and other Indian emigrants secretly began to smuggle Marxist literature into India, and to influence the ideology of the Congress through soliciting, although not very successfully, help from the Congress leaders like C. R. Das and Sampurnanand. M. N. Roy who had developed intimate affinity with Marxist ideology spearheaded the group which was engaged in this attempt. After the Kanpur conspiracy case the Communist Party of India came to be formally organised and considerable Marxist literature came to be published in India.

The impact of the Brussels' Congress of 1927 influenced and inspired Jawaharlal Nehru and, through him, the Congress to adopt socialistic lines. This marked within the country yet another phase of radicalisation in which a number of trade unions and student and youth leagues came to be organised, all over the country. The utterances of the leaders during this period were considerably inspired by socialist ideology. The imperialistic exploitation, economic inequality, utter poverty, and adverse impact of the capitalist system, provided a congenial background for the growth of socialism. However, the presence of Gandhiji and Gandhian ideas, including the ideas which indicated the roots of indigenous socialism in Indian tradition and philosophy, the illiteracy of the general masses, the undeveloped factory-stage civilisation in India, lack of wide knowledge about Marxism and socialism, orthodoxy and faith in religious rituals were still great impediments in the way of the smooth growth of socialism.

2

INDIGENOUS SOCIALISM : ROOTS IN THE WRITINGS OF SOME MODERN INDIAN WRITERS

Liberal Ideology

OF LATE THIS has been increasingly realised that, ideologically, the foundations of the principles and objectives of Indian socialism can be derived from the past, *i.e.*, the ancient social, economic and philosophical traditions of India.[1] It is for this reason that ever since the mid-nineteenth century the socio-economic issues became the central theme of the economists, the socio-religious reformers as well as the political leaders of India. In their writings and speeches some glimpses were provided of the ancient philosophy and culture of India, as well as of its ancient socio-economic order. What is more

[1] Sadiq Ali the General Secretary of the Congress while tracing the evolution of socialism pointed out that there were two major forces which moulded the ideology of the Congress : 'one was our association with England, and the other was the revival of the ancient heritage of India.'

Sadiq Ali, *Towards Socialist Thinking in Congress*, New Delhi, All India Congress Committee, Aug., 1961, p. 4.

Asoka Mehta observed : 'We can draw sustenance from the past for our vision of democratic socialism ; we can trace the roots deep of the fruits and foliage that we seek.' Asoka Mehta, 'Economic Development through Socialism', *Janata*, XIX (30–31), p. 15.

V. K. R. V. Rao formerly member of the Planning Commission observed : 'To my mind, the Indian conception of a socialist society had been greatly influenced by the spiritual heritage of the country—both from the Vedantic concept of the Hindus and the democratic concept of the Muslims. I would, therefore, draw some of my inspiration in a democratic socialist society from the spiritual heritage of this kind.' V.K.R.V. Rao, 'How Do We Plan for a Socialist Society in the Country', *AICC Economic Review*, XV (14–15), Jan. 9, '64, p. 100.

important is that these writers and reformers also gave vent to the socio-economic aspirations of their time.

In this connection we might recall, the trend of economic nationalism in India, more particularly since the beginning of the Swadeshi Movement in 1906. To some extent, behind economic nationalism was the broad ideology laid down in the writings and expositions of the early liberal thinkers like Dadabhai Naoroji, Mahadev Govind Ranade, Romesh Chandra Dutt and Gopal Krishna Gokhale, to name but a few.[2] They emphasised the need to improve the indigenous industries and economic development so as to meet the growing economic aspirations of the new social class—mostly composed of the professional middle classes.

DADABHAI NAOROJI

One of the foremost contributions of Dadadhai Naoroji, with regard to economic ideas, was the 'Drain' theory, which formed the main thesis of his scholarly treatise *Poverty and Un-British Rule in India*. He exposed the fact of imperial exploitation of a nation by a nation with reference to India. The image created by this theory was so great and enduring that the succeeding generation of leaders, including Gandhiji, had not to give a second thought to the reality and the magnitude of exploitation.

Dadabhai's treatise, although couched in sophisticated words may still be regarded as one of the sternest commentaries on the deeds of an imperial country. With regard to the benefits done to India which were constantly harped on by the then British rulers, Dadabhai observed :

> We do pray to our British rulers, let us have railways and all other kinds of beneficial public works by all means, but let us have their natural benefits, or talk not to a starving man of the pleasures of a fine dinner...do not in Heaven's and Honesty's names, talk to us of benefits which we do not receive.[3]

Dadabhai charged the British rulers that they were bent upon not only remitting the wealth of the country to England, but also taking back through their India-earned capital itself her inner wealth

[2] K. P. Karunakaran, ed., *Modern Indian Political Tradition*, New Delhi, 1962, pp. 13–14.

[3] Dadabhai Naoroji, *Poverty and Un-British Rule in India*, London, 1901, p. 195.

as well such as the minerals and other valuables. Thus, the drain was to occupy an unprecedented scale.[4]

It may be recalled that Dadabhai and Karl Marx were contemporaries. Junior to Marx by only seven years in age, he outlived him by about thirty five years. They studied in the same library —the British Museum of London. It is rightly pointed out that Dadabhai devoted himself to the theme of exploitation of a nation by a nation while Marx devoted himself to that of a class by a class.[5] Their anti-imperial and anti-capitalist conclusions appear, therefore to have been derived from the womb of the socio-political conditions in which they were placed.

Dadabhai had attended the Conference in 1905, held in Stockholm, before he came to India to preside over the Calcutta Session of the Congress. By participating in the conference which was avowedly socialistic Dadabhai showed with his characteristic perspicacity that the values of liberalism he cherished in the nineteenth century could be enshrined only in socialism in the twentieth century.[6]

Dadabhai, who had been a leading protagonist of liberal principles and ideologies, had now come to believe increasingly in the canalisation of those ideas through more nationalist and economically expressive channels. That the resolutions for the 'Boycott' of British goods and the launching of the *Swadeshi Movement* were passed under his Presidentship and the strong support and stout advocacy of these were made by him only indicated this trend.

Dadabhai contradicated the theory that India was poor because of over-population which was the stock-in-trade of the Britishers then to shield the fact of exploitation. He also drew the peoples's attention towards 'the moral drain' that the British Government was causing in India.

    [4] *Ibid.*, pp. 227–28.

    [5] 'Dadabhai was called upon to answer the question posed by exploitation under imperialism, was called upon to provide the intellectual scaffoldings for the fabric of nationalism, while Marx was called upon to provide the intellectual scaffoldings for the fabric of working class socialist movement. Both of them had two distinct, two separate, problems and they were able to offer solutions that light up the two most difficult problems of our age.' Asoka Mehta, *Democratic Socialism*, pp. 103–04.

    [6] Asoka Mehta, *The Plan : Perspective and Problems*, Bombay, 1966, p. 37.

INDIGENOUS SOCIALISM

MAHADEV GOVIND RANADE

The passion of M. G. Ranade's life was social reform in India and her economic advancement. He realised greatly the urgency of the social and economic reforms. To achieve that end, he founded The Indian Social Conference—a distinct forum to devote exclusively to the Socio-economic problems in India. Through it he emphasised the need for a social system based on social justice and equity. Although he lamented many of the natural limitations of India in the sphere of agriculture, such as, soil, irregular rain etc., he emphasised greatly the burden of taxation which was almost, in his own assessment, one-third of the total gain of the peasants. According to him the main causes of poverty, were :

(a) system of rural credit involving extortion by money lenders,
(b) paucity of capital, and
(c) land policy of Government, i.e., state monopoly over land.

Referring to the land policy of the government, particularly the trend towards state monopoly of land, he said that it was ruinous for the Indian society.[7] He was greatly concerned with the question of social equality, subjection of women, and the conditions of the depressed classes. He wanted to eradicate these evils so as to build Indian society on a sound social philosophy of equality and justice. To this end, he had pioneered the organization of the *Prarthana Samaj* in Bombay.

Ranade did not throw the responsibility of Indian poverty entirely on the shoulders of the Britishers, but he was judicious enough to acknowledge many of India's own natural limitations ; yet he made no mistake in having a strong dig at the government's policy of omission and commission which kept India low. He strongly criticised the British system of economy that was being copied for India and emphasised that India must have her adaptation according to her own conditions.

Ranade was opposed to the trend of state capitalism, i.e., the concentration of land—the main agricultural means of production— into the hands of the state exclusively.[8]

---

[7] James Kellock, *Mahadev Govind Ranade*, Calcutta, 1936, p. 37.
[8] M. G. Ranade, *Essays on Indian Economics*, Madras, 1906, p. 3.

GOPAL KRISHNA GOKHALE

Gopal Krishna Gokhale, Gandhiji's political 'Guru' and the liberal leader of the National Congress, showed a deep insight into the economic muddle of the time and generated political consciousness in the Congress and the country. He had challenged 'the artificial surplus' shown during the time of Curzon, which had been, according to Gokhale, 'the result of manipulated exchange.'[9] He also challenged the propriety of raising the price of salt by the government.

It has been said about Gokhale that he always sympathised with the 'starving, shrunken, shrivelled-up ryot, toiling and moiling from dawn to dark...entirely voiceless in the Parliament of his rulers and meekly prepared to bear whatever burdens God and man might be pleased to impose upon his back.'[10]

Gokhale lent his strong support to the Swadeshi movement and considered the boycott of the British goods—an agitational reaction against the decision for the Partition of Bengal to be symbolic of both political and economic unrest in the country. He observed :

> ...the true Swadeshi movement is both a patriotic and an economic movement.... The devotion to motherland, which is enshrined in the highest Swadeshi, is an influence so profound and so passionate that its very thought thrills and its actual touch lifts one out of oneself.... But the movement on its material side is an economic one ; and through self-denying ordinances, extensively entered into, must serve a valuable economic purpose, namely, to ensure a ready consumption of such articles as are produced in the country....[11]

ROMESH CHANDRA DUTT

The impact of the writing of R. C. Dutt was also very great on the mind of the Indian people. Few could excel in the mastery over facts that he exhibited, especially in his survey of the economic conditions of India. Sitaramayya the official biographer of the Congress recorded about him :

> He held that the causes of famine were the hazy assessments on land and the destruction of the village industries by free competition with English machinery. He regretted that a

[9] B. Pattabhi Sitarammayya, *The History of the Indian National Congress*, Allahabad, 1935, p. 149.
[10] *Ibid.*
[11] Quoted in Karunakaran, *op. cit.*, pp. 95-96.

country which had organised Village Self-Government 3,000 years ago was being virtually ruled through the Police, the hated link between the district officers and the people.[12]

No wonder, therefore, that the revelation through Dutt's writings, particularly his classic work, *The Economic History of India* brought tears into Gandhij's eyes and 'sickened' his heart.[13] Dutt systematically exposed the land policy of the government which led to the growth of antagonistic classes the peasants and the landlords. In addition, the money-lending class was the offshoot of the government's apathetic attitude towards the agricultural needs of the peasants and their means of subsistence. He also highlighted the extent, and exposed the mechanism of imperial exploitation. All these created an impact on Indian mind, and coming, as it did, from one of the most informed administrators of that time itself, it greatly agitated the public mind.

ASSESSMENT OF THE IMPACT

Referring to the impact of the ideologies of these liberal leaders K. P. Karunakaran points out that these liberal thinkers realised that at least in economic matters the negative approach of the government was not beneficial to India. They advocated for the state assistance or incentive in the spheres of industries and agriculture. And to that extent they stood for the expansion of the role of state (although not for state monopoly). He observes :

... in the interests of an under-developed country like India, the Moderate leaders had no difficulty in reconciling these economic demands with political demands which were in the line with liberalism. Their approach towards this question was pragmatic rather than ideological. Although some of them had a vague sense of social justice and the concept of equitable distribution of income among all the sections of the people, they were not in any sense socialists.[14]

Of course, it will be wide off the mark to suggest that any of the thinkers noted above was conscious of socialist ideology or socialistic approach ; but it is true that economic consciousness generated in the new middle class (mostly of the lower strata) was, to a large

[12] Sitarammayya, *op. cit.*, p. 191.

[13] M. K. Gandhi, *Hind Swaraj*, Ahmedabad, Navajivan, 1958, p. 93.

[14] Karunakaran, *op. cit.*, p. 14.

extent, the work of these men. Through them the Congress also did pave the way for economic regeneration and economic nation-alism in India.

The recent socialist historians of Russia have also acknowledged this fact. Commending their role in generating a socio-economic consciousness in India, Balabushevich and Dyakov observe :

> ...the Congressmen expressed their disapproval of the adverse economic consequences of the colonial rule. This was clearly stated in the works of the first Congress theoreticians—Naoroji and Mahadev Govind Ranade. Naoroji stressed that India's development was being held back because the British were pumping the national wealth out of the country. Ranade indicated that because of the decline in handicrafts India, which had once been an industrial country, was now purely agrarian. Romesh Chandra Dutt, the economist, did much to explain the basis of the demands of the national bourgeoisie.[15]

The extremists and the radicals within the Congress like Bal Gangadhar Tilak and Lala Lajpat Rai were, of course, the main spirit behind the movement of economic nationalism through Swadeshi Movement, especially through the boycott of British goods. With them it was a manifestation of the patriotic cult of nationalism. These trends in the Congress and its ideology led to such an upsurge in the country that it gave a considerable push to the economic aspirations of the people.

Revivalist Ideology

We may now turn to take a stock of the consciousness generated through the socio-religious reform and revivalist movements of the nineteenth century. This had its own relevance in giving direction to the growth of socialism. Firstly, it suggested that the socialist principles and programmes were nothing new and in the ancient socio-economic order the principles of socialism were already present to a considerable extent. Secondly, it acted as a counter against the ideology of Western brands of socialism and drew attention towards their lop-sidedness, un-spiritual basis and too much materialistic concern. Thirdly, the crude method of violent class-war justified under Marxian socialism came to be seriously questioned.

[15] Balabushevich and Dyakov, *op. cit.*, p. 12.

SOCIO-ECONOMIC CONTENT OF THE REFORM MOVEMENTS

The *Brahma Samaj* and the *Prarthana Samaj*, it is true, had not much economic motivation, but through the awakening of social consciousness and the spread of education, such forums did enlighten the ignorant masses considerably and made the people receptive to new ideas. According to B. B. Misra, to some extent, the class which greatly stimulated the revivalist movement was the economically unemployed discontented men of the lower middle classes. To that extent it had some economic content as well.[16]

Raja Ram Mohan Rai, the founder of the *Brahma Samaj* strongly denounced the Hindu caste system and its traditional rigidity. He emphasised the need for liberal and Western education, which went far in softening the crudities of the traditional social life, caste-rigidity, dogmatism and blind beliefs. This created a new social and informed outlook.

From the point of view of the indigenous inspiration to the regeneration of the socio-economic order in India, the revivalist forums, such as the *Arya Samaj*, the Ramkrishna Mission and the Theosophical Society have had more pointed relevance. These movements increasingly looked back to India's traditional heritage, her spiritual basis and her ancient social order. The reformers and philosophers from these folds greatly admired the ancient philosophical as well a institutional bases and did not consider even socialism a novelty.

DAYANANDA SARASWATI

Among such thinkers, the founder of the *Arya Samaj*, Swami Dayananda Saraswati stands out prominently. He was born only six years after the birth of Karl Marx and died in the very year of the death of the latter, *i.e.*, in 1883. While Karl Marx devoted himself to the analysis and solution of the socio-economic maladies flowing from the machine-age capitalism, Dayananda devoted himself to the socio-economic as well as the spiritual depravity of a social order flowing from the orthodox beliefs of a society from within and imperial exploitation from without.

Dayananda was a profound scholar of Sanskrit and developed a deep insight into the Vedic literature and the ancient civilisation.

[16] B. B. Misra, *The Indian Middle Class*, London,1961, p. 371.

He wanted India to 'go back to the *Vedas*.' He worked hard to demolish the image of Brahmins' superiority in society in as much as he tried to uplift the untouchables. Mahatma Gandhi acknowledged his great lagacy in the field of social equality and in the mitigation of the evils of caste-untouchability. If these are at all the concern of the socialists, these were in full measure the objectives of Swami Dayananda and of his organisation—the *Arya Samaj*.

Dayananda's book *Satyartha Prakash* was a strong plea to revive India's culture of the *Vedas* instead of blindly following the ideologies of the West. He derived considerable inspiration from *Manusmriti* and propounded the justification of *Varnashrama Dharma* which some thinkers later on named as socialistic order of the ancient India. His teachings reflect the concept of '*Vaidic Samyavad*'. He also came in contact with the *Brahma Samaj* and the *Prarthana Samaj*, but differed from them, in so far as 'his inspiration was genuinly indigenous and his approach uncompromisingly revivalist.'[17] Thus broadly speaking his philosophy was 'India for the Indians' and it excluded all '...extra-Indians influences, such as Islam, Christianity, and British Government'.[18] He struck at once at the roots of the internal maladies and caste-rigidity as well as the exploitation of India by foreigners. He may be regarded as a pioneer in the field of social equality.

ANNIE BESANT

No less was the contribution of the cumulative ideas of the Theosophical Society, which found in its fold one of the co-authors of the 'Fabian Essays', the Irish born lady, Annie Besant. She made India her field of activity since 1893. Herself a devout socialist at heart, she found in India rich socialistic traditions and found no difficulty in accommodating her original Fabian ideas with those of the Indian revivalist thinkers. Rather her original socialist ideas got tempered with the Indian culture and ware heavily coloured by spiritual theme. She was so profoundly influenced by Indian religion and philosophy that the spiritual and ethical motivation, and not materialistic alone, formed the primary basis of her own socialist ideas.

[17] Misra, *op. cit.*, p. 381.
[18] *Ibid.*, p. 382.

Annie Besant greatly admired the ancient village order of India. She found a corporate life in the ancient village order and its autonomous 'council government'. She pleaded for the revival of the old order so as to improve the position of the peasants who formed the bulk of the Indian society. Her inspiration in this regard came from the study of Kautilya's *Arthashastra*.[19] Probably, one of the objectives of the 'Home Rule League', which she had founded, was also to espouse this cause. She wanted the masses to become conscious of their present condition *vis-a-vis* their condition in the past. She accused the British rule in India of destyoring the ancient village life and its corporate character as well as India's finest art and industries. Behind the plea for 'self-rule' for India, Besant had in her mind the ancient glories of India.[20]

Besant was moved by the poverty of the Indian masses and advocated the economic transformation of society even without the aid of state legislation. For that purpose, she regarded the building up of a sound economic system as vital. It was not just enough to evolve an equitable economic theory, what was required was to make determined efforts for its achievement with a sense of reality and urgency. She reminded :

> You cannot persuade people for the most part to listen very patiently to other sorts of reforms, if they are suffering from pressing physical needs, if their bodies are ill-nourished, if they dwell in slums, if the general conditions of health...are unattainable by them in their daily lives. Disquisition on economics even can hardly interest them unless these Economics point to method of remedy, remedy for which those who speak of it are prepared to work and to bring about in a reasonable time.[21]

The above observation is indicative of her pragmatic approach.

BHAGAVAN DAS

Bhagavan Das, about whom we have spoken earlier, was yet another Indian philosopher within the fold of the Theosophical Society who eulogised the Indian philosophy and the ancient social

---

[19] *Report of the Thirty-second Indian National Congress*, Calcutta, 1917, p. 47.

[20] In a seven-point exhaustive formulation she strongly pleaded the case for 'self-rule' in India.

Annie Besant, *How India Wrought for Freedom*, Adyar, 1915.

[21] Annie Besant, *The New Civilisation*, Adyar, 1928, pp. 84–85.

order. He was a noted scholar of Sanskrit and an original thinker. He was also one of the most prominent exponents of the theme of 'Ancient Scientific Socialism' in India based on the principles of *Varnashrama Dharma*. His pioneer work, *Ancient versus Modern Scientific Socialism* provoked Jayaprakash Narayan to formulate his own 'Marxian' socialist ideas in *Why Socialism?* . J. P.'s main purpose was to repudiate the ideas of Bhagavan Das and others.[22]

THE PRINCIPLES OF MANUSMRITI

As new ideologies from the West came to influence Indian thinking, Bhagavan Das undertook to evaluate them in the context of Indian philosophy and her ancient social order. He reacted sharply to the theories of Capitalism, Fascism and Communism—the doctrines commonly prevalent during the thirties. In contrast to these he eulogised the scheme of Manu as propounded in the *Manusmriti* :

Manu has given us such a technique in his permanent (and not merely five-year or ten-year or twenty-five-year) plan of the Individual Life and the Social Life in combination, for the whole of the Human Race—the only systematic and complete plan...that was known to history until Russian Communism is in the stage of experiment as yet. In that plan are included the fundamental Principles of Planned Education, Planned Family-life, Planned Economy, Planned Defence—Sanitation—Judication, and Planned Religion—Recreation—Art.[23]

Thus it was Manu's social order that appealed to him greatly. However, under the changed circumstances he realised the importance

[22] Also, under the pseudonym 'Shyam Sunder' a series of articles providing stringent criticism of Bhagavan Das's ideas with regard to 'Ancient Scientific Socialism' appeared in the pages of the *Congress Socialist*, the official weekly organ of the C. S. P.
- (i) Shyam Sunder, 'Ancient Socialism', *Congress Socialist*, II (34), Aug. 28, 1937.
- (ii) ——'Ancient Scientific Socialism', *Congress Socialist*, II (35), Sep. 4, 1937.
- (iii) ——'Ancient Scientific Socialism : Static Approach to Dynamic Situation', *Congress Socialist*, II New Series (36), Sep. 11, 1937.
- (iv) ——*Congress Socialist*, II New Series (37), Sep. 16, 1937.

A reply to the series by Bhagavan Das appeared in *Congress Socialist*, III (32), Aug. 6, 1938.

[23] Bhagavan Das, *Ancient Versus Modern Scientific Socialism*, Adyar, Madras, pp. 6–7.

of its adaptation with considerable modifications. The embryonic principles underlying the *Varnashrama Dharma* appeared to him as scientific and universal nature, capable of being applied even to the present mechanised stage of society. He felt that if the *Varnashrama* State, propounded under *Manusmriti*, could be correctly followed the 'conduct of individuo-social and socio-individual life' could proceed smoothly.[24]

In his conceptual evolution it cannot be suggested that Das discovered the principles of socialism in the *Varnashrama Dharma* after he had been confronted with socialist ideology in India during the twenties and thirties, although the timing of the publication of his book as well as its foreword were strongly suggestive of this. His interest in the study of Manu's scheme and his social order can be traced back to as early as 1909, when he had been called upon to address a Theosophical gathering on the subject.[25]

In an evaluation of the *Varnashrama Dharma* and the fourfold division it embraced, he observed that it comprised 'psychologically and universally, the four 'orders', or 'life-stages'.[26] There were two constituents in it the *Varnas* and the *Ashramas*. There was also the third element of *Dharma* (duty). These together fulfilled Manu's scheme of life.

The four *Ashramas* or life-stages were : the student-order, the household-order, the service-order and the ascetic-order. And the four *Varnas* were the teacher, the warrior, the merchant and the labourer. Thus the four *Ashrama*-stages in life alongwith the four *Varnas*, on the basis of four essential vocations or functions in life, constituted the total scheme of Manu's social order.[27] *Dharma* meant performing one's vocational function in life. He observed :

> Such is the Dharma of Manu,...which endeavours to hold together all His progeny, and not only the human kingdom, but the other kingdoms also, so far as may be, in the bonds of soul brotherhood, of mutual love and helpfulness, in the

[24] *Ibid.*, pp. 81–82.
[25] The expanded form of a series of lectures delivered at the Thirty-fourth Annual Convention of the Theosophical Society held at Varanasi from Dec. 27 to 30, 1909 was published later in the form of scholarly treatise in 3 vols. Bhagavan Das, *The Science of Social Organisation*, Adyar (Madras), 1910.
[26] *Ibid.*, I, 105.
[27] *Ibid.*, p. 107.

true spirit of the practical socialism of the joint human family....[28]

While he did not consider any school of socialism to stand in comparison with the *Varnashrama Dharma*, he found the Guild Socialism of the Western conception nearest to the idea. So suggestive it appeared to him that he enlisted an extract from G. D. H. Cole's analysis of Guild Socialism as an appendix to his book on the subject.

With reference to the place of individual and family Das observed :

> ...an individual, as such, is an incomplete personality with unfulfilled destiny, and cannot be regarded as the unit of society. The family is the unit of society. The Family-Home is the first and the best school of true socialism. Without the heart-experience which the Family provides, it is not possible to realise why and how one can and should sacrifice his own ease, health, even life itself, if and as necessary, for any one else. The joint family patently embodies and acts upon the essential principles of socialism, 'To all according to their needs, from all according to their capacities', 'Each for all, all for each'.[29]

Thus the joint family appeared to Das a proto-type of a socialist society and the principles of a joint family likened it to socialism in an embryonic form. This conviction appears to be at the root of Das's thinking.

Das also pointed out that in any scheme of socialism the human nature and the psychological factors were very important. It was necessary that man's spirit was ennobled, which could be possible by discovering the laws of nature and the power latent in man, *i.e.* in 'the Universal Self immanent in all beings'.[30]

BLENDED EMPHASIS ON INDIVIDUAL AND SOCIETY

The socialistic order of society envisaged by Manu, according to Das, had two important characteristics. Firstly, there was a balance struck between the individuo-social and the socio-individual life.

---

[28] *Ibid.*, pp. 110–11. As the above observation was made as early as in 1909, it would not be correct to suggest that socialistic principles in Manu's scheme was an after thought in Das's ideas.

[29] Bhagavan Das, *Ancient vs. Modern Socialism*, p. 60.

[30] *Ibid.*, p. 141.

Secondly, there was a greater emphasis on Society than on political system, *i.e.* State.[31] The state was charged mainly with the responsibility to see that the *Varnashrama Dharma* ran smoothly.

Once *Varnashrama Dharma* was truly followed, equality in wealth and its equitable possession were necessarily to flow from it. In this connection, Das emphasised the need of a sound social order, an order where there were neither rich nor poor but 'one middle class'. Das observed :

> Of course, strict economic or any other equality is impossible, and a monotonous sameness is even undesirable. Evolution is differentiation. But the avoidance of extreme inequality is possible and very desirable.[32]

In order to avoid extreme inequality, it was necessary that multiplication of needs must also be avoided. For that he pleaded :

> Since Capital, in the sense of money as mechanism of exchange, is indispensable, and at the same time excessive accumulation of it in any pair of hands is very dangerous ; since absolute economic equality is impossible, but equitability in the distribution of wealth is necessary ; since without some personal incentive...human beings do not put forth their best, and yet also unrestrained competition is disastrous ; therefore the principles of Ancient Socialism seem to suggest that, in modern conditions, a lower limit or minimum of necessaries, in the way of food, clothing, housing, tools of occupation, should be fixed for all alike, by the Legislature, in accordance with the principle of 'plain living'... (and) 'living wage'.[33]

Das greatly emphasised the need of putting a limit on expenditure and, at the same time, fixing a minimum living wage in society. That implied a process of levelling down of the high-ups in society and levelling up those who lived below the minimum level of existence. A workable and equitable position should be achieved which alone could form the basis of equality in a sound social order. All these were considered to be the virtues of Manu's Code of Law or the 'Ancient Indian Socialism'.

Das has summarised his ideas thus :

> India's slogans should be—not the merely materialist interpretation of History, but 'the Spirituo-Materialist Interpretation of History, since the Universe is obviously

[31] *Ibid.*, pp. 80–84.
[32] *Ibid.*, p. 67.
[33] *Ibid.*, p. 111.

compounded of both Spirit or Mind and Matter, Purusha and
Prakriti ; not Class war,...but 'Class cooperation' through
class-balance and class-reconciliation, not a classless society,
nor a dichotomised Rich-and-Poor Society, nor an infinitely
sub-divided fissiparous Casteful Society, but a 'Society of
Temperamental-Vocational Classes' justly co-ordinated ; not
an utterly homogenous literal Equality in all respects, nor an
utterly heterogenous and grossly iniquitous Inequality, but an
'Equitability' in the partition of different kinds of Work...not
the placing of the necks of whole Peoples under the heels of
single or a few despotic Individuals...nor the crushing of all
Individualities under the steam-roller wheels of Machine-like
Communism or Fascism..., not a sudden and complete National Genius',...not a blind imitation of the latest experiments
going on in any other country, nor a blind clinging to all of
our past without discrimination between its good and its bad...
but a far-sighted and judicious 'Combination of the Old and
the New', 'Respect for old Tradition as well as new Exploration' ; not abolition of Religion and Property and Family, nor
perpetuation of the conditions in which they now are, but
'Purification of Religion, Property, Family',...not unchecked
Capitalism, nor Fascism, nor Bolshevism, but the indigenous
and genuinely philosophical, psychological, 'Ancient time-
tested Scientific Socialism' of the best Indian Tradition.[34]

It was because of such a strong plea by Das to follow the
ancient Indian social order with necessary modifications that J. P.
considered his ideas a serious attempt to provide an alternative to
Western socialism. J. P., however, wholly disagreed with his ideas
during the thirties.[35]

The main criticism against Das was that he did not comprehend
the 'basic ideas of Marxism, viz., the materialist interpretation of
history, the theory of state, the classless society.'[36] With regard to
Manu's or Das's suggestion of fourfold division, J. P. maintained
that it was arbitrary, because social division was an organic process
of society and not a matter of individual choice. The suggestion of
Das that man in a missionary zeal could help the society grow
smoothly and the belief that class-struggle was not necessary appeared
to the critics as thoroughly impracticable ideas. The critics regarded

[34] *Ibid.*, pp. vii–ix.
[35] Jayaprakash Narayan, *Why Socialism ?*, Benaras, The All India
Congress Socialist Party, 1936, pp. 111–26.
[36] *Ibid.*, p. 111.

Das's ideas as a 'static approach to dynamic situation'.[37]

SWAMI VIVEKANANDA

From the fold of the Ramakrishna Mission, Swami Vivekananda emerged to give expression to the socialistic ideas on traditional Indian lines. Probably he was the first Indian thinker to claim in clear terms that 'I am a socialist.' Ever since Bhupendra Dutta depicted him as the first socialist of India in 1929, attempts have been made to trace the roots of socialistic ideas into his writings and speeches.[38]

During his visit to Europe, Vivekananda cultivated intimate knowledge of schools of socialism prevalent then, including Anarchism.[39] He showed a close insight into the origin of socialist doctrine and the original use of the term 'socialism'. He wrote in one of his letters :

> The doctrine which demands the sacrifice of individual freedom to social supermacy is called socialism, while that which advocates the cause of the individual is called individualism.[40]

Vivekananda maintained that in India there has been an eternal subjection of individual to society and self-sacrifice by dint of institution and discipline. The emphasis on society, however, did not mean the lessening of individual's liberty ; liberty was integral to the freedom of the society itself. He considered that liberty was essential for the growth of the individual and it should be permitted not only in the spheres of thought and expression but also in the spheres of food, dress and marriage. In the Indian traditions there has been, a discreet balance between the two.

The socio-economic objectives of Swami Vivekananda appear to have arrested not as much attention as his spiritual and Vedantic teachings. But his concern for the poverty of India was great. A significant aspect of this concern was revealed in Romain Rolland's account of Vivekananda's life. Rolland pointed out that his real

[37] *The Congress Socialist,* New Series (36), Sept. 11, 1937, p. 9.

[38] Atindra Nath Bose, 'Swami Vivekananda : the First Socialist of India', *Janata,* XIII (I), Jan. 26, 1938, p. 27 ; also, see the preface of his collection works : *Caste, Culture And Socialism,* Almora, Advaita Ashrama, 1947, p. i.

[39] He met Kropotkin in Paris in 1900 and also met Plekhanov's partymen in England. Kropotkin was a great anarchist and Plekhanov was a Russian communist. *Ibid.*

[40] *The Complete Works of Swami Vivekananda,* IV, 421.

motive behind going to America was to seek help for the poor in India. He revealed :

> It was the misery under his eyes, the misery of India that filled his mind to the exclusion of every other thought. It consumed him during sleepless nights. At Cape Comorin it caught and held him in its jaws. He dedicated his life to the cause of uplifting unhappy masses. 'It is now my firm conviction that it is futile to preach religion amongst them, without first trying to remove their poverty and their sufferings. It is for this reason—to find more means for the salvation of the poor India—that I am now going to America.'[41]

This was fully indicative of his deep concern with India's poverty and anxiety to remove it by seeking help from the Western countries.

SOCIALISTIC IMPLICATIONS OF THE ORIGINAL CASTE SYSTEM

As a revivalist Vivekananda devoted himself spiritedly to the understanding of the original caste (Varna) system and found it fundamentally not only glorious institution but also socialistic in its very nature. He observed :

> In Indian social order, 'I am born for the caste, I live for the caste...' In other words, in the present day language ... the western man is born individualistic, while the Hindu is social-istic, entirely socialistic, ... so, I have no voice in my marriage, nor my sister. It is the caste that determines all that.[42]

Vivekananda, however, admired the caste system only in the original form and not in the degenerate form in which it existed in the present society. He pitied that not one among a million under-stood what caste was. Caste to him was not a hereditary system, it was purely functional and vocational in character. Since, the modern concept of caste had degenerated and was determined by birth alone, he advocated the destruction of such a caste system. He warned that the *Brahmins*, the *Kshatriyas* and the *Vaishyas* have had their day, and rightly so, but the coming time are now for the *Shudras*. Not that *Shudras* should vocationally and by their knowledge or valour or wealth (the respective qualities of the first three classes) rise to the level of those classes in order to have their sway, but that

---

[41] Quoted in *The Diary of Mahadev Desai*, Ahmedabad, Navajivan Publishing House, 1953, I, 151.

[42] Vivekananda, *Caste, Culture And Socialism*, p. 7.

they would dominate even as *Shudras.*[43]

THE POWER OF THE MASSES

Vivekananda was fully conscious of the strength and the importance of masses, *i.e.* the poor and the downtrodden classes in society. He considered the masses the source of all strength He pointed out :

Whether the leadership of society be in the hands of those who monopolise learning, or wield the power of riches or arms, the source of its power is always the subject masses ... But such is the strange irony of fate ... that they from whom this power is directly or indirectly drawn ... soon cease to be taken into account by the leading class.[44]

Equally conscious he was of the role and the importance of the labourers in society. Referring to them he observed :

If the labourers stop work, your supply of food and clothes also stops ... They have worked so long uniformly like machines guided by human intelligence, and the clever educated section have taken the substantial part of the fruit of their labour... The. lower classes are generally awakening to this fact and making a united front against this, determined to exact their legitimate dues ...

When the masses will wake up, they will come to understand your oppression on them, and by a puff of mouth you will be entirely blown off.[45]

---

[43] He prophetically declared : 'a time will come, when there will be the rising of the *Shudra* class, with their *Shudrahood* ; that is to say, not like that as at present, when the *Shudras* are becoming great by acquiring the characteristic qualities of the *Vaishya* or the *Kshatriya ;* but a time will come, when the *Shudras* of every country, with their inborn *Shudra* nature and habits—not becoming in essence *Vaishya* or *Kshatriya* or socially higher in status in society, but remaining as Shudras—will gain absolute supremacy in every society. The first glow of the dawn of this new power has already begun to slowly break upon the Western world ; and the thoughtful are at their wits' end to reflect upon the final issue of this fresh phenomenon. Socialism, anarchism, nihilism, and like other sects, are the vanguard of the social revolution that is to follow. As the result of grinding pressure and tyranny, from time out of mind, the Shudras, as a rule, are either meanly servile, licking dog-like the feet of the higher class, or otherwise are as inhuman as brute beasts.'

Vivekananda, *Caste, Culture And Socialism,* p. 89 ; also, quoted in, Karunakaran, *op. cit.,* p. 418.

[44] *The Complete Works of Swami Vivekananda,* IV, 403–04.

[45] Vivekananda, *Caste, Culture And Socialism,* pp. 93–94.

He was greatly pained at the lot of the poor and regretted that religion should have been made a cloak to shield its existence. The poor needed to be awakened to the realisation of their miserable conditions. 'They sink lower and lower every day, they feel the blows showered upon them by a cruel society, and they do not know whence the blow comes.' He warned the upper and the rich classes in India not to take pride in their birth or past glory, but to see the trends of time. He warned the rich and upper classes in the strongest terms :

> In this world of *maya*, you are the real illusions, the mystery, the real mirage in the desert, you, the upper classes of India ! You represent the past tense, with all its varieties of form jumbled into one. That one still seems to see you at the present time, is nothing but a nightmare brought on by indigestion. You are the void, the unsubstantial non-entities of the future. Denizens of the Dreamland, why are you loitering any longer ? Fleshless and bloodless skeletons of the dead body of past India that you are—why do you not quickly reduce yourselves into dust and disappear in the air ? Aye, in your bony fingers are some priceless rings of jewel treasured up by your ancestors and within the embrace of your stinking corpse are preserved a good many ancient treasure-chests. So long you have not had the opportunity to hand them over. Now ... in these days of free education and enlightenment, pass them on to your heirs, aye, do it as quickly as you can. You merge yourselves in the void and disappear, and let New India arise in your place. Let her arise—out of the peasant's cottage, ... out of the huts of the fishermen, the cobbler, and the sweeper. Let her spring from the grocer's shop, from beside the oven of the fritter-seller. Let her emerge from the factory, from marts, and from markets. Let her emerge from the groves and forests, from hills and mountains.[46]

Thus he maintained that the upper and rich classes were fundamentally antagonistic to the poor, and therefore, in eventual shape of things to come they were bound to lose against them.

On at least two important points Vivekananda's thinking struck a curious note of similarity with the Gandhian ideas propounded later. One was the need for diffusion of power and the other was the distrust of machine and machine-made products. Referring to the former, he observed :

Accumulation of power is as necessary as its diffusion, or

[46] *Ibid.*, pp. 97–98.

rather more so. The accumulation of blood in the heart is an indispensable condition for life—its non-circulation throughout the body means death ... If this diffusion be withheld, the destruction of that society is, without doubt, near at hand.[47]

This was an evidence that Vivekananda stood for a plural decentralised socio-political order, which has of late been greatly advocated by the socialists.

Referring to machinery and materialism he observed :

Machines never made mankind happy, and never will make. He who is trying to make us believe this will claim that happiness is in the machine, but it is always in the mind.[48]

The maladies of the machine-age civilisation of the West which exercised the minds of Marx and other socialists appeared to Vivekananda as totally blind alley, and hence, fundamentally mistaken. What was distinctive of India was that she never regarded material comforts alone as the real objective of life. He considered it a point of vital difference between the Indian and the Occidental approaches to the real goal of life. He pointed out :

...They (Indians) know that behind this materialism lives the real divine nature of man which no sin can tarnish, no crime can spoil, no lust can taint ; which fire cannot burn, nor water wet, which heat cannot dry, nor death kill ; and to them this true nature of man is as real as is any material object to the senses of an Occidental.[49]

Vivekananda's entire socio-economic approach to human problems was oriented by his deep conviction in the spiritual goal of India.

VEDANTIC IDEALS

Vivekananda did not preach any violent social reform, and instead, he only emphasised the need to revive the Indian society on its old foundation of universal salvation and equality, which had been laid down by the seers and philosophers of India, such as Sankaracharya, Ramanuja and Chaitanya.[50]

He particularly made a strong plea to follow the old Vedantic philosophy and revive the pattern of original, communal and

[47] *The Complete Works of Swami Vivekananda*, IV, 391.
[48] *Ibid.*, p. 151.
[49] *Ibid.*, p. 153.
[50] *Ibid.*, p. 314.

collective sort of Indian living. The Vedantic philosophy, as we shall see, gave a direction to the growth of socialism in India and later some of the Indian socialists including Sampurnanand and Nehru derived great inspiration from Vivekananda's Vedantic teachings.[51]

Vivekananda was opposed to untouchability and believed in the social as well as the religious equality of all men. He was not 'enamoured of a mere economic equality ; rather he stood for a cultural and spiritual fraternity in which there would be not only economic socialism and political freedom, but also moral and intellectual kinship. In short, he did not believe in levelling down, but rather in levelling up.'[52] Thus his motto had been 'From caste to socialism through culture.'[53] He knew well that unless social inequalities were done away with and privileges were given up, class conflict would be inevitable and the upper classes might be 'blown off' completely. He warned that any delay in it would be 'dangerous'.[54]

Although Vivekananda had full knowledge about socialism and the other Western ideologies, he did not choose to affix himself to any dogma. He sincerely believed in the objectives of equality, social justice and welfare of the workers and the poor. He desired the abolition of untouchability and the uplift of the low and downtrodden in society. He was one of the greatest revivalists in India who manifested a deep socialistic concern, 'at a time when Lenin was not known to the world and Russia was still under the heels of the Tsar.' He declared prophetically that socialism in some form or the other was coming on the board. He has been described, therefore, as the 'first socialist' of India.[55]

MAHATMA GANDHI

The formative influences on Gandhiji were derived largely from his family environment. Born in a family of saintly leanings, he

[51] *Ibid.*, p. 314.

[52] Sampurnanand, *Memories And Reflections*, Bombay, Asia Publishing House, p. 10 ; Nehru, *Discovery of India*, pp. 339–41 ; also, Nehru, *Autobiography*, p. 426.

[53] Vivekananda, *Caste, Culture And Socialism*, p. iii.

[54] *Ibid.*, p. iv.

[55] Atindranath, Bose, 'Swami Vivekananda—The First Socialist of India', *Janata* XIII (i), Jan. 26, 1958, p. 28.

grew up 'with an unusually sensitive conscience'.[56] In his very child-hood he was convinced of the essential goodness of man's nature and recollected some sweet reminiscences of human nature.[57] He recorded :

> One thing took deep root in me—the conviction that morality is the basis of things, and that truth is the substance of all morality.... It began to grow in magnitude everyday, and my definition of it also has been ever widening.[58]

Non-violence and Truth were the complementary ideals of his life. He felt that non-violence was such an essential condition of truthful living that it could not be compromised, not even for short-circuiting the process of achieving the freedom of India. Naturally, therefore, in the correctives that he suggested for the socio-economic inequities in society also, the moral fervour recurred again and again.

The men who inspired him most were Tolstoy and Ruskin, and a host of Indian writers and philosophers. Tolstoy impressed upon him the value of physical labour to earn one's daily bread. Inspired by his lofty ideals, Gandhiji founded a 'Tolstoy Farm' in South Africa. He derived from Tolstoy further inspiration for non-violence, non-possession and renunciation in life. The mission to work for the eradication of untouchability from the Hindu society might also have been one of the lessons of Tolstoy's writings.[59]

In Ruskin's *Unto This Last* he found some of his deepest con-victions reflected, and on reading it, he resolved to transform his life after its ideals. Ruskin's denunciation of the lust for wealth and advocacy for productive labour, *i.e.* labour producing 'honey, not spider's web', greatly appealed to him.[60]

There were numerous socio-economic problems with which Gandhiji was confronted in India. As correctives to these problems, Gandhiji put forward certain suggestions and remedies which have,

[56] P. Spratt, *Gandhism*, Madras, The Huxley Press, 1939, p. 8.

[57] M. K. Gandhi, *An Autobiography*, Ahmedabad, Navajivan Publishing House, 1959, p. 157.

[58] *Ibid.*, p. 25.

[59] Derek Kahn, 'Gandhi, Tolstoy and Nonviolence', *Congress Socialist*, I New Series (46), Nov. 7, 1936, pp. 7–8. Also, *Congress Socialist*, I New Series (48), Nov. 21, 1936, pp. 7–9.

[60] V. Lakshmi Menon, *Ruskin And Gandhi*, Varanasi, Sarva Seva Sangh Prakashan, Feb. 1965, pp. 25–26.

of late, been described as the 'Gandhian Socialism' or the 'Indian Way to Socialism'. This may be noted that the expression 'Gandhian Socialism' was coined at a much later stage in the socialistic thinking, by his devout followers and critics alike, but such expression truly originated with his own utterances and the claim that he was a 'socialist' himself.

The word 'socialist' or 'socialism' did not appear in his book *Hind Swaraj*, which he claimed even till the late thirties to have carried all his essential ideas. It was only after his confrontation with the doctrines like communism and socialism, during the twenties and thirties that he often used the expression himself, for his own socio-economic ideas. His claim of being a socialist and communist, however, appears to have been an attempt to impress upon the people generally that there was no novelty in those doctrines. The Indian philosophy and the ancient social order also envisaged socialistic order. He felt that way he could detract the people from being swayed by the Western ideologies.

It is significant to note, that although Mahatma Gandhi spent a number of years in England in 1890s and studied the works of Tolstoy and Ruskin while in South Africa, the theme of Utopian or Christian socialism did not in any way alter his fundamentally Indian way of thinking. Not that he was ignorant of the labour conditions when he wrote *Hind Swaraj* in 1908, but that he was fully alive to the miserable plight of the workers. Even then he considered industrialisation and mechanisation the basic cause of the misery. He observed in *Hind Swaraj* :

> Now thousands of workmen together meet for the sake of maintenance work in factories or mines. Their condition is worse than that of beasts. They are obliged to work, at the risk of their lives, at most dangerous occupations, for the sake of millionaires.[61]

The above observation is fully indicative of the fact that he was neither ignorant of the labourers nor of the millionaires. Yet, even with such keen insight, he was not a convert to the Western schools of socialism. His whole life in South Africa was devoted to the cause of the indentured labourers, and in India also he devoted himself initially to the service of the peasants and the factory labourers. Curiously, however, he manifested no interest in socialism

[61] Gandhi, *Hind Swaraj*, p. 36.

as advocated then. In an address to a mammoth gathering of the labourers in Madras in 1920, he impressed upon them the need to understand the human relations and to learn through proper education 'how far labour can impose its will on the masters.'[62] Coming even so close to the theme of the socialists and knowing well that 'strikes are now in the air to-day throughout the world,'[63] he preferred not to adopt their terminology or to commend the use of strikes.

The earliest knowledge he gathered about the communists in India was in the year 1929 when he interviewed some communists in the Meerut Jail.[64] He had not read any Marxist literature till 1932, rather even till much later period.[65] Even after his study of *Das Kapital* and other communist literature during his prison confinement in 1942, he maintained that the 'communism' of his conception was the only thing that could bring relief to the suffering humanity.[66]

What is being driven at here is that Gandhiji's confrontation with the socialists and communists in India, during the thirties should be taken as the earliest period, wherefrom, 'Gandhi vs. Socialism' or 'Gandhian Socialism' became the theme of intellectual discussion. He elaborated his own ideas and objectives, largely on the 'Eastern Principle' or the ancient scriptural knowledge. And yet, he described his ideas as 'socialism' or 'communism'.

THE SOCIO-ECONOMIC PROBLEMS

Some of the problems that appear to have arrested Gandhiji's notice in India, after his return from South Africa, were typically those that the communists and the socialists claimed as their own. While it would be a long diversion to go depicting all such problems, a few significant problems may be noted here.

[62] *Speeches And Writings of M. K. Gandhi*, Madras, G. A. Natesan and Co., 1922, p. 785.

[63] *Ibid.*, p. 786.

[64] M. K. Gandhi, *Towards Non-violent Socialism*, Ahmedabad, Navajivan Publishing House, 1957, p. 157.

[65] Mahadev Desai, his Secretary asked : 'Bapu, you must read Marx and reply to his argument so as to make a permanent contribution to literature for our young men.' Bapu replied, 'You are right. I also have some such feeling.' *The Diary of Mahadev Desai, op. cit.*, p. 9.

[66] K. G. Mashruwala, *Gandhi and Marx*, Ahmedabad, Navajivan Publishing House, 1960, p. 105 ; the above book contains an article on 'Gandhiji's Communism' by Pyarelal.

While working among the peasants, workers and the masses of Indian society, Gandhiji was greatly affected by the problem of poverty of the masses. The disparity between the rich and the poor appeared to be so great as to command his immediate attention. He realised, probably as clearly as a socialist did, that labourers were not paid their due wages, rather not even their living wage, and were being 'exploited' by the capitalists for their profit-motive only.[67]

He knew that the peasants in India were equal sufferers who were progressively becoming landless. The zamindars exploited their labour for their own ends. Even though the peasants were the tillers of the soil, they were deprived of its natural fruit. His concern was also with that section in society, which had no job, either in the factory or in the field, i.e. with the vast section of the unemployed labour in India which was being driven to starvation and beggary. The problem was not only limited to the poverty of a class, but also wide enough to cover the masses as a whole. This prompted Gandhiji to take up the cause of the masses and not only of classes as such.[68] Gandhiji keenly realised that the real problem of socialism was to bring about equality in society. Indian society, as it stood then, appeared to have been devoid of this ideal in all spheres. He found caste and communal cleavages in the Indian social order. To him, therefore, the urgent task was to bring about social equality in India.

He also found huge economic inequality and antagonistic relation between the capital and labour. Realising all these clearly, he observed in no less socialistic terms than those of the socialists that :

A violent and bloody revolution is a certainty one day unless there is a voluntary abdication of riches and the power that riches give...[69]

Hence economic equality or at least an equitable socio-economic order was the burning need of the time.

Gandhiji's study of the works of Dadabhai Naoroji and Romesh Chandra Dutt and his experiences of the British imperial policies in India convinced him that the capitalist mode of production on a large scale inevitably implied greater industrialisation and imperial

[67] Gandhi, *My Socialism*, p. 11.
[68] *Ibid.*, p. 27.
[69] *Ibid.*, p. 26.

exploitation. Mass scale production brought at once the problem of procuring raw materials and preserving markets for the ready consumption of goods. He found India to be a victim of such a system. Even before he read Marx and socialist literature, it appears, the nature of imperialism and all that it implied remained fully exposed before him.

A significant problem that engaged his attention was the use of big machines and factories on a vast scale in India. The factory-scale production brought its own problems. Millions of hands were dispensed with and the prospect of staggering unemployment of able-bodied persons loomed large. Gandhiji himself put the problem of big scale machinery thus :

> What I object to is the craze for machinery, not machinery as such...Men go on 'saving labour' till thousands are without work and throng on the open streets to die of starvation... Today machinery merely helps a few to ride on the backs of millions. The impetus behind it all is not the philanthropy to save labour, but greed. It is against this consititution of things that I am fighting with all my might....[70]

The problems confronting the modern industrial civilisation, according to Gandhiji, was largely created by big machines. He did concede, however, that some machines might be useful, such as Singer's sewing machine but the factories making such machines must be nationalized and controlled be the state. Some of the problems to which Gandhiji devoted himself were poverty, unemployment, the plight of the labourers and peasants, the social and economic inequality, the imperial exploitation and the problems posed by a machine-age civilisation. These problems, he thought, concerned the socialists too. But the manner in which Gandhiji undertook the task was somewhat different. To him, the ultimate task was not just the mitigation of the socio-economic maladies but also the avoidance, as far as possible, of the degeneration of civilisation and the spiritual degradation.

Gandhiji realised that the socio-economic maladies and inequities of a society were largely the products of the degenerate human nature. The extent to which the human nature could be softened and made amenable to certain values in life, to that extent Gandhiji believed, the socio-economic maladies to be mitigatory.

[70] Gandhi, *Towards Non-Violent Socialism*, p. 28.

He had full faith, however, in the reform of the human nature, hence in the possibility of establishing a socialist society of his own vision. Referring to the Western socialists, he observed : 'when some reformers lost faith in the method of conversion, the technique of what is known as scientific socialism was born.'[71] For himself, Gandhiji fully believed in the method of conversion. He was also convinced that the economic equality, or the material well-being of all, was intimately related to the human nature and its sociability.

Thus the out and out economic concern of the socialists at once became an ethical problem to Gandhiji. No wonder, therefore, that his 'socialism' was couched in spiritual terms and based on the possibility of reform in the human nature.

Believing, as he did, in the fact of social and economic inequality, Gandhi suggested the adoption of the principle of 'trusteeship' in society. Along with it, he also advocated the doctrine of 'renunciation' or 'voluntary poverty'. The twin principles of trusteeship and voluntary poverty were suggested under the over all conviction that correctives to the socio-economic maladies were possible only through a certain disciplining of the human nature. Unless the crudities and the material craze in human nature were softened and tamed to an appreciable degree, a possible or workable corrective to the socio-economic maladies could never be fully evolved.

What was instinctively Gandhian in his suggestions was that he completely disagreed with Marx in his philosophical approach to what man was. With regard to this difference it has been pointed out that

> ... according to Gandhiji the basic principle is life and not matter. Even what we perceive as insentient matter has its being in and by life ; it has no existence independent of it ; at any rate, in the absence of life none can testify to its existence. The universe rises, exists and disappears in life, which alone is....[72]

Gandhiji believed in the existence of soul or of the *Atman* and his belief was firmly anchored to the philosophical knowledge of the *a priori* existence of God—the all-pervasive Life-Force and the ultimate Truth and Reality. This fundamental difference with Marx,

[71] Gandhi, *My Socialism*, p. 3.
[72] Mashruwala, *op. cit.*, pp. 43-44.

who considered matter itself to be the primary entity, combining and giving effect to the consciousness of the being, was at the root of the correctives advocated for the socio-economic maladies. The correctives suggested were ethical and spiritual.

Gandhiji derived another corrective from the ancient social order of India, *i.e.* from the *Varna Dharma*. Like the revivalists, he was convinced that the *Varna Dharma*—implying four-fold division— was based on the socialistic principles of society. The *Varna Dharma* was a testimony to the communal and cooperative order of the Indian society and to the sense of duty (dharma) with which one affixed oneself to life. Gandhiji observed :

> Every person is born with certain definite limitations which we cannot overcome. From a careful observation of those limitations the law of Varna was deduced. It establishes certain spheres of action for certain people with certain tendencies. This avoided all unworthy competition, whilst recognising limitations, the law of Varna admitted of no distinctions of high and low ... my conviction is that an ideal social order will only be evolved when the implications of this law are fully understood and given effect to.[73]

Gandhiji thought *Varnashrama Dharma* ensured 'hereditary skill' and 'limited competition' and it was the 'best remedy against pauperism.'[74] He further maintained that '*Varnashrama Dharma* defines man's mission on this earth ... for the purpose of holding body and soul together ...'[75]

The other solutions put forward by Gandhiji were :

(1) The principle of bread labour,
(2) Decentralisation of power,
(3) The ideal of cooperation, and
(4) Panchayat Raj.

These principles, if followed together in society, could ensure the smooth working of a social order on the basis of equality and justice.

The ideal of society that could be achieved through the solutions or correctives put forward by Gandhiji, was described by him as *Sarvodaya*—the welfare of all. It has already been pointed out that Gandhiji's concern was not only with a class but with the masses as

[73] *Modern Review*, LVIII (3), October 1935, p. 413.

[74] M. K. Gandhi, *Sarvodaya*, Ahmedabad, Navajivan Publishing House 1958, p. 57.

[75] *Ibid.*, p. 56.

a whole. He considered both the poor and the rich to be afflicted with similar maladies—the poor by their poverty and the rich by their lust for wealth, and he pitied both. His ideal, therefore, was *Sarvodaya*, and described it as his concept of 'socialism'.

THE IDEAL OF SARVODAYA

The term *Sarvodaya* was originally used by Gandhiji as the title to the Gujarati rendering of Ruskin's book *Unto This Last*, which in turn also partly supplied, the ideological inspiration for the ideal of *Sarvodaya*.[76] It has been described by some commentators as the 'absolutist version' of the utilitarian principle : 'the greatest good of the greatest number.'[77] But, the comment is not wholly apt ; Gandhiji himself pointed out the difference :

> The greatest good of all inevitably includes the good of the greatest number, and therefore, he (the votary of *Ahimsa*) and the utilitarian will converge in many points in their career, but there does come a time when they must part company, and even work in opposite directions. The utilitarian to be logical will never sacrifice himself. The absolutist will even sacrifice himself.[78]

The difference was indeed vital. Gandhiji conceived *Sarvodaya* as a spiritual ideal, whereas utilitarianism, generally understood, was a philosophy of material and worldly welfare ; at least, it was largely wedded to the realities of life.

Sarvodaya as a spiritual ideal flowed from the firm belief in truth, non-violence and love—the absolute and the sterling virtues of a life believing in God, soul and morality. It was on that basis that this ideal, like the Platonic concept of state, demanded severe tests and virtues from men. *Sarvodaya* envisaged the need for non-possession, voluntary poverty, earning one's bread through physical labour and such other disciplined conducts in life.

On the economic side, *Sarvodaya* envisaged economic equality, equitable distribution of income and above all the spirit of trusteeship, *i.e.* using one's wealth for the good of all. It further implied that land belonged to the tiller only, and to none as an absolute property.

---

[76] Gandhi, *Sarvodaya*, pp. 3-4.
[77] Ganesh Prasad, 'Sarvodaya—a Critical Study', *Indian Journal of Political Science*, XXI (1), Jan.-Mar., 1960, p. 48.
[78] Gandhi, *Sarvodaya*, p. 4.

On the social side, it required the eradication of all forms of social inequality, caste system and untouchability. It also implied the revival of the ancient principle of the *Varnashrama Dharma*.

On the political side, it required a diffusion of power through village panchayats. The *Panchayat Raj* was in fact almost a synonym for the term *Sarvodaya*.[79] It required an active participation of the people in regulating their affairs. He compared *Sarvodaya* with true democracy of a decentralised order in which the men at the bottom level were to play the pivotal role. He observed :

> In this structure composed of innumerable villages, there will be ever widening, never ascending circles. Life will not be a pyramid with the apex sustained by the bottom. But it will be an oceanic circle whose centre will be the individual always ready to perish for the circle of villages, till at last the whole becomes one life composed of individuals, never aggressive in their arragence but ever humble, sharing the majesty of the oceanic circle of which they are integral units.[80]

This clearly envisaged a political order in which the individual was to become the corner-stone, and yet, a fully integral unit within the social whole. This also underlined the necessity of decentralisation of power in a political set-up.

Thus *Sarvodaya* was an ideal mansion propped up on many pillars and each pillar was anchored to a rock-like foundation. It is this picture of Gandhian *Sarvodaya* that has often been referred to as the 'Gandhian Socialism' or the 'Indian Way to Socialism.'[81]

Gandhiji exhibited almost a platonic indifference to the question whether or not his vision could be actually realised in life. He always replied that Euclid's definition of a point could not be ideally attainable, but that alone did not prove its futility.[82]

It is difficult to agree with the suggestions of some orthodox socialists that Gandhiji did not understand the concept of antagonistic classes in society. On the contrary, there are ample evidences in his writing to suggest the fact of such a realisation.[83]

---

[79] *Ibid.*, p. 5.

[80] *Ibid*, p. 70.

[81] Kamala Gadre, *Indian Way to Socialism*, New Delhi, Vir Publishing House, 1966, pp. 27–32.

[82] M. K. Gandhi, *Voluntary Poverty*, Ahmedabad, Navajivan Publishing House, 1961, p. 18.

[83] Gandhi, *My Socialism*, pp. 11-12.

Gandhiji lived at a time when the factory-scale capitalist mode
of production was not only begun in India but was growing in
considerable dimensions. It did not occur to him that concentration of wealth in the hands of a few need any more to be proved
through academic dissertation ; that was a stark reality. He found
it everywhere and took it for granted. Hence, the terms—the value,
surplus value, capital formation, monopoly, etc., did not receive
much attention from him. He was fully conscious that selfish profit-
motive was the main source of wealth accumulated by the capitalist.
He went even further to suggest that all rich men generally adopt
questionable means.[84] He was equally alive to the fact that land
remained undeservedly concentrated into the hands of a few landlords as their private property. He knew that peasants were the
tillers of the land, and yet, the fruit was largely misappropriated
by the landlords. There could be no mistaking about these, whether
he derived such a knowledge through his studies of Marx, or through
his own keen observation, is beside the point here. Gandhiji, however, calculatedly advised against the forcible overthrow of the
capitalist class or the expropriation of the landlords from land.
This was considered enough by the socialists, during the thirties, to
disown him as a 'reactionary'.

The whole strategy of Gandhiji was applied to avert any bloody
revolution between the antagonistic classes, and it is at this point
that Gandhian ideas took decidedly a different turn from the line
that the socialists generally persued during the thirties and forties.
His methods were basically the methods of moral persuation, trusteeship of wealth, *Satyagraha* and non-cooperation with evil.

Thus, if any thing was distinctively Gandhian in the solution
to the problem of antagonistic class interests in society it was the
corrective he suggested and, more particularly, the methodology he
engineered to that end. Pointing out the broad differences between
the Marxian socialism and Gandhian socialism, Kamla Gadre
observes :

> Just as Gandhian socialism differs from the militant socialism
> of the West, so also it differs from Marxism which is often
> confused with socialism. Marxism is based on materialism.
> It finds the key to all social changes in the material basis of
> human life ; Gandhiji, on the other hand, held that the basis

[84] *Ibid.*, p. 24.

of social progress is not matter but mind. Marx proves the inevitability of socialism on economic arguments ; Gandhiji on ethical grounds. Multiplication of wants is a worthy objective according to Marx ; sublimation of wants is Gandhiji's ideal. Class-war and expropriation of private property are the Marxian steps to socialism ; but the Gandhian way is the way of *satyagraha* and trusteeship.[85]

While it may be questioned whether Marx did or did not mean all that was imputed to him under the above citation, the Gandhian position as assessed by her, was more or less a correct appraisal.

THE TWIN PRINCIPLES OF TRUSTEESHIP AND NON-POSSESSION

If Gandhiji disapproved of the forcible overthrow of the capitalists and the dispossession of the landlords from the land, he did not approve of their existence in the form they did either.

He advocated a theory of trusteeship—an ideal that he derived from the Gita. Since 1903, his study of the Gita impressed upon him the ideals of *aparigraha* (non-possession) and *samabhava* (equability).[86] Of course, he took inspiration from the English Law also which impressed on him the ideal of equity. He considered the concept of 'trustee' was inherent in the traditional genius of India and in the Indian philosophy and culture. Thus non-possession and trusteeship were the corollaries of each other. He explained :

> Supposing I have come by a fair amount of wealth—either by way of legacy, or by means of trade and industry—I must know that all that wealth does not belong to me ; what belongs to me is the right to an honourable livelihood, no better than that enjoyed by millions of others. The rest of my wealth belongs to the community and must be used for the welfare of the community. I enunciated this theory when the socialist theory was placed before the country in respect to the possessions held by zamindars and ruling chiefs. They would do away with these privileged classes. I want them to outgrow their greed and sense of possession, and to come down in spite of their wealth to the level of those who earn their bread by labour.'[87]

Gandhiji clearly indicated that whatever be the means of amassing wealth, its use must be limited by the condition of

[85] Gadre, *op. cit.*, p. 27.
[86] Gandhi, *Autobiography*, p. 195.
[87] Gandhi, *Trusteeship*, p. 5.

'honourable livelihood' and 'no better than that enjoyed by millions'. He asked the rich to 'come down' to earn their right to bread through physical labour. The theory of trusteeship, therefore, was intended to serve as a double-eged sword—to cut off the grounds for the socialists to preach class-war in society and to deprive the rich of their sense of possession and the greed for wealth. The psychological factor introduced through this theory [was not of less importance. It impressed upon the rich the questionability of amassing wealth and made them suffer the complex of adverse public reaction against the excessive possession of wealth. The fact that force was not to be used against them did not imply that social pressure could also not be made to bear upon them. Gandhiji emphatically declared that 'if the rich do not become trustees of their own accord, force of circumstances will compel the reform unless they court utter destruction.'[88] Therefore, he was not even averse to the idea of statutory trusteeship', provided the people at the bottom initiated the move through their village panchayats.'[89]

Gandhiji stressed equally on the need to evolve the spirit of renunciation or non-possession. This he also described as 'voluntary poverty'. He considered it to be the native genius of India to live by abdication of riches. He advised everyone not to bother about the 'morrow' and not to be crazy about hoarding. Voluntary poverty was a 'blessed' thing ; it ensured simple living and high thinking ; it was largely a matter of discipline and control over palate. Even more than things possessed, the important thing was the spirit behind possession. He reminded that 'you will take for your house not many mansions, but the least cover you can do with. And similarly with reference to your food and so on.'[90]

Voluntary poverty involved the idea of doing away with the superfluities and not the essentials of life.[91] Keeping anything without need was a sort of an act of theft.[92] The principles of trusteeship and voluntary poverty taken together were intended to keep the path of life straight and smooth. Trusteeship from without and voluntary poverty

---

[88] M. K. Gandhi (edited by V. B. Kher), *Econonomic And Industrial Life And Relations*, Ahmedabad, Navajivan Publishing House, 1957, I, pp.191–92.

[89] Gandhi, *Trusteeship*, pp. 6–8.

[90] Gandhi, *Voluntary Poverty*, p. 5.

[91] Gandhi, *Sarvodaya*, p. 92.

[92] Gandhi, *Voluntary Poverty*, pp. 14–15.

from within were intended to squeeze the volume of inequality in society to the minimum equitable level of existence. Sheer dispossession of private property, violently or non-violently, could not achieve the goal of equality, until the urge for possession also was subdued. The Gandhian correctives were aimed at both.

FAITH IN THE POSSIBILITY OF REFORM

As has already been indicated Gandhiji fully believed in the essential goodness of human nature. He considered the Western socialism to have been fundamentally different from his own, in so far as, it believed in the essential selfishness of human nature, whereas he believed in its essential goodness. He believed that an individual could be reformed, and similarly a society too. Pointing out the difference between Gandhism and Western socialism, Rajendra Prasad observed :

> Socialism does not give any importance to the reform of the individual apart from society. It aims at organizing society and binds the individual to that order. We all know that society is composed of individuals...Gandhism maintains that society can be reformed only by reforming the individual and bettering his lot.[93]

It was this conviction that made Gandhiji to work and preach differently from the socialists who professedly believed in the inevitability of class-war. For himself, he believed only in the possibility (not inevitability) of class-war, and, probably, more so in the possibility of its avoidance, provided a certain disciplined conduct of life was evolved and pursued.

Yet, the whole thing hinged on the possibility of its not behave success, supposing the reform did not succeed, the rich did as expected, and did not become the real 'trustees'. What was to be done—was the moot point ; particularly when the door to class-war was firmly bolted. As an answer to this problem, Gandhism stood and stands unique in its own way.

GANDHIAN METHODOLOGY

At the outset, it may be suggested, Gandhiji believed that the way out to the above problem was incorporated in the principles and

---

[93] Rajendra Prasad, *Legacy of Gandhiji*, Agra, Shivlal Agrawal and Co., (P) Ltd., 1962, p. 57.

institutional bases of the ancient Indian social order. The intelligent revival of the old order could go a long way to find the needed remedy. Gandhiji asserted :

> Class war is foreign to the essential genius of India, which is capable of evolving communism on the fundamental rights of all on equal justice....Our socialism or communism should, therefore, be based on non-violence and on harmonious co-operation of labour and capital, landlord and tenant.[94]

In this connection he largely derived his inspiration from the native genius of India and reminded :

> Let us not be obsessed with catchwords and seductive slogans imported from the West. Have we not our distinct Eastern tradition ? Are we not capable of finding our own solution to the question of capital and labour ? What is the system of Varnashrama but a means of harmonizing the difference between high and low, as well as between capital and labour ?...I have been a sympathetic student of the Western social order and I have discovered that underlying the fever that fills the soul of the West there is a restless search for truth...Let us study our Eastern institutions...and we shall evolve a truer socialism and a truer communism than the world has yet dreamed of.[95]

Therefore, Gandhiji put more reliance on the revival of the principles behind the ancient social order and in the pursuit of the Eastern traditions.

He also advocated the method of *satyagraha* or civil resistance as an alternative to class-war. It had two basic aspects the one to non-cooperate with the evil in society in whatever form, and, the other, to fight non-violently against the social system which generates that evil. Non-cooperation was to rouse the consciousness about the 'wrong' in the opposite party or person, and the *satyagraha* was the 'weapon of love' which the civil resister was to wield against the other party or person, after 'having flung aside' the sword of violence.[96] These provided according to him, more effective weapons to bring about the desired end without any class-war.

Gandhiji believed that *satyagraha* could be launched not only on an individual basis but even on a mass basis. It is beyond our scope to go into its whole strategy ; what is important is to bear in mind that

[94] Gandhi, *Sarvodaya*, p. 94.
[95] *Ibid.*, pp. 95–96.
[96] *Ibid.*, p. 81.

the mass-method, at least, in the context of that period, was novel
and had remained confined to the armoury of the social reformers.
It was later that socialists discovered its effective use for the cause
of socialism. It was one enduring contribution of Gandhiji to the
field of socialist methodology.

SOCIALISTIC IMPLICATIONS OF THE PROGRAMMATIC
ASPECTS OF GANDHIAN THINKING

Gandhiji, being an idealist, as well as a realist suggested many
constructive programmes, the significance of which was lost upon the
socialists during the thirties. Among these were the use of Khaddar
and the spinning wheel, the eradication of untouchability, the revival
of village panchayat and cottage industries and such others.[97]

The implications of a few of the programmes mentioned above
may be indicated here so as to provide an insight into their socialistic
importance. No less a socialist than G. D. H. Cole observed about
Khaddar :

(It was) not a mere fad of a romantic eager to revive the past
but a practical attempt to relieve the poverty and uplift the
standard of the Indian villages.[98]

It may also be noted that its impact on the Lancashire mills
and its workers was so devastating that when Gandhiji visited
England in 1931, he was surrounded by the unemployed workers,
women and children, with grievances against the launching of the
Khaddar movement by him.[99]

J. B. Kripalani, explained the socialistic implication of Khaddar
thus :

The essence of socialism consists in its theory (right or wrong)
of surplus value. It is through this surplus value that the
exploitation of the masses is carried on. Surplus value takes
the forms of profit, rent, and interest. An industry or business
that leaves no surplus value, that is, has no room for profit,

[97] Richard B. Gregg, *Which Way Lies Hope ?*, Ahmedabad, Navajivan
Publishing House, 1957, pp. 185–206. Gregg provides a comparative study of
Gandhian programmes vis-a-vis capitalism and communism and establishes
the superiority of the former.

[98] Quoted in Hiren Mukerjee, *Gandhiji—A Study*, New Delhi, Peoples
Publishing House, 1960, p. 216.

[99] Tendulkar, *op. cit.*, III, p. 155.

rent or interest, must be considered socialistic.[100]

And, that way he maintained that 'the whole of Khadi industry is a socialistic experiment and a socialistic venture.'[101]

To Gandhiji, the basic tool of Khaddar, that is *Charkha* or the spinning wheel was only a symptomatic aspect of his broad philosophy of non-violence and love. A true *Satyagrahi* could not do without *Charkha* and *Takli*. He observed :

> Life based on non-violence....must be reduced to the simplest terms consistent with high thinking...For non-violent defence... society has to be so constructed that its members may be able as far as possible to look after themselves in the face of an invasion from without or disturbances within...the 'takli' or at most the spinning wheel and the loom are the simplest possesions for the manufacture of cloth. Society based on non-violence can only consist of groups settled in villages in which voluntary cooperation is the condition of dignified and peaceful existence ...If the 'Charkha' can bear the ample interpretation I have put upon it, it becomes the most effective weapon in the armoury of Satyagraha. The weak thread from the wheel binds the millions in an unbreakable cord.[102]

Hence *Charkha* was considered integral to his broad philosophy of non-violence and love. It was conceived also as the instrument or the weapon of the non-violent *satyagrahi*.

Similarly, the fight against untouchability was a vital programme of Gandhiji's social philosophy. It has been compared with 'Tolstoy's attempt to purify Christianity, his association with the Stundists, the Doukhobors, and other peasant non-conformists.'[103] Julius Braunthal, a British socialist, compared it with the Negro question in the USA which was frankly conceived to be an economic and socialistic issue.[104] Gandhiji knew that such social cleavages, like untouchability, could make it impossible for India to rise in the scale of civilisation, and if 'untouchability stays Hinduism goes.'

[100] J. B. Kripalani, *Gandhian Thought*, New Delhi, Gandhi Smarak Nidhi, 1961, p. 6.

[101] *Ibid.*, p. 7.

[102] Quoted in N. N. Mitra, *The Indian Annual Register*, Calcutta, The Annual Register Office, Jan.–June 1940, I, 224.

[103] Derek Kahn, 'Gandhi, Tolstoy and Non-violence', *The Congress Socialist*, I, New Series (48), Nov. 21, 1936, p. 7.

[104] Julius Braunthal, 'The Negro Question in the U. S. A.' *Congress Socialist*, II (14), April, 10, 1937, pp. 9–10.

Eradication of untouchability, therefore, was the vital need towards achieving the socialist objective of equality. The social philosophy of Gandhiji could not permit scope for caste, colour, sex, or any other such social discrimination.

Thus, programmatically also, the constructive programmes of Gandhiji had great socio-economic significance which the Indian socialists did not realise during the thirties. Curiously enough, however, the government did not fail to notice its far reaching consequences from the beginning.[105] Referring to the substitution of the 'labour' franchise by the 'spinning' in the constitution of the Congress and to the proposal for creating an All-India Village Industries Association, at the suggestion of Gandhiji, a top authority of the Government appraised the situation thus :

> ...a 'labour' franchise shall be substituted for a 'spinning' franchise...This reorganisation seems primarily intended to bring Congress into close connection with rural areas, a point of considerable importance if taken with the proposals for the Village Industries Association.[106]

The said authority took note of the critic's point of view that Gandhiji 'was devoting undue attention to social rather than political question.' He reported that his constructive programmes might lead to the infiltration of his ideas into the villages and, thereby, to bring the villages closer to him and the Congress workers.[107] Thus, it had considerable political significance.

In short, it may be suggested that the Gandhian ideas were full of socialistic significance, although the yardstick for such assessment could not be had from among the traditionally existing ones, such as, Utopianism, Marxism, or Communism. Gandhian ideas were unique, and, largely, indigenous in nature.

We shall see, as we proceed, that in the vision of Indian socialism, particularly since Independence, Gandhism provided the brighter phase of the socialist coin while the other phase, Marxism, lost its lustrous glitter.

[105] See File No. 3/16/34 Poll., Govt. of India, Home Deptt. ; the above file contains a letter of M. G. Hallett, Secretary to the Government of India to all Local Governments and administrations.

[106] *Ibid.*, para 4.

[107] *Ibid.*, para 9.

3

THE PIONEERS OF INDIAN SOCIALISM

I. Ideology Of The Trade Union Leaders

IN ONE OF the earliest books available with regard to socialism in India, published in 1919, it has been pointed out that socialism in the Western sense had not yet touched the depth of Indian society, however, the trend of its future growth in India appeared to be well-nigh certain.[1] Sampurnanand has also opined that before 1922 not much was known about socialism, and the available literature was scanty.

It was only after 1922 that some Marxist publications were started, and shortly after the Kanpur Conspiracy Case was over the Communist Party of India came to be organised. Some secret Marxist literature was also used to be smuggled in India through M. N. Roy. These generated the initial consciousness towards Marxian or Western socialism. Some even hold the view that the Kanpur Conspiracy Case was itself responsible for generating such consciousness in India.[2]

The initial impact of the communist ideology was manifest in the fold of the trade union movement. Of course, the lead even in this sphere was given by the intellectuals and the political leaders, most of whom were intimately related with the Indian National Congress itself.

Jawaharlal Nehru, who has often been described as the first socialist in the Congress, conceded that the trade unions were the

[1] D. Pant, *Socialism, Its Embryonic Development in India*, Lahore, 1919, p. 112.

[2] J. C. Dikshit, 'Communism in Indian Labour Movement', *The Indian Worker*, XII (45 and 46), Nov. 2, 1964, p. 14.

pioneers of socialist ideology in India. Hence, at the outset, it will be appropriate to refer to the socialistic ideas as they percolated through the trade union forums.

Some philanthropic type of labour organisations existed in India since 1875. The men who played prominent part in organising these bodies apart from the political leaders, were the humanitarians like S. S. Bengalee, P. C. Mazumdar, Sasipad Banerjee and N. M. Lokhandey. It was only since the organisation of the Madras Labour Union in 1918, under the guidance of B. P. Wadia, that the real period of trade unionism began in India. Besides Wadia the pioneers were men like Joseph Baptista, Lala Lajpat Rai, N. M. Joshi, V. V. Giri and Dewan Chamanlal.

WADIA AND BAPTISTA

B. P. Wadia was a theosophist and was greatly influenced by Annie Besant. It has been revealed that he got the initial impetus to organise Labour Unions on British model from Besant herself. He disliked the too much materialistic bias in the Indian labour movement. Joseph Baptista was also clearly inclined towards the ethical and spiritual values of life and the ideology of the British Fabianism. As the Chairman of the reception committee of the first AITUC Session in 1920, he observed :

> ...the supreme need of the moment is really for some light from the East to illumine the darkness of the West ; for the humanising spiritualism of the East, to chasten the brutalising materialism of the West.[3]

Again, in his presidential address to the second session of the AITUC, he pleaded with conviction that the Indian labour should neither follow the too much individualistic line, nor the Bolshevik design, but stick to the golden path of Fabian socialism. Thus on both Wadia and Baptista, Marxism or communism had no impact.

LALA LAJPAT RAI

The same trend had been manifested in other leaders also. Lala Lajpat Rai, during his exile in America, had come in contact with a host of European and American radicals and socialists includ-

---

[3] *Report of The First Session of AITUC*, p. 17. Also quoted in Sinha, *op. cit.*, p. 49.

ing M. N. Roy and his wife. He, however, was a staunch critic of the communist doctrine and had been greatly influenced by the ideology of the British Labour Party. He was also been one of the initial organizers of the Arya Samaj in Punjab, to the socio-economic ideas of which he thoroughly subscribed. Thus complex influences worked upon him and convinced him about the superiority of the spiritualistic ends of the Indian life as against the materialistic goals of Western civilization. He was full of praise for the ancient ideal of emphasising the spiritual needs of the soul more than the material needs of the body.[4] He was conscious of the degeneration and degradation of the Indian Society, which had fallen from its ancient concept of duty, *i.e.* 'dharma'. While he was not categorical about the solution that could be employed in the Indian conditions, yet he did move on progressive lines. He wrote in a letter :

> How to get rid of the existing demoralisation, build up life and society on a true basis of Dharma with substantial justice, social, political and economic to all, I do not yet know. One thing, however, I am certain, viz., that you cannot build up a society like that with competition as foundation. What we can do is to preach the gospel of cooperation, and try to put it in practice as far as possible by giving right ideas and organising for purposes of cooperation among the poorer classes of our countrymen, the peasants and the workers. All classes of people must feel that salvation will come from within, with co-operation, mutual help and mutual trust, and not from without...[5]

This was indicative of his progressive ideas, and it also emphasised the need for cooperation as the basis of organizing society. It may be recalled that his realisation that competition could not be the basis for solution, or that the salvation to the socio-economic maladies could be had only through cooperation were such ideas which were not different from those emphasised by Mahatma Gandhi himself.

On his return to India in 1920, he was naturally looked upon with hope and inspiration by the working classes. The First Session of the AITUC which took place in that year, met under his presidentship. In the course of his address, he observed :

---

[4] Lala Lajpat Rai, *India's Will to Freedom*, Madras, Ganesh and Co., 1921, p. 76.

[5] *Ibid.*, pp. 81–82.

This modern world is characteristically a world of machinery of steam, gas and electricity. This is a world of mass production, of organized capital, organized industry and organized labour. Organized mass production involves the organization of capital, and the organization of labour on a scale never heard of before. So far organized capital has had its way. It has ruled the world for the last 150 years, and the world today is groaning under its burden. It has destroyed many an old civilization, enslaved religion, chained science and placed in bondage all the forces of nature and human intellect.... It is only lately that an antidote has been discovered and that antidote is organized labour.

We in India have been rather slow to find and apply this antidote. The reasons are obvious. We were politically impotent and economically helpless.

There is no one in India who believes that the European and Russian standards of labour can be applied to India of today. If there were any, I would remind him or them of the message of Lenin to Bela Kun wherein the former warned the latter against the danger of applying Russian standard to Hungary prematurely. For the present our greatest need in this country is to *organize, agitate and educate. We must organize our workers, make them class-conscious, and educate them in the ways and interests of commonweal.*[6]

The two obvious themes of the address cited above are the critical analysis of the evils of world capitalist system and the need in India for independent labour organization. For this he wanted a free access to socialist literature of the world and had a dig at the government for preventing such an access to the Indian people.

He reminded the Labour Unions of the 'hoary civilisation' and the 'mighty spiritualism' of India and made them aware of the destruction that the Western capitalist system had brought about for the country. Even though engaged in labour welfare which usually requires the growth of industries, he showed disbelief in too much industrialisation of the Indian society. He observed,

India will not be a party to any scheme which shall add to the powers of the capitalist and the landlord and will introduce and accentuate the evils of the expiring industrial civilisation into our beloved country.[7]

[6] Quoted in Karunakaran, *op. cit.*, pp. 425–26, 433–34.
[7] Lala Lajpat Rai, *The Political Future of India*, New York, B. W. Huebsch, 1919, p. 201.

He criticised Marxism for holding the inevitability of the capitalistic stage of development for every country. He was convinced that Indian conditions were different and therefore, labour and capital were both to cooperate as equal partners.

N. M. Joshi was another labour leader of that time and also the first nominated delegate (by the government) to represent the Indian labour at the International Labour Conference in Washington in 1919. He was a great admirer of the ideals of the British Labour Party and even wanted to organise an Indian Labour Party on similar lines. He developed personal contact with the British Labour Party leaders and came in contact with a number of communists in England and America, yet he remained convinced of the ideals of moderation, as represented by the British Labour Party. He chiefly relied upon the strategy to use the Central Legislature for ameliorating the labourer's miserable plight, and to that end, he even desired to keep the labour organizations separate from the Congress and its nationalist leaders. A similar moderate attitude was displayed by both V. V. Giri and Dewan Chamanlal also, who were among the recognised labour leaders in the Congress.

In short, during the initial period of trade unionism in India after the First World War, spiritual ends as well as material objectives were together advocated as the objectives of the labour organizations and the AITUC. The tilt of emphasis was primarily on the spiritual rather than on the material goal ; secondly, the ideology of the British Labour Party and Fabianism, i.e., of moderation and constitutionalism, inspired Indian socialism more than the ideology of Marxism or Communism.

TRADE UNIONISM SINCE 1927

N. M. Joshi and Dewan Chamanlal were inclined more to work through close cooperation with the government, and they objected to the affiliation of the AITUC with the League, against Imperialism and the Pan-Pacific Trade Union Secretariat, which they regarded as communist-sponsored organizations.[8] This was the beginning of a rift within the Labour fold and the trend towards

[8] League against Imperialism was formed at the Congress of Oppressed Nationalities which met at Brussels in 1927, and Jawaharlal Nehru served for some time on the executive committee of that body ; Pan-Pacific Trade Union Secretariat was a communist-sponsored and communist-dominated body.

rift which started since 1927, grew further ever since. Jawaharlal Nehru pioneered the formation of the Indian League against Imperialism and was elected the president of the AITUC in 1928. As he was considered by them to have Marxist leaning, the trend of split within the labour fold came to a climax. Finally, it broke into two wings : the AITUC (the parent body) as the left, and the Indian Trade Union Federation (ITUF) as the right wing. The latter wing was founded and led by Joshi and Chamanlal.

It is only since 1928, *i.e.*, the election of Nehru as the president of the AITUC that radical ideology on socialist lines, inclining it a little towards Marxian or communistic lines, came to be advocated through the forum of the trade unions. Jawaharlal then, to an extent, gave expression to radical socialist ideology, although he was not a convert to Marxism, as such. During this period he found valuable support from Subhash Chandra Bose also.

Jawaharlal's return from the Brussels Congress of 1927, therefore, marks the real turning point in the growth of a little radical socialist ideology both in the Indian National Congress and in the Indian trade union movement. It is for this reason that he has often been described as the pioneer of socialism in India.

However, before we turn to Jawaharlal Nehru and his socialist ideas, a reference need be made to Subhas Chandra Bose, who gave him valuable support in the trade union movement as well as in the Congress.

SUBHAS CHANDRA BOSE

Subhas Chandra Bose, the radical leader from Bengal and a representative of the militant cult of Indian nationalism, gave valuable support to Nehru in his radical as well as socialistic ideas. Ever since the Madras Congress of 1927, he supported Nehru in piloting the 'Independence' Resolution and lent support in forming the Indian League for Independence. During this period he, along with Nehru, was among the two radical left-wingers who made a whirlwind tour of the country organizing and addressing various youth leagues, students and workers unions, all over the country. After Nehru had resigned the presidentship of the AITUC, following his election as the President of the Congress in 1929, Bose took up the presidentship of that body himself.

Ideologically, however, Bose appeared as not having been influenced by Marxist or communist ideology as much as Nehru then was, but he was decidedly a left-winger and a radical. He had also positive sympathy for socialist ideology, if that was not to be a copy of Russian Communism or Marxism. He considered Nehru's views to be 'fundamentally wrong', in so far as the latter had limited the choice of the world between communism and fascism alone, with preference to the former over the latter.[9] For himself, he conceived some sort of synthesis between the two as the probable ideal. He described his own ideal as *Samyavada* implying by it a synthetic doctrine of equality.

He also discarded Gandhism as an alternative to socialism or communism. To him it appeared that Gandhiji gave a new method of passive resistance and *satyagraha*, but did not give any programme for social reconstruction, as communism did. In that context even Gandhism was no alternative to socialism.[10]

But Bose expected some good from the birth of the CSP in 1934, although, like Nehru, he did not join it. He, however, considered that 'the instinct that has urged the formation of the party is right.'[11]

An important aspect of Bose's thinking was his deep inclination towards or affinity with the Indian history and culture of the past. It has been pointed out that he conceived Indian socialism as a 'synthesis of matter and spirit, of material and spiritual values, which is the basic spirit of Indian culture.'[12] He also hoped that 'it may be that the form of socialism which India will evolve will have something new and original about it, which will be of benefit to the whole world.'[13] Bose realised that the socialist thought from the West was influencing India, but it was because the past had been forgotten. He observed :

...we have lost the the thread of our own history.... It would ...be folly to rely for enlightenment of thought on Russia. We

[9] Subhas Chandra Bose, *The Indian Struggle*, Bombay, Asia Publishing House, 1964, p. 313.

[10] *Ibid.*, p. 316.

[11] *Ibid.*, p. 283.

[12] Anil Roy, 'Netaji's Political Philosophy', *Janata*, VIII (33), Sept. 13, 1953, p. 7.

[13] *Ibid.*

64

shall build our own society and politics according to our own needs...socialism did not derive its birth from the books of Karl Marx. It has its origin in the thought and culture of India.[14]

Bose even drew a ten-point programme for a Socialist Party in India, which could be of use for its future programme and action.[15] From these programmes it can be gathered that even though he was a radical leader of that time, who generally sympathised with the socialist ideology, he basically thought on similar lines, which we have referred to earlier as indigenous roots of Indian socialism :

It will seek to build up a new social structure on the basis of the village communities of the past, that were ruled by the village 'Panch' and will strive to break down the existing social barriers like caste.[16]

The above programme clearly indicated that Bose had deep affinity with the ancient bases of Indian social order, and he also wanted to strive for social equality, the absence of which was at the root of the socio-economic maladies in Indian society.

He was certain that the ideology like communism could not flourish in India, and the most important reason he cited was its anti-national approach. One of his significant observations was that

...the materialistic interpretation of history which seems to be a cardinal point in Communist theory will not find unqualified acceptance in India, even among those who would be disposed to accept the economic contents of Communism.[17]

With all his affinity with the Indian culture and the past heritages of India, Bose was modern in his approach. He was closely acquainted with the Western currents of socialism. Unfortunately, owing to his deep involvement in the radical politics of the time and the struggle for independence, he was probably deprived of the chance of giving any detailed and calculated thought on socialism, for which he had evidently cultivated strong sympathy. He maintained that 'salvation of India as of the world depends on socialism.'[18] But, like Nehru, he also considered that independence was a prior issue to that of socialism or any other 'ism'.

[14] *Ibid.*
[15] Bose, *op. cit.*, p. 312.
[16] *Ibid.*, p. 312.
[17] *Ibid.*, p. 315.
[18] L. N. Sarin, *Studies of Indian Leaders*, Delhi, Atma Ram and Sons, 1963, p. 114.

II. Jawaharlal Nehru

FORMATIVE INFLUENCES

Born in 1889, Jawaharlal Nehru grew in his own estimation, in a family environment of a 'petite bourgeoisie.' He was tutored privately by English governesses at home and, at the tender age of fifteen, sent to England for better and higher education. His father Motilal Nehru was a first rate lawyer deeply influenced by the English ways, its modes and manners of civilisation and its language. This initial westernisation of Jawaharlal, through English education, familial environment, and above all, contact with the British morals and manners inculcated in him from the beginning a great admiration for the Western ideologies in many spheres.

One of the earliest family tutors of Jawaharlal, Ferdinand T. Brooks, was a theosophist, who revealed to him the contents of many Hindu scriptures—the *Upanishads*, the *Bhagvadgita*, and *Dhammapada*, apart from other theosophical literature containing mysterious secrets of life and the universe. He was also greatly affected by the speeches of Annie Besant, and, while yet a boy of thirteen, he was accepted as a member of the Theosophical Society.

In May 1905, Nehru left for England for education but a series of events occurred which greatly agitated and affected him. Those were the Russo-Japanese War and the Partition of Bengal of 1905, the 'Self-Rule, (Swaraj) resolution of the Indian National Congress of 1906, and the Swadeshi movement that followed in its wake. The radicalisation that flowed from these developments in India, touched him, as it touched many other Indian youth of his times.

It was during this period that he came in contact with the ideas of Fabian socialism and developed interest in persons like George Bernard Shaw, Bertrand Russell and the British economist, Keynes. He also read about nationalist leaders like Mazzini, Cavour and Garibaldi. It is important to recall, however, that he developed interest in 'Utopian socialism' only, and not in 'Scientific socialism' at this stage, and even this 'was all very academic'. Probably, his interest was due to a vague feeling that in such socialist ideologies there was implied the idea of anti-colonialism.[19] Thus, the initial inspiration towards to socialist ideology appers to have been incul-

---

[19] Tibor Mende. *Conversations with Nehru*, Bombay, Wilco Publishing House, 1958, p. 13.

cated in him because of his feeling that socialism was a theory and practice which helped in denouncing colonialism, a burning urge of the Indian youth then.

On his return to India in 1912, Nehru joined Allahabad Bar, found the political climate 'dull', partly because of the split of the Congress in 1907 into the radicals and the modrates, and partly due to the long term imprisonment of Bal Gangadhar Tilak and the externment of Lala Lajpat Rai. The moderates in the Congress pinned hopes on 'the Minto-Morley schemes of councils'.[20] Nehru's own inclination was more towards the radicals in the Congress ; this was indicated in his letters to his father around 1908. One reason for his dislike of the moderates was that 'they did not think in terms of economics; except in terms of the new upper middle class which they partly represented and which wanted room for expansion.'[21]

Nehru had developed a modern and scientific attitude through education and contacts, and wanted that social, economic and religious outlook of life ought to change under scientific knowledge of the West. Hence, he was critical of the Hindu religious nationalism and revivalism. In this respeet, probably, he was the first socialist who came with strong Westernised inspiration and denounced the habit of 'looking back'. He wanted both Hinduism and Islam to look to things from the point of view of newer ideas and forces. Thus modernism as a basic ingredient was injected into the Indian politics through him in a more consistent and concentrated form. He himself expressed this trend, 'India was in my blood and there was much in her that instinctively thrilled me...yet I approached her almost as an alien critic, full of dislike for the present as well as for many of the relics of the past that I saw. To some extent I came to her via the West....'[22]

It was broadly under this frame of mind that he found India compulsorily dragged in the War, for she 'was forced to toe the line of her imperialist mistress.' It was during the War, that Home Rule League was started and there was a renewed life in the Congress. Mahatma Gandhi had also come back from Africa and joined the

[20] Nehru, *Autobiography*, p. 27.

[21] Quoted in, Dorothy Norman, *Nehru*, Bombay, Asia Publishing House, 1965, I, 27.

[22] Nehru, *Discovery of India*, p. 37.

Indian politics. The moderates and the extremists arrived at a compromise and the Lucknow Congress of 1916 met under some new hope and inspiration. It was, broadly after this, and more particularly after the Rowlatt Act, the Jallianwala Bagh massacre, and the Khilafat Movement that Nehru found himself drawn in the very vortex of the national struggle. It was during this period that he came in contact with Gandhiji who had started taking active interest in the affairs of the nation.

While making an assessment of the role of the moderates and the extremists in the Congress Nehru made a significant observation which is very much suggestive of his socialistic leanings. He wrote about the essential difference between the Moderates and the Extremists. The former were a prosperous party of the Haves and some hangers-on of the Haves, and the Extremists had a number of Have-nots also and, as the more extreme party, naturally attracted the youth of the country, most of whom thought that strong languge was a sufficient substitute for action. *But neither the Moderates nor the Extremists had anything to do with real Have-nots, the workers and the peasants.*[23] It was in such a mood, when he was not yet reconciled fully to the moderates or the extremists in the Congress and was looking forward for some form of aggresive action, although not clear as to what form of action he contemplated then, violent like the Bengal terrorists or some other, that the success of Gandhiji in Champaran and Bolshevik Revolution in Russia thrilled him with new hope. He is reported to have expressed himself that 'I was simply bowled over by Gandhiji, straight off.'[24] What he admired in Gandhiji was his service to the cause of peasant and workers of India, a cause dear to all socialists. To him, Gandhiji signified :

> Get off the backs of these peasant and workers,...all you who live by their exploitation ; get rid of the system that produces this poverty and misery.[25]

INSPIRATION FROM BOLSHEVIK REVOLUTION AND GANDHI

The Bolshevik Revolution also inspired Nehru to some extent. Although not much precise information about the Revolution was available in India, Nehru did feel, even at this stage, sympathy for

[23] Nehru, *Glimpses of World History*, p. 673.
[24] Quoted in Norman, *op. cit.*, I, 42.
[25] Nehru, *Discovery of India*, p. 361.

Lenin. He derived from the Revolution the urge to work and think more and more 'in terms of social change'. Any calculated leaning in him towards Marxist-Leninist idology at this stage, however, cannot be suggested. In his conversations with Tibor Mende, he made a clear confession that Gandhism more than Bolshevism served as the initial inspiration to him, in the the early twenties. He said :

> Gandhi was always talking of the underdog. He was doing it in his own way ; not in the Socialist way, not in the class-struggle way, but just always talking about the underdog ; especially of the peasants of India. So, our thinking became more and conditioned to the peasantry of India ; not so much to the industrial workers, though to some extent to them too. It was rather to the peasants and very much against the land-lords and the rest...Now, the Russian example did not come in much ; it helped us in thinking. We thought we could learn much from it—but merely to adapt our thinking, but not to change it basically.[26]

Thus, the Gandhian influence was great on Nehru and the Russian impact was *only a filler to his thought then, hence not basic to his thinking*. Gandhiji appeared to him to have stirred up the masses of India to its bottom-most ladder, which the Congress had not yet touched. The politics of the masses began with the introduction of Gandhiji and the Gandhian methods in the Indian politics, and towards these Nehru was greatly attracted. It was because of such hopes that Nehru participated in the call for the First Non-Co-operation Movement under the stewardship of Gandhiji. He was convinced then that Gandhiji's method was distinctive of India and it suited the national genius. He is reported to have said :

> We (Congressmen) had so much faith in Gandhiji and in Gandhiji's methods. Every other method was either approved or disapproved, we thought that they might suit other countries, but we felt that we were on the right path.[27]

Thus, broadly up to the close of the War, a vague sort of Fabian and British economic ideas, strong feeling of anti-colonialism, scientific and modern attitude on social and economic issues, strong urge for aggresive action, deep admiration for the social works of Gandhiji, inspiration from the Bolshevik Revolution, injected in Nehru the initial urge to imbibe socialist theory and practice.

[26] *Ibid.*, p. 18.
[27] *Ibid.*, p. 17.

Since 1920 a new phase of thought dawned upon Nehru, as he came to acquire a first hand experience about the conditions of the Indian peasantry. After his chance visit to Pratapgarh where he came to see for himself the 'seminaked' sons of India. Here was a turning point in his life. He came to realise the miseries of the peasants, and the exploitation that the zamindars and the *taluqdars* were perpetrating upon them. It was during this new realisation that the first Non-Co-operation Movement was started. At this stage :

> The Punjab and the Khilafat wrongs were the topics of the day, and non-co-operation, which was to attempt to bring about a righting of these wrongs, was the all-absorbing subject.[28]

An important aspect of the Non-Co-operation Movement, as led by Gandhiji, was its religious and spiritual mooring. It was also considered as sort of 'revivalist' movement. Gandhiji often referred to *Rama Rajya*. To all these Nehru was mentally opposed, but as it had a practical and pervasive appeal to the masses. he found himself 'powerless to intervene'.[29] Nevertheless he admired the moral and ethical side of the movement. He observed :

> I did not give an absolute allegiance to the doctrine of non-violence or accept it for ever, but it attracted me more and more, and the belief grew upon me that, situated as we were in India and with our background and traditions, it was the right policy for us. *The spiritualisation of politics, using the word not in its narrow religious sense, seemed to me a fine idea.*[30]

The italicised part of the observation is significant in so far as it indicated, even at that early stage, his admiration for the ethical and spiritual side of the Gandhian methods, which found fuller culmination in his thinking later. Although, he was modern and scientific in outlook and had derived inspiration from the Western socialism primarily, he did not obliterate the ethical and spiritual side of the human values.

From the point of view of the growth of socialist ideas in Nehru the most important event, after the First Non-Co-operation Movement, was his visit to Europe in 1926-27. In Europe, he was widely

[28] Nehru, *Autobiography*, p. 63.
[29] *Ibid.*, p. 72.
[30] *Ibid.*, p. 73.

accepted as a representative of the Congress and attracted wide notice. He visited many countries including Italy, Switzerland, England, Belgium, France, Germany, Holland and Russia. The two most important experiences that proved consequential in his socialist thinking were derived from his participation in the Brussels Congress in February 1927 and the October Day Celebrations that very year in Moscow. During the period Nehru was deeply engrossed in the problems of imperialism. Being a young leader of colonial India, he leaned towards communism in the hope that it could be helpful in weakening or destroying the imperialist system. He observed :

> ...I turned inevitably with goodwill towards Communism, for, whatever its faults, it was at least not hypocritical and not imperialistic. It was not a doctrinal adherence, as I did not know much about the fine points of Communism.[31]

While he was in Europe, he also took upon himself the initiative to write to the Congress for participating in the ensuing Brussels Congress of the Oppressed Nationalities. His interest in the Congress was due to his conviction that it would help primarily in the destruction of imperialism, wherein he must have visualised the germs of India's freedom also. Eventually, Nehru represented the Indian National Congress at the Brussels Congress. He was elected there to serve on the executive of the League Against Imperialism, which comprised distinguished socialist personalities, like Madam Sunyat Sen, Romain Rolland, Gorky, Virendra Chattopadhyaya and others. The Brussels Congress provided him with an insight into the labour conditions of Europe and the communistic and socialistic trends of the time. Above all, it made him aware of his own sense of responsibility towards the cause of the oppressed classes in Indian society, and the growing need, to correlate the national movement with the socialistic urge of the time.

His visit to Russia was also of great bearing. It dispelled many of the illusions about Russia then. He was interested in Russia not only because of the great Marxist socialist experiment that was going on there, but also because Russia was a close neighbour to India and in some manner its conditions were similar to those of India. He observed : both are vast agricultural countries with only the beginnings of industrialisation, and both have to face poverty and illiteracy. If Russia finds a satisfactory solution for these, our work

[31] *Ibid.*, p. 163.

in India is made easier.[32]

After his return, he wrote a series of articles concerning his experiences in Russia, which were published in the *Hindu*—a nationalist daily of Madras, and later, published in a book-form under the title, *Soviet Russia*. This outlined many aspects of Soviet life including its Constitution, social life, literature, laws and prison system.

But, probably his visit was not an unmixed pleasure to him ; he formed rather a low opinion about the tactical maneuverings of the communists in Europe including those in Russia. This was indicated, apart from his later writings, in a letter addressed to Virendra Chattopadhyaya, as early as in November, 1927. He wrote :

> In one of your letters you say somewhere that you had received reports from Moscow that I had not behaved as I should probably because of parental and family influence. It is difficult of course for me to judge of the extent of these influences but so far as I can remember I did nothing and refrained from doing nothing in Moscow because of parental influence. I suppose opinions differ as to what I might have done there. I myself was quite clear in my mind as to what I should do and I was also conscious of attempts made to make me do things which I did not think desirable. The attempts were justifiable but the manner of them sometimes produces the reverse impression. No one likes to be jockeyed into doing anything and I felt that some such attempt was made. Anyway I wish our friends in Moscow would realise that greatly as I appreciate much that they have done any attempt to lead me by the nose is apt to bring about a contrary reaction. The communist party may believe in the strictest discipline within its ranks but I am not member of (the) party *nor am I likely to be one, even should I come to accept the principles of communism.*[33]

Later he observed :

> ...Communists often irritated me by their dictatorial ways, their aggressive and rather vulgar methods, their habit of denouncing everybody who did not agree with them.[34]

On his return to India in 1927, he brought home an intimate understanding about the socialist and the communist thought and movement in Europe, and the universal urge of the oppressed peoples to end the colonial bondage everywhere. Although he had not

[32] Norman, *op. cit.*, I, 130.
[33] 'An Unpublished Nehru Letter', *Link*, 6 (49), July 19, 1964, p. 12.
[34] Quoted in Norman, *op. cit.*, I, 126.

formed a very favourable attitude towards the communists and had not contacted any strong ideological bond with communism or Marxism. He expressed Marxist views on different occasions between 1927 and 1933 with regard to important socialistic issues, such as imperialism and colonialism, capitalism, class-struggle, industrialisation, poverty of the masses, economic equality, etc. In 1933, a booklet entitled, *Whither India* appeared containing the essentials of his socialist understanding at that stage. For the enunciation of the socialist ideas ; this booklet might be regarded as the first of its nature from amongst the Congress leaders.

His ideas, which largely contained analysis and interpretation of socialist ideas of the West, including Marxism, appeared to some to be so radical as to be verging towards communism itself. An interesting role in this connection was played by the Publicity Department of the then Government of the United Provinces, which depicted Nehru as a communist with a view to alienting him from those Congressmen of that time who apprehended such an ideology and movement. This was done through a pamphlet entitled *Communistic Likes And Dislikes.*[35] Herein, Nehru was described as 'a high priest of communism in India.'[36] The pamphlet contained excerpts from his utterances of that time as well as from *Whither India* ? It was obviously a propaganda move against Nehru, for, when the high ups in authority came to learn of such a move, they advised to stop such attempt forthwith and not to identify him or any other socialist in the Congress with communists. Such attempts, it may be recalled, might have been responsible in confusing the public in correctly assessing Nehru's socialistic ideas during the very vital period of the formation of the C.S.P.

The C.S.P. was formed while Nehru was still in prison following his re-arrest in 1934. But before his arrest, when he was approached in this regard, he agreed to finance and cooperate with the party in general, but declined to join it.[37] He had his reservations with regard to the need for forming a separate party. He maintained that the Congress platform itself could gradually be

[35] File No. 7/13/34 Poll, Government of India, Home Dept.
[36] *Ibid.*, p. 3.
[37] Thomas A. Rusch, *Role of Congress Socialist Party in the Indian National Congress*, 1931–42, an unpublished dissertation submitted to the University of Chicago, 1955–56. p. 149.

used to propagate socialist ideas. Probably, he did not like the formation of the C.S.P., and yet at the same time, did not oppose it strongly. His attitude toward it has been described by Sampurnanand as one of 'amused contempt'.[38]

During his prison days between Feb. 1934 and Feb. 1935, he wrote the major part of his writings collected in *Towards Freedom* which contained his commentaries on some Gandhian ideas and vindicated his own position *vis a vis*. With regard to socialism, he criticised Gandhian understanding about it, and pointed out its outmoded nature and its essentially 'religious' approach. He wrote therein :

> He (Gandhiji) suspects also socialism, and more particularly Marxism, because of their association with violence. The very words 'class-war' breathe conflict and violence and thus repugnant to him. He has also no desire to raise the standards of the masses beyond a certain very modest competence, for higher standards and leisure may lead to self-indulgence and sin....
>
> That outlook is as far removed from the socialistic, or for that matter the capitalistic, as anything can be.[39]

Nehru also criticised the Gandhian concept of trusteeship of the capitalists and regarded it as a 'religious' attempt 'to improve the individal internally, morally and spiritually and thereby to change the external environment.[40] He considered Gandhian ideas retrogressive in so far as Gandhiji wanted 'to go back to the narrowest autarchy, not only of a self-sufficient nation, but almost a self sufficient village.'[41] Similarly, it appeared to him, that the *Khadi* movement launched by Gandhiji was 'an intensification of individualism in production, and...a throwback to the preindustrial age.'[42] Thus on the whole, he considered Gandhian ideas, particularly in relation to the socialist ideology growing then, to be out-dated and impracticable. He wondered :

> With all his keen intellect and passion for bettering the downtrodden and oppressed, why does he support a system, and a system which is obviously decaying, which creates this misery

---

[38] Sampurnanand, *Memories and Reflections*, p. 72.
[39] Norman, *op. cit.*, I, 376.
[40] *Ibid.*, p. 377.
[41] *Ibid.*, p. 378.
[42] *Ibid.*, p. 379.

and waste ? He seeks a way out, it is true, but is not that way
to the past barred and bolted ? And meanwhile he blesses all
the relics of the old order which stand as obstacles in the way
of advance—the feudal states, the big zamindaris and taluk
daris, the present capitalist system. Is it reasonable to believe
in the theory of trusteeship—to give unchecked power and
wealth to an individual and to expect him to use it entirely for
the public good ? Are the best of us so perfect as to be
trusted in this way ? Even Plato's philosopher-kings could
hardly have borne this burden worthily.[43]

Thus, is no uncertain terms he repudiated Gandhian ideas with
regard to trusteeship, advanced as an alternative to socialism. For
himself, Nehru remained a Westernised socialist and described his
objective as 'the establishment of a socialist order, first within
national boundaries, and eventually in the world as a whole, with a
controlled production and distribution of wealth for the public good.[44]
This indicated the universal outlook of his socialist vision, as well as
his soft approach on the issue of nationalisation. He was probably
inclined to think in terms of 'controlled' regulation of production and
distribution only, and not much beyond it.

When Nehru came out of prison, he was confronted with the
issue of the Government of India Act 1935. In a statement in
London, in January, 1936, he described the said Act as a 'trivial
thing, not touching the fringe of India's real problem, which was
economic' and maintained that the 'vital changes were impossible
within the constitution which mortgaged India to vested interests.'[45]

In some press statements in London, Nehru expressed his views
with regard to some aspects of his socialist thinking also. He
pointed out :

One of the biggest of India's problems was unemployment,
most of it in the peasant class which had started with the
suppression of the old forms of Indian industry and the
introduction of new methods from outside. A large portion
of the unemployed reverted to land and no outlets had been
provided for a hundred years under British rule.[46]

At this stage Nehru clearly expressed himself for 'socialism
completely'. But how it should be applied to India depended on

[43] *Ibid.*
[44] *Ibid.*, p. 378.
[45] *Hindu*, Jan. 29, 1936, p. 11.
[46] *Ibid.*

many factors and the time at which it could be applied depended on the strength of the peasantry. He maintained :

> The land problem could be solved by collectivisation, which would involve expropriation, but in order to have a peaceful settlement, one should go as far as possible to win over the vested interests, though India's resources would not make any direct compensation for expropriation possible.[47]

He also emphasised the need for reduction of rent and the spread of education, sanitation and other benefits. He expressed himself 'personally' in favour of large-scale industrialisation too. In one of his letters to Lord Lothian about the same time, Nehru indicated his determined opposition to capitalist system. He wrote therein :

> I do not see how we can move along socialistic lines in a society which is based on acquisitiveness and in which the profit motive is the dominant urge. It thus becomes necessary to change the basis of this acquisitive society and to remove the profit motive, as far as we can.... That involves a complete change-over from the capitalist system.[48]

TRANSFORMATION OF SOCIETY

In his *Autobiography*, which was published in the same year, Nehru indicated his preference for socialism, and in the context of Fascism, even for communism.[49] He drew the attention towards 'the economic changes that were rapidly taking place the world over,' and pointed out that 'We must realise that the nineteenth-century system has passed away, and has no application to the present-day needs.'[50] He had come to realise that if the changes could not be brought about without challenging the basis of the old society and the vested interests, the challenge was unavoidable. But he had no intention necessarily to injure others ; a compromised settlement was definitely preferable, if it could only be feasible. He was also conscious that change in the social order was to be effected after weighing the 'costs of it in material as well as in spiritual terms.'[51] Yet he fully realised that 'A clash of interests seems inevitable.'[52]

[47] *Ibid.*
[48] *A Bunch of Old Letters*, p. 143.
[49] Nehru, *Autobiography*, p. 591.
[50] *Ibid.*, p. 586.
[51] *Ibid.*
[52] *Ibid.*, p. 588.

76

He only 'feared too much violence' and considered it 'injurious and waste of effort.'[53] At this stage, Nehru fully appreciated Marx's extraordinary degree of insight into social phenomena, which was due to the scientific method that Marx adopted.

THE LUCKNOW CONGRESS

The same year, Nehru was elected President of the Congress for the second time. The choice of him as the President had several consideration. '...The basic motive...arose from the rift between conservatives and radicals which threatened to wreck the party. Gandhi knew that Nehru was the one person who could bridge the growing gap between socialism and Gandhism. As the godfather of the Congress Socialist Party, Nehru was entirely acceptable to the Left. As Gandhi's favourite son he was tolerated by the Old Guard, most of whom were colleagues of atleast fifteen years standing. Thus he was uniquely suited to the task of reconciliation.'[54] He observed :

> I am convinced that the only key to the solution of the world's problems and of India's problems lies in socialism, and when I use this word I do so not in a vague humanitarian way but in the scientific economic sense. Socialism is, however, something even more than an economic doctrine, it is a philosophy of life and, as such also, it appeals to me...I work for Indian independence because the nationalist in me cannot tolerate alien domination. I work for it even more because for me it is the inevitable step to become a socialist organization and to join hand with the other forces in the world who are working for the new civilization.[55]

At the C. S. P.'s Faizpur Session in 1936, Nehru was personally present as a fraternal delegate and exhorted the socialists to think out the method through which socialism could be adopted under Indian conditions.[56]

Nehru had another opportunity to address the Faizpur Session of the Congress as its President. In pursuance of the earlier decision

[53] *Ibid.*, p. 593.

[54] Michael Brecher, *Nehru : A Political Biography*, London, Oxford University Press, 1959, p. 214.

[55] *Nehru on Socialism* (selected speeches and writings), New Delhi, Perspective Publications (Pvt.) Ltd., 1964, pp. 66–67.

[56] B. Pattabhi Sitaramayya, *Congress Ka Itihas*, Hindi edn., New Delhi, Sasta Sahitya Mandal, 1948, II, 16.

SOCIALISTTHOUGHT IN MODERN INDIA

at the Lucknow Congress a comprehensive agrarian programme was launched there through a resolution of the Congress. The resolution aimed at many programmatic issues such as, reduction of rent, exemption of uneconomic holdings from rent or tax, assessment of agricultural incomes on a progressive scale, abolition of feudal dues, levies and forced labour, introduction of cooperative farming, appointment of special tribunals for looking into the peasant debts, organising the peasant unions, and such other programmes. The resolution comprised a thirteen-point comprehensive programme for peasant welfare.[57] A remarkable shift of emphasis, however, was reflected in the Faizpur Address of Nehru.

> We cannot understand our problems without understanding imperialism and socialism. The disease is deep-seated and requires a radical and revolutionary remedy, and that remedy is the socialist structure of society. *We do not fight for socialism in India today for we have to go far before we can act in terms of socialism.*[58]

STRESS ON DEMOCRACY

Nehru's stress now had also changed from that on socialism to that on democracy, an ideal which the Congress held dear to itself, He explained :

> The Congress stands today for full democracy in India and fights for a *democratic state, not for socialism.* It is anti-imperialist and strives for great changes in our political and economic structure. I hope, that the logic of events will lead it to socialism for that seems to me the only remedy for India's ills.[59]

It appears, Nehru's clear assertion that the Congress was not to fight for socialism at that stage was positively a concession to the 'rightists' within the Party. Adoption of socialist ideology had almost created a 'deadlock' on this issue between the Lucknow and Faizpur Sessions. To some extent, Nehru himself realised that the achievement of freedom had a positive priority over any other issues, including socialism.[60] Hence he put greater emphasis on democracy

[57] *Indian National Congress,* Faizpur, 1936, (Resolution No. 12), pp. 96–97.

[58] Faizpur Presidential Address, reproduced in, *Nehru on Socialism,* op. cit., p. 92.

[59] *Ibid.*

[60] Norman, *Nehru,* I, 576.

and political freedom than on socialism.

THE ELECTION MANIFESTO OF 1937

The Election Manifesto with which the Congress came forward to face the electorates for the first time in 1937, had been adopted at the Bombay meeting of the Executive Committee in August 1936. The draft of the Manifesto was proposed by Rajendra Prasad and seconded by Narendra Deva. It rejected the new Act and upheld that the real objective of independence could not be achieved through legislatures. The Manifesto reiterated its old Karachi Resolution and programmes of 1931. It further pledged to secure a decent standard of life for the industrial workers and evolve a suitable machinery to settle their disputes with the employers. The pledges broadly depicted a socio-economic programme of the Congress which, even through it was not of a radical nature, was broad enough to orient the Congress on socio-economic lines. Nehru was enthusiastic about it and observed :

> We went to that forgotten creature, the Indian peasant, and remembered that his poverty was the basic problem of India. We identified ourselves with him in his suffering and talked to him of how to get rid of it through political and social freedom.[61]

In the same context he also pleaded for rejecting the 1935 Act and for its replacement by *panchayati raj*—meaning by the expression 'a grand *panchayat* of the nation, elected by all our people.'[62]

EXPERIENCE IN PLANNING

Shortly after it Nehru got another forum to manifest his socialist ideas and programmes. In 1938, he was made the Chairman of the National Planning Committee, set up by the Congress, and no fewer than twentyseven sub-committees were formed within it. Nehru described his work as Chairman to be 'fascinating' and yet he realised that any effective planning could be done only in a 'free India.'[63]

An important confession that Nehru made in this regard was

[61] *Ibid.*, p. 481.
[62] *Ibid.*
[63] B. N. Ganguli, 'Nehru and Socialism', *The Economic Weekly*, XVI (29, 30 & 31), July, 1964, p. 1217.

the difficulty in finding out an ideology acceptable to all the members as a common basis for planning. The assortment of men which composed the committee could not evolve an agreed social theory. He pointed out :

> ...we did not start with a well-defined social theory, our social objectives were clear enough and afforded a common basis for planning. The very essence of this planning was a large measure of regulation and cordination. Thus while free enterprise was not ruled out as such, its scope was severely restricted.[64]

The main objective of planning was to further industrialization. Agriculture and social services were also to follow in its trial.

In 1946 *The Discovery of India* elucidated Nehru's approach towards Marxism and socialism. It was considerably modified from that of *Whither India* ? In this work Nehru put his phiolosophy of life. 'Essentially, I am interested in this world, in this life not in some other world or a future life. Whether there is such a thing as a soul, or whether there is a survival after death or not, I do not know ; and, important as these questions are, they do not trouble me in the least. The environment in which I have grown up takes, the soul (or rather the *atma*) and a future life, the *Karma* theory of cause and effect, and reincarnation for granted. I have been affected by this and so, in a sense, I am favourably disposed towards these assumptions. There might be a soul which survives the physical death of the body, ... Presuming a soul, there appears to be some logic also in the theory of incarnation.'[65]

But at the same time Nehru made it clear that he did not believe in things like 'soul' or 'incarnation' as a 'religious' faith. He also did not believe in the concept of 'personal God'. The only thing he believed in was in the mysteries of nature, and to an extent, in 'the conception of monism', *i. e.* the *Advaita* philosophy of Vedanta.[66] He fully appreciated the 'ethical approach to life' and Gandhiji's emphasis on right means. This line of thinking was very important because, later on, it became his 'Basic Approach'[67] even with reference

---

[64] Nehru, *Discovery of India*, p. 404.

[65] *Ibid.*, p. 13.

[66] *Ibid.*, p. 14.

[67] In 1958 an article entitled 'Basic Approach' appeared in the *AICC Economic Review,* in which Nehru showed his inclination towards Vedantic philosophy in some positive terms.

to socialism and Marxism. Nehru also acknowledged the impact of Marx and Lenin on his mind. It helped him see history and current affairs in a new light. He admired the achievements of the Soviet Union and considered that it 'had advanced human society by a great leap'. And yet, he pointed out that 'I am too much of an individualist and believer in personal freedom'[68] and do not like regimentation.

In the *Discovery of India* a significant aspect of Nehru's line of thinking was that he was inclined to think more and more in terms of the mysteries of nature. As referred to above, he was now inclined not only to think of the 'mysteries' of nature but also to accept 'something' beyond the elements of mind or matter. On this score Marxism provided him no satisfactory answer. 'It did not satisfy me completely, nor did it answer all the questions in my mind, and, almost unawares, a vague idealist approach would creep into my mind, something rather akin to the Vedanta approach.'[69] And at the same time, Nehru showed his dislike for metaphysical and speculative thinking. 'Most of us accept also certain metaphysical conceptions as part of the faith in which we have grown up. I have not been attracted towards metaphysics ; in fact, I have had a certain distaste for vague speculation. And yet I have sometimes found a certain intellectual fascination in trying to follow the rigid lines of metaphysical and philosophic thought of the ancients or the moderns. But I have never felt at ease there and have escaped from their spell with a feeling of relief.'[70] In short, neither Marxism nor metaphysics was wholly acceptable to him. He did not bother about finding any *a priori* philosophical base or about the fine points of socialism. '...While I accepted the fundamentals of the socialist theory I did not trouble myself about its numerous inner controversies. I had little patience with leftist groups in India, spending much of their energy in mutual conflict and recrimination over fine points of doctrine which did not interest me at all. Life is too complicated and, ...too illogical, for it to be confined within the four corners of a fixed doctrine.'[71]

From the point of view of the socialist ideas of Nehru, the post

[68] Nehru, *Discovery of India*, p. 15.
[69] *Ibid.*
[70] *Ibid.*, p. 13.
[71] *Ibid.*, p. 17.

independ period was essentially one of thinking, not so much on the theories, objectives and methodologies of socialism, as on its applicability. His post-Independence ideas with regard to the fundamental issues with which this study is primarily concerned, have been integrally treated in the chapters that follow. We need indicate here only that the applicability of socialism to Indian conditions, received fresh thoughts from him and its mechanism was thoroughly reoriented to suit Indian conditions, as he understood them. In doing so a slight shift in the shades of meaning of socialism can also be traceable, but it was in no sense a radical departure from the past.

Basically, Nehru's socialistic ideas remained rooted in the thinking of his pre-Independence years. If anything he now came to realise, it was the spiritual and the ethical aspect of life and its values. In an assessment of Nehru's socialism, this ethical inclination was fully discernible.

> Pandit Nehru's socialism was born out of a deep attachment to the values of ethics and social justice. He had no intellectual commitment whatsoever to its mechanics as prescribed in the Marxist text-books. While Pandit Nehru had great respect for many of the abiding insights of Marxist thought, he did not subscribe uncritically to any of its dogmas.[72]

SOCIALIST IDEAS : TRENDS IN THE PRE-INDEPENDENCE PHASE

With regard to the fundamental issues under socialism, Nehru's pre-independence mode of thinking may be described.

OPPOSITION TO IMPERIALISM

Nehru was strongly opposed to imperialism both in theory and in practice. In his analysis of the growth of imperialism, he observed, 'Industrialism has resulted in greater production and greater wealth, in the concentration of wealth in a few countries and a few individuals, and a more unequal distribution of wealth. It has resulted in a struggle for raw material and markets, and has thus brought into existence the imperialism of the last century. It has caused wars and has given rise to colonial empires of to-day. It has laid the seed of future wars. And recently it has taken the shape of an economic imperialism which, without the possession of territory,

---

[72] M. L. Dantwala, 'Economic Ideology of Jawaharlal Nehru', *The Economic Weekly*, XVI (29, 30 & 31), July 1964, p. 1209.

is as efficient and potent in exploiting other countries as any colonial empire of yesterday.'[73]

He further emphasised that, as the necessary result of industrialism, imperialism is not a peculiar phenomenon of the British race alone, it is fully ingested in the very system of capitalist development.[74] The modern form of imperialism does not follow the old method of territorial expansion, but the subtler way of economic imperialism.

The same theme appeared in his article *Whither India ?*, wherein he presented a somewhat Marxist approach to the methods of production, class organizations and imperialism. He observed : 'Capitalism has led to imperialism and to the conflicts of imperialist powers in search for colonial areas for exploitation....'[75] It was that process which was reflected in the 'push to Asia' mentality, leading to colonial expoitation of Asia.[76]

APPROACH TOWARDS CLASSES

Nehru also appears to have strongly believed in the incompatibility of interests of the various classes in society, viz , the interests of the princes, the zamindars, the professional classes, the agriculturists, the industrialists, the bankers, the lower middle classes, the workers, the foreign capitalists, and so on. He observed : 'Nothing is more absurd than to imagine that all the interests in the nation can be fitted in without injury to any. At every step some have to be sacrificed for others.'[77] Thus, he recognised not only the different class interests in society but also the irreconciliability of the conflicting interests. Without 'a sudden change called revolution', probably, the antagonistic class interests could not be eliminated altogether.[78] He, however, did not imply by the term revolution 'any necessary connection with violence.'[79]

CLASS WAR

On the closely related theme of class war in society he adopted,

[73] Norman, *op. cit.*, I, 155.
[74] *Ibid.*, pp. 155–56.
[75] *Whither India*, reproduced in *Nehru on Socialism*, collections, New Delhi, Purspective Pub. Pvt. Ltd., 1964, p. 214.
[76] *Ibid.*, p. 22.
[77] *Ibid.*, p. 12.
[78] *Ibid.*, p. 14.
[79] Norman, *op. cit.*, I, 159.

to some extent, the Marxist and communist points of view. He observed : 'We are ofen accused of preaching the class war and of widening the distance between the classes. The distance is wide enough, thanks to capitalism, and nothing can beat the record of capitalism in that respect. But those who accuse us are singularly unseeing and ignorant of what goes on around them. Is it the socialist or the communist who separates the classes and preaches discontent or the capitalist and imperialist who by his policy and methods has reduced the great majority of mankind into wage slaves who are worse even in many ways than the slaves of old ? The class war is none of our creation. It is the creation of capitalism and so long as capitalism endures it will endure.'[80] Obviously the class-war to which he referred intended to prove the existence of class antagonism in society. He regarded it not as the projection of the socialists' vision of the future but a fact of history and a continued reality of socio-economic order in the capitalist society. This may, however, be noted that he did not advocate for engineering or accelerating the process of bringing about any class war. He merely recognised it as a fact.

EQUALITY

Nehru was highly critical of the Indian social order in so far as it had not cared to solve effectively the problem of social inequality. And he considered that it was because of this failure that India 'fell and remains fallen.'[81] He was a strong critic of caste considerations in social and public life.

As a socialist, he pointed out that he was no believer in 'kings and princes...or... the modern kings of industry.'[82] He emphasised the need to achieve economic equality in society. He observed : 'today politics have ceased to have much meaning and the most vital question is that of social and economic equality.'[83] The achievement of such objectives and programmes appeared to Nehru possible only with the adoption of socialist ideology. Hence, he had sympatheti-

[80] 'Presidential Address to the Nagpur Session of the AITUC', *Ibid.*, p. 179.
[81] *Indian National Congress*, Report of the 44th Annual Session, Lahore, 1929, p. 24.
[82] *Ibid.*, p. 31.
[83] *Ibid.*, p. 24.

THE PIONEERS OF INDIAN SOCIALISM

cally leaned towards Marxism and the Western brand* of socialism. But he felt that socialism in India must be adopted to suit Indian conditions, and to that extent, he wanted 'socialism to be practical as well as indigenous.'[84]

MATERIALISTIC AND ECONOMIC CONCERN OF SOCIALISM

During the pre-Independence period Nehru regarded socialism as largely an economic doctrine :

> (It) aims at the control by the State of the means of production—that is, land and mines and factories and the like—and the means of distribution, like railways, etc., and also the banks and the similar institutions.[85]

He appreciatively depicted Marxism as a scientific and logical theory which brought to light the antagonistic nature of different class-interests in society on the basis of prevailing modes of production. Nehru realised that socialism dealt with external economic forces in society, and thus, indeed, it was a materialist theory.

But, the materialism of Marx, Nehru held, was a philosophical expression and antithetical to the Hegelian terminology of idealism. Since Marx dealt with the facts in a scientific way, as they worked in different stages in history, his theory was often termed as 'materialistic.'[86]

From what Nehru wrote in the *Discovery of India*, about his 'favourable' dispositions towards the concept of soul and Vedantic philosophy, it cannot be suggested that he ever subscribed to the concept of 'materialism' himself ; he developed appreciation for 'spiritualism' even during the pre-Independence phase of his thinking. What was definitive about the belief was that economic elements were essential and vital parts of a socialist state or society. About 'idealistic' and 'spiritualistic' elements of life, there was a vague appreciation only—neither positive assertion nor positive denial.

His concern with many issues like the nationalisation of industries indicated that socialism to him was basically a materialist theory having an economic content. Socialism to him was largely an economic and worldly theory dealing with production, distribution,

---

[84] M. N. Das, *The Philosophy of Jawaharlal Nehru*, London, George Allen & Unwin Ltd., 1961, p. 161.

[85] Nehru, *Glimpses of World History*, p. 543.

[86] *Ibid.*, p. 546.

class-conflicts, inequality and such other problems. His interest in planning had also been prompted by his belief that socialisation of the means of production would lead to greater industrialisation and growth of national wealth. Marxism and even communism naturally took him far on this track of thought. The Materialistic Conception of History appealed to him as scientific and logical. It was devoid of the superstitions and religious approach towards the facts of history and life.

PLACE OF INDIVIDUAL

With regard to the place of individual in socialist state, Nehru maintained that individual freedom has got to be correlated with the social structure. He was 'too much of an individualist', as has been pointed out earlier, to concede to a regimented structure of socialist state or society in which the individual were to function as a robot.

Immediately after his release from the prison in 1945, Nehru realised that 'one of the fundamental problems of the day everywhere is how to coordinate the two conceptions of a central socialised organization of society and the state with the greatest amount of individual freedom.'[87] It appears, therefore, that even before Independence he fully realised the need to correlate the individual freedom with a socialistic structure of state. At no point he appears to have accepted the wholesale subordination of the individual to the state or society.

He however, realised that in a complex 'social structure individual freedom had to be limited', 'but some limitation was to be imposed only with regard to 'lesser liberties' and only with a view to protecting the 'larger freedom.'[88] Hence the problem was not of absoluteness but one of finding out a discreet balance between the need to limit and the need to protect. The socialist state or society of his vision was thus confronted with this complex problem of finding out the workable coordination.

His belief in the freedom of the individual, led him to be firmly anchored to his faith in democracy and to an extent also democratic methods.

[87] Norman, *op. cit.*, II, 164.
[88] Nehru, *Discovery of India*, p. 15.

STATE

With regard to state, Nehru appears to have shown no interest in the Marxian concept of the withering away of the state. He defined socialism in terms of 'the control by the state' of the means of production and distribution. And, in practice also, he found the machinery of the state strengthened in the Soviet Union as well as in other communist states. He realised the necessity of a state even as a coercive institution, using violence and force. He observed :

> Violence is the very life blood of the modern State and social system. Without the coercive apparatus of the State taxes would not be realized, landlords would not get their rents and private property would disappear.[89]

He maintained that state had a positive role in society and all states existed 'because of offensive and defensive violence.' He further maintained that even if we assume that the worst forms of violence will be gradually removed from the state, 'it is impossible to ignore the fact that both government and social life necessitate some coercion.'[90] He realised the importance of state in all eventualities and to him it appeared as a perpetual necessity.

MEANS AND ENDS

'As to the methodology for tramsforming the existing social order into socialist state, Nehru pleaded for evolving a radical approach. Probably, he was convinced of the eradication of antagonistic class-interests and of the fact that the achievement of social and economic objectives of socialism could not be possible without some radical and revolutionary method. He emphasised the need for 'developing action and not to depend on the method of petitioning and sweet reasoning' alone.[91] To what extent he was inclined towards violence in this period was not clear, but Gandhiji did sense in him, at least in principle, some sort of a wavering attitude with regard to 'unadulterated non-violence.'[92]

Nehru had repeatedly made it clear that personally non-violence

[89] Nehru, *Autobiography*, p. 540.

[90] *Ibid.*, p. 542.

[91] In an address to the Poona Youth Conference, 1928 ; Quoted in, Bibek Brata Sarcar, *The Socialist Movement in India From* 1919 to 1947 (an unpublished dissertation for Ph.D. degree, Delhi University), p. 90.

[92] *A Bunch of Old Letters, op. cit.,* p. 58.

was a method of expediency and policy to him and not a creed of faith or dogma. He said : 'I have made it clear on many occasions that non-violence is no infallible creed with me and although I greatly prefer it to violence, I prefer freedom with violence to subjection with non-violence.'[93] Nehru realised that coercion could not be avoided as clash of interests sometimes became inevitable. Neither in personal life nor in national life coercion could wholly be avoided. He pointed out : 'I have no doubt that coercion or pressure is necessary to bring about political and social change in India. Indeed our non-violent mass movements...have been powerful weapons to exercise this pressure.'[94] The example of coercion or pressure that he cited above was indicative that he had no love for violence, but no abhorrence of it either. In his letter to Gandhiji, after the Chaurichaura incident, he pointed out that in a mass movement of national scale a few individual and isolated incidents of even violence could never be ruled out.[95]

Nehru realised also that 'the vast changes that socialism envisages cannot be brought about by the sudden enactment of a few laws. But some basic laws and powers are necessary to give the direction of advance and to lay the foundation of the structure.'[96] In effecting, and even not in effecting, any change he suggested both material and spiritual costs involved therein should be taken full account of. In the process 'a clash of interests seems inevitable. There is no middle path. Each of us will have to choose our side.'[97]

Nehru pinned much hope on the methodology of planning. Planning through democratic means was an indispensable element of his method of social reconstruction. He had been especially attracted towards the method of democratic planning since 1927. It appealed to him because it was both democratic and regulative. It could also avoid unnecssary violence.

DEMOCRATIC SOCIALISM

The objectives that inspired Nehru to adopt and ventilate socialist ideas during this period were manifold. He considered

---

[93] *Nehru on Socialism, op. cit.*, p. 37.
[94] *Ibid.*
[95] Norman, *op. cit.*, I, 83.
[96] Nehru, *Autobiography*, p. 588.
[97] *Ibid.*

socialism to be helpful first, in destroying imperialistic hegemony over India ; secondly, in broadening the outlook of those nationalists who thought in the 'narrowest nationalist' term ; thirdly, eradicating the poverty and the misery of the downtrodden and the 'have-nots' in society ; and finally, in providing a scientific and sociological base for the socio-economic aspirations of society.

Nehru fully appreciated democratic values and democratic methods. As such, he was an ardent champion of the cause of liberty, equality and people's participation in the affairs of the nation. Narendra Deva, in his total evaluation of Nehru's socialism, during the pre-Independence phase, described it as 'Democratic Socialism.' No better assessment of Nehru's ideological position with regard to socialism of the pre-Independence period be presented than the one done by Acharya Narendra Deva. This assessment has a pointed relevance as Narendra Deva regarded during this period his own ideas as more or less similar to Nehru :

> I think it would be wrong to appraise Jawaharlalji's activities as those of an individual who is working to the end of establishing a socialist state and on this ground to criticise him adversely. Though he is a professed socialist, his activities are largely guided by ideals of democracy and economic betterment of the masses. He is not wedded to any particular 'ism' nor is he temperamentally fit to be the leader of a group. He believes in some of the fundamental principles of scientific socialism, yet he is not prepared to swear by everything taught by Marx and Lenin. He does not subscribe to any rigid ideology... The history of the last twenty-five years has taught him that materialism is still a vital force...his first flush of love for socialism has received a check in recent years.... He believes in ethical social conduct and has a deep sense of human values. He has faith in ideas of social progress. He believes in planning life for democracy and freedom. He is against totalitarianism and wants to find an equation between individual liberty and planned economic order. He holds that the economic freedom for the masses is not possible without the common ownership of the means of production but that this end should be achieved with as little sacrifice of personal freedom as possible...Pandit Nehru will not agree with the advocates of free enterprise. He would freely admit that planning is possible only through the state and its bureaucracy...coercive force will be necessary to enforce the decisions of the State. ...he would try to check the evils of socialist planning by developing democratic techniques.

Jawaharlalji does not belong to any orthodox school of socialism. But if I were asked to sum up his social philosophy in a neat phrase, I would say that it is *'democratic socialism'*. (emphasis ours).[98]

While Deva's assessment about Nehru's socialism was largely correct, on at least two points, it was not fully comprehensive. These were that neither any reference to Gandhi's impact on Nehru's ideas nor Nehru's 'favourable' disposition towards Vedantic approach was indicated by him. It is, however, true that these trends in Nehru were dominant ; yet, during the post-Independence period, these two were the most significant seeds that struck strong roots in his thinking. Although Nehru never became a full-fledged Gandhian or Vedantist himself, he never became a full-fledged Marxist either. In bits he appeared to be all.

III. Narendra Deva

Narendra Deva, was born in 1890 at Sitapur in Uttar Pradesh.[99] Deva's father was a talented lawyer with scholarly habits who later shifted to Faizabad, and developed saintly leanings and interests in the philosophy of Vedanta. He knew three languages, English, Hindi and Persian and maintained a small library at home. It was in this environment and under the personal care of his father that Deva received his early schooling. Even as a boy, he read the *Ramayana*, the *Mahabharat*, the *Bhagavad Gita* and many other scriptures. He had memorised also a part of *Rudri* as well as the *Gita*.[100] During his school-days at Faizabad he developed interest in Bengali language. He was a brilliant student and often topped in his class. For obtaining Master's Degree in Sanskrit he shifted to Allahabad and had the privilege to reside in the Hindu Boarding House. It was here that Deva was influenced by the nationalist fervour of his times. He described the Hindu Boarding House as the centre of radical thinking under the leadership of 'Sunderlalji', a nationalist student leader of that time.

Deva became sympathetic to the radical school of thinking. The Partition of Bengal, the Japanese victory over Russia, and the

---

[98] Narendra Deva (edited by Yusuf Meherally), *Socialism and The National Revolution*, Bombay, Padma Publications Ltd., 1946, pp. 205-207.

[99] His original family name was 'Avinashilal'.

[100] Deva, *Rastriyata Aur Samajvad* p. 675.

radical speeches of Tilak greatly influenced him. At the age of ten he attended the Lucknow Congress in 1899 with his father and came in touch with the political events of his time. As he grew in age, his interest in political events developed. In 1906, he attended the Calcutta Session of the Congress. There he had the chance of listening to his political idol Lokmanya Tilak and seeing other stalwarts of the Congress. It has been said of him, that then was 'born the leftist in him.'[101] He indeed was keenly aware of the controvercy involved between the moderates—led by Pherozeshah Mehta, Gokhale and Surendranath Bannerji, and the extremists—led by Tilak, Bipin Chandra Pal and Aurobindo Ghose. He fell for the latter group.

Deva's fascination for the radicals and the extremists in the Congress grew in him ever since then. His interest in Aurobindo Ghose was reflected in his being a regular reader of *Bande Matram* featuring Sri Aurobindo's radical ideas, and also of *Arya* published from Pondicherry. 'Fabian and revolutionary traditions as embodied in the works of Mazzini, Sydney Webb, Bluntschli and Marx, provided the main-spring of his political outlook and private character. Among our countrymen A. K. Coomaraswamy, Aurobindo Ghosh, Hardayal, Lajpat Rai and Syed Hyder Raza impressed him with their writings. He was unmistakably on the Marxian track.'[102]

Deva had served as a Secretary of the Home-Rule League while he practised in Faizabad, and, probably, become a member of the AICC also around that time. He has often been described as the 'Grey eminence of Indian Socialist Party', and, by some, also as 'the father of Indian socialism'. He worked closely with Nehru in the agrarian movement of his province and it was largely at Nehru's instance that he joined the Kashi Vidyapith as a teacher. Nehru considerably relied on his valuable comradeship and on many occasions invited him to serve on the Congress Executive Committee and on other Congress bodies.

Ideologically, Narendra Deva was regarded as among those few intellectuals in the Congress who had had deep insight into the Marxist theories and the role that economic factors played in

[101] G. S. Bhargava, *Leaders of the Left*, Bombay, Meherally Book Club, 1951, p. 26.

[102] Bhargava, *op. cit.*, p. 27.

moulding the social structure. The fact that he remained less conspicuous in Indian politics till 1934 was probably due to his reluctance to take much vocal share in the proceedings of the Indian National Congress and also due to his conscious attempt at not propagating his personal ideas. By nature, he was modest and tried to avoid the public focus.[103]

As early as 1929, in a letter to Nehru, Deva emphasised the need to evolve a clear-cut ideology with regard to economic programme in the country.[104] He was aware that, in the absence of such an economic ideology, much could not be done.

Deva's close affinity with Nehru was greatly reflected in his Presidential Address to the first socialist gathering at Patna in 1934, wherein he observed at the very outset : 'My task is made all the more difficult by the absence of our beloved friend, Pandit Jawaharlal Nehru whose absence today we all so keenly feel and whose valuable advise and guidance would have been of immense value.' Deva concluded his address again with a reference to Nehru and on a note of hope that he would 'hail with delight' the birth of the C. S. P. As has already been indicated, he himself acknowledged that his line of thinking was more or less similar to that of Nehru.[105] In 1930 Jayaprakash Narayan met him at Kashi Vidyapith. Both were mutually attracted towards each other. Later, when J. P. was entrusted with the Labour Research Department of the Congress, they often had the chance to meet together and discuss their mutual socialist ideas.

In 1936 Narendra Deva was nominated by Jawaharlal Nehru to the Congress Working Committee. He also became the President of the U. P. Provincial Congress and, in that capacity, he fought the 1937 election for the membership of the U. P. Legislative Assembly. The Congress had decided in favour of office-acceptance under the Government of India Act 1935. Like Nehru and other prominent socialists, he pleaded in the Assembly for rejecting the 1935 Act, and setting up an 'Assembly', representing the will of the people of India. He maintained that it could be possible only when India was made completely free.[106]

[103] Deva, *Rastriyata Aur Samajvad*, p. 687.
[104] Deva's letter to Nehru, *A Bunch of Old Letters, op. cit.*, p. 73.
[105] Deva, *Rastriyata Aur Samajvad*, p. 689.
[106] Deva, *Socialism and the National Revolution*, p. 97.

In 1939 Deva presided over the All-India Kisan Sabha held at Gaya. He showed keen awareness of the problems of the class of peasantry and exhorted them to organize themselves independently of the Indian National Congress. At the same time, he also advised them to maintain close relation with it. He urged strongly for mitigating the miserable plight of the peasantry due to heavy taxation, indebtedness, exploitation by the landlords, fragmentation of land into small uneconomic holdings and such other problems. His address fully indicated that the cause he championed was not limited to the working class or the proletariat class alone, but was comprehensive enough to include the peasantry. He, however, cautioned the peasants against the narrow and sectarian attitudes.

During the 1942 Revolution, he was arrested and along with Nehru kept in the Ahmadnagar Fort. He was released in 1945. In 1946 Deva joined in the efforts to revive the C. S. P. At its Kanpur Session in 1947, he used his influence in persuading his colleagues and the rank and the file within Party not to decide at that stage for complete secession from the Indian National Congress even though the word 'Congress' was decided to be dropped. It was now designated simply as the 'Socialist Party'. In 1948, however, he pleaded for secession from the Indian National Congress. In 1949 Deva presided over the Seventh Annual Conference of the Socialist Party and was chosen to preside in 1952 also, but owing to ill health he could not do so. Again, in 1954, the Presidentship of the P. S. P. was thrust upon him for he was the main source of inspiration to the party. In 1955 Deva was entrusted with the task of drafting the Policy Statement of the P. S. P. It has been described as his last 'testament' to his Party. Indeed, it is a specimen of his deft draftsmanship.

During this period, Deva served as the Vice-Chancellor of the Lucknow University and the Banaras Hindu University and took keen interest in the student movement in the country. His popularity among the students was wide and abiding. The two 'passions' of his life, it has been said, were 'teaching and fighting for his country's freedom.'[107] For these two passions, he found two spheres of activities : one in the field of education and the other in politics.

[107] Raghukul Tilak, 'Acharya Narendra Deva As I Knew Him', *Vigil*, XII New Series (4), Feb. 16, 1957, p. 7.

The days he spent in the Kashi Vidyapith were cherished by him as 'the happiest and most fruitful period of his life.'[108] His knowledge of Buddhist philosophy and Pali language was of wide recognition. During his visit to China as a cultural ambassador of India, he kept the Buddhist literature by his side wherever he went even for a short visit.[109] His treatise on *Buddhadharma Darshan* will remain a lasting testimony to his scholarly genius. It has also been said of him that he was 'one of the greatest orators' of his time, and 'a scholar by nature and politician by necessity'.[110]

BASIC UNDERSTANDING ABOUT SOCIALISM

Narendra Deva's first major speech of theoretical importance was his Presidential Address to C. S. P. of Patna in 1934. The speech was primarily an interpretation of Marxism with regard to some common 'misconceptions' about it as well as its essential ideas. The way he approvingly elaborated some of the Marxist ideas, was enough to indicate that he had developed deep Marxist leanings at that stage, To some extent he was also influenced by Lenin. He often cited Lenin to prove the 'decadent' stage to which capitalism had reached in the form of imperialism. In the capitalist order of economy, he maintained, like Lenin, that antagonism between capital and labour was inevitable.[111] He made it clear that his affinity with socialism or Marxism was mainly because it was a better solution than Fascism to solve the problem of class antagonism.[112] It was significant however that he did not mention anything about 'communism' and 'communists' in his whole Address except just once as a passing comment in course of criticism of Fascism as an ideal. Thus Marxism, and to an extent even Leninism, appeared to have impressed him during this period, but he did not identify Marxism with communism or Bolshevism. He only advised the Congress socialists to 'study the (Russian) experiment and form our own conclusions.'[113] The methodology of planned economy in the Soviet system of course appealed to him, as it had appealed to Nehru

[108] *Ibid.*

[109] Chandra Bhal Tripathi, 'Reminiscences of Acharya Narendra Deva', *Janata*, XII (5), Feb 23, 1957, p. 6.

[110] *Ibid.*, p. 8.

[111] Deva, *Socialism and the National Revolution*, p. 14.

[112] *Ibid.*, p. 16.

[113] *Ibid.*, p. 19.

and he noted with appreciation the Soviet achievement in this field.

Deva did not think that Marx had undermined the importance of mind in his Materialistic Conception of History, nor the Marxism was necessarily opposed to spiritual values.[114] With regard to economic equality, he pointed out that Marx did not conceive of it in absolute terms ; for, absolute equality, Marx realised was absolutety impossible and even 'absurd'. What Marx advocated with regard to it was primarily the abolition of 'classes.'[115] On the issue of class-struggle and class-war in society, he fully agreed with the Marxist proposition that antagonism between capital and labour in a capitalist order of society was bound to preserve the germs of class-struggle, and eventually also of class-war, until the means of production were brought under the social or collective control. In this connection, like Lenin, he preached the necessity of making the classes conscious of their class-interests, because ultimately the class-solidarity alone could 'win power for them.' The propaganda and the organizational work, he maintained, could initially be done only by the class of revolutionary intelligentsia and not by other classes in society.[116]

OPPOSITION TO IMPERIALISM

Deva was strongly opposed to imperialism. He regarded it as the culmination of the logic of a capitalist order of state and society. He maintained that capitalism initially started with free competition and led ultimately to monopoly system, in which the means of production including capital were concentrated into fewer hands. This led to what Lenin termed 'Finance Capitalism'. He quoted Lenin himself on that point :

> When capitalism enters the stage of imperialism monopoly and finance capital becomes dominant, the export of capital acquires special importance and international monopoly combines of capitalists are formed which divide up the world.[117]

Realising well that India was kept in bondage because of the logic of imperial necessities of Britain, he foresaw clearly that socialism retained the clue to achieving India's freedom as well. Socialism was basically a theory and movement directed towards the

[114] *Ibid.*, p. 20.
[115] *Ibid.*, p. 22.
[113] *Ibid.*, p. 7.
[117] *Ibid.*, p. 14.

bringing about of the destruction of capitalism and imperialism every where. Thus to him, it appeared that independence of India itself necessitated the adoption of socialist ideology. This was a similar fascination as the one which attracted Nehru towards socialism.

METHODOLOGY OF SOCIALIST TRANSFORMATION

For bringing about socialism in society, Deva realised that some sort of 'social revolution' would be necessary. While inaugurating a symposium on socialism in 1937, at Patna, he observed, 'Though capitalism is fading rapidly day by day socialism cannot evolve as a matter of course. An earnest effort should be made to bring about a social revolution and combat in an organized way Fascism which is naked form of capitalism.'[118] Thus 'social revolution' appeared to him as a prelude to the socialist transformation of society.

Along with social revolution, he also exhorted the people in general and the Congress in particular for launching an 'economic struggle' and for accelerating the process of political movement itself. He pointed out that unless the workers and the peasantry 'are organized on the basis of their class demands and unless their economic struggle is linked up with the movement for complete independence', any relutionary change desired by the National Congress could not be brought about.[119] Throughout the colonial decades Deva emphasised the need for 'social revolution' and 'economic struggle.' But it was significant that he did not subscribe to the theory that a violent overthrow of the capitalist or imperial system was inevitable. Probably, he did not imply by the expression 'revolution' or 'struggle' any wanton destruction and violence. He took utmost care to emphasise that Communist and Bolshevik methods of ruthlessness and violence should not be equated with Marxism Marx, he maintained, was one of the greatest humanists and Marxism was one of the most humane theories.[120]

At the same time Deva indicated to Gandhiji, as late as in 1945, that personally he was doubtful if freedom of India could be achieved without the use of some violence.[121] Hence, probably,

[118] *The Indian Nation*, dated 24-4-1937, p. 9.
[119] Deva, *Socialism and the National Revolution*, pp. 72-73.
[120] Deva, *Rastriyata Aur Samajvad*, pp. 447-49.
[121] *Ibid.*, p. 691.

violence was not completely ruled out by him so far as the struggle for national independence was concerned. Whether or not it was also essential for bringing about the socialist transformation of society can only be a matter of inference, and not of positive assertion.

In this connection, it may be recalled, that Deva had deep and abiding faith in the democratic values of life. He pointed out the 'socialist desire to build up a powerful anti-imperialist front to achieve independence of the country and to establish a democratic regime wherein the economic life of the country would be organized on socialist lines.'[122]

OBJECTIVE OF SOCIAL DEMOCRACY

Deva maintained that the C. S. P. was a Party which stood for the Lenin's ideal of 'social democracy', i. e. 'economic emancipation' as well as 'democratic freedom.'[123] He also considered Marxism itself to be a fully democratic ideal.[124] The ideal of the C. S. P. or the Congress socialism was only an 'Indian transliteration' of the Russian ideal of 'social democracy'. Under it, two objectives were to be achieved integrally : one, the economic emancipation and, other, the political democracy. Thus, from the beginning Deva regarded socialism as inherently democratic. Therefore the terms 'revolution' and 'struggle' were not undemocratic ideals in his thinking.

Deva was, however, strongly opposed to capitalist democracy, wherein property dominated state. He emphasised the need to evolve a society in which the state would dominate property. That could be possible only when the state was to take over the means of production under its own control, in the interest of the whole community.[125]

He also maintained that planned economy was necessary, but, in itself, it meant nothing. He reminded that even German economy under Hitler's rule was a planned economy but it did not achieve democratic civilization. Planned economy must be directed towards building 'an equal society', otherwise democratic institutions would disappear.[126]

[122] Deva, *Socialism & National Revolution*, p. 115.
[123] *Ibid.*
[124] Deva, *Rāstriyata Aur Samajvad*, p. 295.
[125] Deva, *Socialism & National Revolution*, p. 102.
[126] *Ibid.*, p. 158.

RESERVATION ABOUT GANDHIAN TECHNIQUE

During this period, particularly around the early 'forties, Deva was not enthusiastic about the Gandhian technique of *satyagraha*. He pointed out that 'the Gandhian technique is defective and incomplete and we cannot reach our objective of complete independence by adhering to that technique.'[127] It can naturally be inferred that for the achievement of socialist objectives or bringing about the 'struggle', that he envisaged, Gandhian method was equally unsuited.[128] He advised that the socialists should 'not bother about an immediate struggle but engage...in activities calculated to transform the Congress organization into a fit instrument of revolutionary struggle.'[129]

EMPHASIS ON SOCIETY

Deva was fully conscious that in the new conditions society had acquired or was acquiring a place of fundamental importance. He reminded that it should be realised that the present age was the age of society and not of individual. In the sphere of economic policies and collective processes, society had acquired a place of pre-eminence. Individual retained no meaning in isolated existence, separated from the society. In the changed set-up, he could fulfil himself only by fulfilling the objectives of a social life. As the philosophy of each age changes, in the newer age, socialism was bound to be accepted by the bulk of society.[130]

He laid great emphasis on society, no doubt, but that did not imply that he subordinated the individual to a totalitarian or ruthless state. To such an attempt he was dead opposed from the beginning. It only meant that individual in a socialist state must concede to the ways of socialised and collective living.

Not much indication was given by Deva whether or not he personally believed in the theory of the withering away of the state. But he appreciably enunciated that concept, in the context of Marxism.[131]

[127] *Ibid.*, p. 123.
[128] Deva, *Rastriyata Aur Samajvad*, p. 691.
[129] Deva, *Socialism and National Revolution*, p. 124.
[130] Deva, *Rastriyata Aur Samajvad*, pp. 452–53.
[131] *Ibid.*

IV. Sampurnanand

Sampurnanand was born 1889, in a lower middle class family in Varanasi. The family environment under which he grew impressed upon him from the beginning a cultural, religious and philosophical outlook of life. Like all youths of the early 'twenties Sampurnanand was greatly stirred by the nationalist fervour of the time. Events like the Boer War and Japanese victory over Russia greatly enthused him. The Partition of Bengal agitated him greatly.

Sampurnanand started his career as a teacher with different assignments in a number of institutions, till he became a teacher in a college at Indore. After three years services in that college he got another assignment as the Head Master of the Dungar College at Bikaner.[132] During this period, he devoted himself to literary works and wrote a number of books. While he was still in Bikaner, the call of Mahatma Gandhi for Non-cooperation came. He resigned his post, and threw himself into the vortex of the national politics. He came back to Varanasi to organize the Non-cooperation Movement in 1921. It was here that he came in contact with Bhagavan Das, the President of the Varanasi District Congress Committee. During this time he also came in contact with a number of important leaders of the Congress including C. F. Andrews, Madan Mohan Malviya, Shiv Prasad Gupta and many others. Around this period, he was greatly influenced by Gandhiji's magnetic personality ; particularly, the technique of non-violent struggle attracted him greatly. He has recorded : 'We did not become saints, all of us, but those who had the rare good fortune of feeling the Mahatma's touch were different men ever after. His alchemy turned dross into gold As some people said, it was the culmination of scores of previous births to have joined the Congress in that year.'[133]

In December 1921, Sampurnanand was arrested while leading the movement for recruiting volunteers for the Congress in open defiance of the act which prohibited it. And it was not till July 1922, after the withdrawal of the Non-cooperation Movement, that he was released from the prison. He had, however, decided to

---

[132] Both the colleges at Indore and Bikaner were under the control of princely states of India. Thus he got opportunity to know the conditions in the princely states also.

[133] Sampurnanand, *Memories and Reflections*, p. 31.

devote his services to the cause of national struggle and the Congress. He continued to serve as the Editor of the *Maryada*—a nationalist journal, and a task that he had accepted ever since his return to Varanasi in 1921. In 1922 he became a member of the AICC also.

In 1923, he joined the Kashi Vidyapith as a professor of philosophy. The Vidyapith was a nationalist and private institution and had on its staff important luminaries like Bhagavan Das, Sri Prakasa, Narendra Deva and many others of repute and recognition. The Principal of the Vidyapith was Bhagavan Das towards whose ideas, Sampurnanand was somewhat attracted. Especially, the views of Das with regard to the *Varna Ashrma Dharma* appealed to him. He agreed with him that it was the nearest to perfect approach, evolved in the context of its time for conducting a human society on the basis of spiritual and material equity.[134] Certainly the old system was out-dated and inadequate, but he thought that its principles were still commendable and could be used as the basis for the future organization of the social order.[135]

Sampurnanand also admired, without subscribing to all aspects of its content, *The Outline Scheme of Swaraj for India* referred to as the 'Das-Das Report'.[136] It contained a picture of what 'Swaraj' for India should mean. Also, the *Gandhian Constitution for Free India* appealed to him greatly wherein its author had depicted a Gandhian picture of the future India based on 'the background of Indian traditions and thoughts contained in the *Ramayana*, the *Mahabharat*, the *Manusmriti*, Kautilya's *Arthashastra* and Shukracharya's *Nitisara*.[137]

MARXIST IMPACT

It was around this period that he came in contact with the Marxist literature. At that time much was talked about the communists and their anti-religious attitude. However, to Sampurnanand the communist appeared as the sworn 'enemies of imperialism and

---

[134] Sampurnanand, *Samajvad*, 6th edn., Varanasi, Bhartiya Gyanpitha, p. 70.

[135] *Ibid.*, p. 74.

[136] Sampurnanand, *Memories and Reflections*, p. 50 ; *The Outline Scheme of Swaraj for India* was written jointly by C. R. Das and Bhagavan Das and was published in 1923.

[137] *Ibid.*, p. 51.

friends of the underdog.'[138] The latter realisation evoked 'admiration and sympathy' for them. To some extent he indeed was influenced by his study of the Marxist and communist literature. He himself conceded that the memorandum that he presented, to the Gaya session of the Congress in 1922, had some Marxist impact upon it.[139]

Sampurnanand worked in close collaboration with Jawaharlal Nehru in the political activities of the Congress. He also served as the Secretary of the U. P. Provincial Congress Committee in 1926, and thrice he held that position in his life. In 1926, when the Congress decided to participate in the elections, he was elected to the provincial legislature. In the wake of the determined opposition to the Simon Commission, along with other Congressmen, he resigned from the Legislature in 1929.

In 1930 Sampurnanand prepared a pamphlet entitled *When We are in Power*. The pamphlet contained a few socialist programmes which he exhorted the Congress to adopt them as its objective. Some of the programmes included therein were :

1. Abolition of Zemindari with compensation.
2. Consolidation of holdings.
3. Nationalisation of key industries and principal means of transport.
4. Fixation of minimum wages and maximum hours of work.
5. Provision of work or maintenance, also old-age pensions.
6. Every woman to have leave on full pay, one month before and after accouchement.
7. Food and free elementary education to be provided by the State to every child whose parents cannot afford this.
8. Total Prohibition.
9. No Salt Tax.[140]

In April 1934, there appeared another pamphlet, *A Tentative Socialist Programme for India*.[141] In the above pamphlet Sampurnanand exhorted the socialists of India to form an All-India Socialist Party to organize and focus the country's attention towards socialistic programmes. 'It is strange irony of fate that while there are a large number of socialists, many of them sincere Marxists in India, there is no All-India Socialist Party to organize and focus their

[138] *Ibid.*, p. 19.
[139] *Ibid.*, p. 41.
[140] *Ibid.*, p. 73.
[141] Sampurnanand, *A Tentative Socialist Programme*, appears as an enclosure in the File No. 41-1-34 Poll, Government of India, Home Department.

activities with a definite programme known to the country. There are no doubt very active socialist groups in many provinces but for various reasons they have so far not been able to gain for socialism place that which rightly belongs to it as the system of principle and policies which alone can bring peace and prosperity to the country and permit it to co-operate with the other nations for the common good of humanity.'[142]

The pamphlet also contained a fifteen-point socialistic programme. This was in conformity with the programme already mentioned in his earlier pamphlet *When We are in Power.* It is obvious that he had come to concede some of the programmes that the communists were also propagating then.[143] No wonder therefore that the Government took notice of his programmatic ideas and kept an eye on his socialistic inclinations and activities.

AS A FOUNDER OF C. S. P.

In 1934 with his initiative a socialist party was formed at Varanasi. Only a couple of days after, the socialistically inclined Congress from different provinces met at Patna with avowed intention to form an All-India Congress Socialist Party. In that move Sampurnanand indeed played a leading role and thus became one of the founders of the C. S. P. At first Conference of the C. S. P. at Bombay held in October in the same year, Sampurnanand presided over the Conference. He also became a member of the Executive Committee of the Party. He mentioned about those activities thus :

I must say that this committee consisted of men with whom it was a pleasure to work. The sense of comradeship generated by work in the Party was something rarely noticed in the Congress Committees. We were not only fighters for freedom but apostles of a new age, a new orientation of human life, a new mission and the hostility to which we were subjected by most of the old leaders cemented our bonds of comradeship still more firmly.[144]

Sampurnanand, could not continue long in the C. S. P., although ideologically he kept himself close to it for a long time. On the issue whether or not the Congress should have paticipated

[142] Sampurnanand, *A Tentative Socialist Programme*, p. 1.
[143] Abolition of intermediary classes and nationalization of key industries were and are the major planks of the communists.
[144] Sampurnanand, *Memories and Reflections*, p. 75

in the elections under the much opposed Government of India Act 1935, the C. S. P. as a whole and Sampurnanand did not see eye to eye. The C. S. P. was opposed to it but he was among those who held the view that 'there was no reason why an attempt should not be made to bend our economy the socialist way, within the narrow limits provided by the Constitution.'[145] He strongly urged for participating in the election. Eventually, he resigned from the C. S. P. over that non-ideological issue and was elected to the provincial legislature of U. P. Between 1938 and '39 he served as the Minister of Education in the provincial government. From 1946 to 1951 served as a Minister of Finance and Labour in the U. P. Government and again as a Minister of Home and Labour from 1951 to 1954. He became the Chief Minister of that province in 1955 and remained in office till 1960. Shortly after the 1967 Election he retired from the post of the Governor of Rajasthan. He died after a prolonged illness.

He was one among those few thinkers, who was more concerned in enquiring and establishing the first principles of Indian socialism than launching straight way an uncharted movement towards its achievement. He advocated a Vedantic philosophical base for Indian socialism, and did not think it necessary for India to toe the beaten lines of the Marxists or communists.

Sampurnanand's first major work with regard to socialism, was *Samajvad*, published in 1936. Later, a portion of the revised edition of that book appeared in English under the title *Indian Socialism*. A booklet, carrying the similar title as his first work *Samajvad*, appeared in 1961. This contained three scattered articles from him.[146] His book on philosophy, entitled *Chidvilas*, was written on the suggestion of Gandhiji to enunciate the Vedantic and philosophical point of view *vis-a-vis* the Marxist. It was because of his leanings towards the philosophy of Vedanta that, in the fold of the C. S. P., he was often dubbed as 'Vedantic Socialist'.[147] Another important book *The Individual And the State* appeared in 1949. This contained some of his important political ideas. *Memories And Reflections*, one of his most valuable works, appeared in 1962. Recently a compilation of

---

[145] *Ibid.*, p. 83.
[146] Sampurnanand, *Samajvad* (booklet), Uttar Pradesh, Publication Bureau, Jyestha 1857 (1957), p. 39.
[147] *Ibid.*, p. 24.

his speeches and writing has appeared as *Sfut Nibandha*. Apart from these he has written a number of other books on different subjects.

IDEOLOGICAL TRENDS (PRE-INDEPENDENCE PERIOD)

Sampurnanand had come under the impact of the Marxist theory since the early twenties, although his deep philosophical and religious background of the childhood days appeared never to let its hold on him to permit adoption of wholesale Marxist ideology. In the first edition of his book *Samajvad*, he barely exposed Marxian concept of socialism without indicating his own disinclination towards that theory. Rather for over a decade, from 1922 to 1934, he gave evidence to suggest that their had been Marxist impact on him. To some extent the impact of M. N. Roy's ideas on him was also noticeable.

On the eve of the Gaya session of the Congress in 1922 Sampurnanand prepared a memorandum on the Congress programme, wherein he pleaded strongly for council-entry against the views of those followers of Gandhi who favoured boycott of the Legislature. But the council-entry, he suggested, was just to wreck the government from within—a strategy advocated by M. N. Roy. Then Roy described the move by him as a 'clear voice of one of those true revolutionaries to whom belong the future leadership of our movement.'[148] Sampurnanand himself also acknowledged that the 'memorandum had the stamp of my studies of communist literature.'[149]

The two pamphlets *When We are in Power* and *A Tentative Socialist Programme for India*, referred to earlier, envisaged somewhat radical programmes. In the latter pamphlet while exhorting the Marxists and socialists to organize an All-India Socialist Party, he wrote : 'The capitalists and upper bourgeosie are actively engaged in entrenching themselves behind various pseudo national organizations. It is we alone who are allowing our case to go by default. It is because I feel this most strongly that I have drawn up this tentative socialist programme which I am forwarding to you. In certain respects it is an advance on my book referred to above (*When We Are In Power*)...*It is based on Marxism but does not attempt to*

---

[148] Cited by G. D. Overstreet & M. Windmiller, *Communism in India*, Bombay, Purennial Press, p. 47.

[149] Sampurnanand, *Memories and Reflections*, p. 41.

follow Leninism. In fact, the very existence of Leninism proves that Marxism is elastic and lend itself to the conditions prevailing in the particular country to which it is sought to be applied. I have consistently tried to keep before my eyes, India's cultural, historical, political and economic background.' (emphasis ours)[150]

The above lines were unmistakably inspired by the strong urge in Sampurnanand to organize a socialist party on non-Leninist and yet on Marxist lines. He differentiated Marxism from Leninism, that is from the Soviet brand of communism. In his book *Samajvad* he tried to expound Marxian Socialism as he understood it then. In the introduction to the very first edition of that book he acknowledged his favourable disposition towards Shankracharya's *Advaitvad.* He felt, however, that there was no fundamental conflict between the Marxist proposition of dialectical materialism and Shankar's philosophy of *Advaitvad.*[151] At the same time he pleaded that those who find inadequacy in Marxian socialism, such as lack of spiritualism, should try to explore the extent to which socialism could be adjoined with spiritualism. His treatment of Marxism, therefore, was under the overall context of the Indian philosophical propositions, particularly the philosophy of Vedanta.

APPRECIATION OF MARXISM

He approvingly analysed the Marxist theory that the private control over the means of production, whether in terms of land or in terms of capital and labour, should be brought under social control. He maintained that the theory of surplus value was the basis of capitalism.

With regard to class-struggle also, he maintained that it was an old phenomenon of society and it existed ever since a class of persons exerted control over the means of production. Since the time of the *Puranas* the law prevailed that the strong should rule over the weak. The nature of state has always been coercive and it has always used its force in order to justify its own system ; it has been an instrument through which the ruling class dominated other classes. He emphasised that the working classes must control the state, without which socialism could never come into existence.[152]

[150] Sampurnanand, *A Tentative Socialist Programme,* p. 2.
[151] Sampurnanand, *Samajvad,* p. 8.
[152] *Ibid.,* p. 229.

METHODOLOGY OF CHANGE

Regarding the method to be adopted for winning control over the state Sampurnanand held the view that constitutional means or legislative methods could not bring the desired results. The socialists, therefore, rightly adopted the method of revolution and history also supported it. Whether it should be violent revolution or non-violent was not material in the sense that non-violent method was always preferable but only if it could succeed. But often it were the violent revolutions that were successfully launched in the world. What was important was not the means but the attainment of the objectives.[153] The objective of socialism was the establishment of a classless society that could be possible only when the power was vested among the exploited classes of the workers and peasants. Thus, under socialism, revolution was not a question of choice but one of compulsion. It was not the creation of the socialists but the logical culmination of the principle of ownership by a small class of persons to the exclusion of other labouring classes of the means of production at a given stage in society. Class-struggle was a perpetual phenomenon. In the technology-oriented civilisation, this had reached a phase of white heat in which class-war appeared imminent and a historical logicality.[154]

V. Jayaprakash Narayan

Jayaprakash Narayan, popularly known as J. P., played the most prominent role in propagating the socialist ideas in India, as well as in founding the Congress Socialist Party and organizing its provincial-level parties all over the country. He was the leading figure among the socialists who had been locked-up in the Nasik Central Jail in course of the Civil Disobedience Movements of 1930 and 1932. Here, he indoctrinated some of his comrades with Marxist and socialist ideas.

J. P. was born in 1902 in an average middle class family of a village in Bihar. His political life began in 1921 while he was still a college student at Patna. Like many youths of his time he came out from the college at the stirring call of Gandhiji to play his part in the First Non-Cooperation Movement of that year. Consequently

[153] *Ibid.*
[154] *Ibid.*, pp. 162–63.

he lost his merit scholarship, which he had been receiving at the college. Shortly after that, in 1922, he went to America for study and earned for his maintenance, through various works including manual labour on farm, factory, hotel and shop. He spent about seven years in America and studied at four different universities in turn— California, Iowa, Wisconsin, and Ohio. It was in Wisconsin that he came in contact with Marxist ideas. In the company of a Jew friend Avrom Landy and through the Mexican-born leader of the American Communist Party, Manuel Gomez, he derived the first lesson of Marxism and communist theory as well as practice, in so far as he lent assistance to Gomez in fostering a labour movement in America.[155] It was at this stage that he developed interest in Marxian ideology and tried to 'devour' the existing Marxist literature in company of a few friends. He wrote about it : '...it was in land of resilient and successful capitalism, in the United States of America... that I became a convert to Marxism, or more precisely, to Soviet Communism as it was then. It was at Madison, Wisconsin the home of La-Follete progressivism then, that in the company of Jewish and European born fellow students I drank deep at the fountain of Marxism. I think we left nothing unread of Marxism that was available....The pungent writings of M. N. Roy that found their way from Europe into the communist cells, particularly of Asian students, completed the conversion to Marxism.'[156]

INITIAL WORK THROUGH THE CONGRESS

After J. P.'s return to India in 1929, hardly had he made up his mind as to the future course of his life, when Jawaharlal Nehru, the then Congress President decided to use his services in organizing the Labour Research Department of the National Congress. His Marxist leanings and the labour work through the National Congress proved to be complementary pursuits, and these further increased his interest in socialist theory and practice. The radical trend of the time coincided with his youthful Marxist leanings. He was inspired by the goal of complete Independence adopted by the Congress at its Lahore Session in the very year of his return. Around

---

[155] Rambriksha Benipuri, *Jayaprakash*, Muzaffarpur, Benipuri Prakashan, 1967, pp. 56–57.

[156] J. P. Narayan, *From Socialism to Sarvodaya*, Kashi, Akhil Bharat Sarva Seva Sangh Prakashan, 1959, p. 10.

this time, for a while, J. P. was split within himself on the issue of joining the Communist Party of India. But its anti-nationalist stand impelled him to decide otherwise. He even thought in terms of founding a separate communist party and tried to explore its possibilities. He also established some contact with M. N. Roy, and was considerably influenced by him.[157] But, obviously, he did not get enough support in this move and the idea was nipped in the bud.[158]

ROLE IN C.S.P.

In 1932 J.P. was arrested, and sent to the Nasik prison where he found company of some young leaders. Among these were: Yusuf Meherally, Achyut Patwardhan, Asoka Mehta, M. R. Masani, S. M. Joshi, N. G. Gore and M. L. Dantwala. These men often met in study-classes and group discussion within the forewalls of the prison itself. Some Marxist literature was also smuggled into their cells.[159] It was in this environment that the idea of organizing a distinct socialist party on national scale, although not separate from the Congress, was first mooted.[160]

It was at the first gathering of the Congress socialists at Patna, on the eve of the Patna session of the National Congress that J. P. was elected the Organising Secretary of the newly formed party. In that capacity he made a whirlwind tour of all parts of the country and, wherever he went, he propagated socialist ideas on more or less Marxist lines. His major theme at that stage was to explain Marxian socialism to the people and to refute the views of those who considered socialism an ideology, foreign and uncongenial for India.

In one of his speeches at Madras on 27 July 1934, of which the government took serious note, J. P. declared : 'I want to present to you two theses. The first is that every honest congressman...who wants to bring about complete independence of India, not merely in name, but complete independence for the

[157] J. P. Narayan, *Swaraj for the People*, Varanasi, ABSSS, 1961, p. II.

[158] Rusch, *op. cit.*. p. 151.

[159] *Ibid.*, p. 147.

[160] Besides the Nasik group men, Narendra Deva, Sampurnanand and Rammanohar Lohia to name but a few, played leading role in founding the Congress Socialist Party in 1934.

majority of the Indian people, that is, for the worker, for the peasant, for the poor of this country, must accept socialism as his basic principle of thought and action. The second thesis is this that if we want that our great movement for national independence should go on, should advance...then today we must accept the socialist programme'.[161] While elaborating his views on the above lines, he pointed out that political democracy based on adult franchise, representative system, and private ownership of the means of production, was failing everywhere. What was required was 'economic democracy' and 'economic freedom.' For him, at that stage, 'economic freedom' was 'another word for socialism.'[162] He also refuted the view that socialism as an ideology could be 'foreign' to any territorial areas. He observed : 'If there is a capitalistic system of organization in China, in Japan, in Australia or in any part of the world, no matter what its traditions have been before, socialism is bound to grow there, and you see it growing there...India today is the part of the most highly developed capitalistic system in the world.'[163] He further pointed out that, if in such backward the efforts of places as Uzbek-Turkistan socialism has been established through the Soviet Communist Party, on similar lines the possibility of socialism in India could not be ruled out.

J. P. also criticised the Gandhian and the Congress method of non-violence. He considered it a 'great blunder', and urged the people to develop a mass movement-comprising the working classes and the peasants-against the government.[164]

In 1934, J. P. was elected the General Secretary of the C.S.P. at its First Session held at Bombay and, subsequently, at the Third Session of the Party held at Faizpur in 1936 he was elevated to the position of its Chairman. Thus, during the initial and formative period of the C.S.P., he played a singularly important role.

J. P. drafted the Faizpur thesis of the party in 1936 and the Meerut Thesis, adopted by the Party earlier, also bore his unmistakable stamp. In the Faizpur Thesis he laid down that the chief task of the C.S.P. was 'the creation of a powerful National

---

[161] File No. 36/3/34/Poll, Government of India, Home Department, p. 3 ; the government version of the speech is fully reproduced in the above file.

[162] *Ibid.*, p. 4.

[163] *Ibid.*, p. 9.

[164] *Ibid.*, p. 11.

Front against Imperialism.'[165] While elaborating the task indicated by the Meerut Thesis in different spheres, he pleaded that working class was 'potentially the most revolutionary class' and 'it is our task as socialists to see that it assumes its historic role.'[166] It is interesting to recall that while he did acknowledge that 'the working class and the peasantry' had led important 'militant struggles against imperialism.'[167] but the king-pin of the struggle was said to be the working class itself, and not the peasantry as such.

At this stage J. P. was largely responsible for initiating the United Front policy i.e., alliance between the Congress socialists and the communists, even against strong opposition by his colleagues like Rammanohar Lohia, Achyut Patwardhan, M. R. Masani and Asoka Mehta. He himself conceded later that the policy had 'disastrous consequences.'[168] But ever since then he came to realise increasingly that the Communist Party was 'not a free agent but a tool of Moscow.'[169] Besides that realisation, there were certain other developments taking place in Soviet Russia which also powerfully influenced his thinking. He observed : 'These were the infamous trials of renowned Russian Communist leaders.'[170] Thus he drifted away from communism, and that was once for all.

In 1939, J. P. was arrested and sentenced to one year's imprisonment, following an alleged seditious speech he made at Jamshedpur. It was during this term of imprisonment that he opposed Gandhiji's programme for individual satyagraha as he thought that the time 'was ripe for a final onslaught on the foreign power.'[171] He was kept in Deoli Detention camp, and it was here that the government procured a letter from him in which he had advocated the use of violence. Gandhiji, however, took exception to that letter, and pleaded with J. P. for the reconsideration of his philosophy, which deserved 'severest condemnation.'[172]

On the eve of the Ramgarh session of the National Congress in 1940, J. P. presented, through Gandhiji, a draft resolution on 'An

[165] *All India Congress Socialist Party*, 1937, p. 21.
[166] *Ibid.*, p. 25.
[167] *Ibid.*, p. 21.
[168] Narayan, *From Socialism to Sarvodaya*, p. 16.
[169] *Ibid.*
[170] *Ibid.*, p. 17.
[171] Bhargava, *op. cit.*, pp. 34–35.
[172] Sampurnanand, *Memories and Reflections*, pp. 109–10.

Outline Picture of Swaraj.'[173]   Although, the draft was not considered by that Congress, Gandhiji published it in the columns of *Harijan* and expressed his general agreement with most of the programmes envisaged therein.[174]

This might be suggested as the beginning of that phase in J.P.'s life and ideological evolution when he moved closer towards the Gandhian line of thinking.   Referring to this phase of his thinking Bimla Prasad observed that the 'fascination for Gandhian ideas' was clearly discernible in him.   He also added that the 'ardour for Gandhism' J. P. manifested since 1948 appeared to have grown in him 'as early as 1940, if not earlier', and, perhaps, in the beginning rather unconsciously.[175]

During the Quit India Movement of 1942 J. P. was imprisoned and kept in the Hazaribagh Central Jail.   But he miraculously escaped from this Jail 'to stem the ebb-tide of the August Struggle.'[176] He, along with Rammanohar Lohia and others, engaged himself in underground activities and led the freedom struggle while most of the Congress leaders were in Jail.   During this period he organized the 'Azad Dasta' and wrote three letters to the Freedom Fighters, and a fourth was addressed to the Americans.[177]   The letters were powerful exhortation on the people for carrying through the struggle for freedom and not to desist from the use of subversive and insurrectionary methods.   Throughout the colonial period J.P. often 'advocated the use of arms in the struggle for freedom, contrary to the stand of Gandhiji.'[178]   He acknowledged as late as 1944 that 'I am no believer in non-violence.'[179]   According to historian of the P.S.P., 'Throughout the colonial period, he was a convinced believer in the class-struggle and insurrectionary methods for achieving national as well as socialist aims.'[180]

[173] Reproduced in, Narayan, *Socialism, Sarvodaya and Democracy,* pp. 37–39.

[174] *Ibid.*

[175] *Ibid.,* p. xv, xxii.

[176] Bhargava, *op. cit.,* p. 35.

[177] J. P. Narayan, *Towards Struggle,* Bombay, Padma Publications Ltd., 1946, pp. 19–62, 223–39.

[178] Narayan, *Socialism, Sarvodaya and Democracy,* p. xvi.

[179] J. P. Narayan, *Inside Lahore Fort,* Madras, Socialist Book, 1959, pp. 101–02.

[180] Harikishore Singh, *A History of the PSP,* Lucknow, 1959, p. 17.

111

CLOSER TO GANDHIJICLOSER TO GANDHIJI

But, eventually, J. P. was arrested, tried and convicted in the Lahore Fort. An insight into his thought, and his response to the events outside and inside India, can be easily had from the pages of his diary notes published under the title *Inside Lahore Fort*. He approvingly noted Stalin's act of dissolving the comintern which 'had become a nuisance', and added that 'It was only another Bolshevik tradition liquidated.' As the objective of World Revolution had long been given up, he justified its liquidation fully.[181]

The pages of the Diary were strongly suggestive that while J.P. fully abhorred the habit of parochialism and clanishness and revival of the ancient village order of self-sufficiency and primitive economy, he did feel however that village must become the real unit of decentralised political system. He observed :

Not only economically should the village become a unit (of) a large whole, but also politically. It appears to me that if our political life is to be rehabilitated, the village must become once again a self-governing unit in a very real sense of the term. In fact, unless this is done the village cannot perform even the economic functions of the type of unit envisaged here. In the field of politics, if our political institutions are to strike deep roots and command basic loyalties, if they are to be the faithful expression of our corporate existence, the village Panchayats must be revived in all their glory and with all their old authority.'[182]

The passage above, may be taken as the forerunner of his thought-currents that prompted J. P. later to come forward, with a strong plea for the reconstruction of the Indian polity and a communitarian way of life.

In his diary notes, J. P. also indicated his faith in planned economy and the need for reconciliation between centralisation. and decentralisation. He was convinced at this stage, that for planned economic development, the necessity of a large measure of centralisation is obvious ;[183] yet he indicated his preference for planning through democratic method, and considered that reconciliation of centralisation or planning with democracy was very essential.[184]

[181] Narayan, *Inside Lahore Fort*, p. 1.
[182] *Ibid.*, pp. 3-4.
[183] *Ibid.*, p. 5.
[184] *Ibid.*, pp. 109–10.

Many passages of the diary further suggested that he was drawing closer to Gandhiji and his ideas. He made a particular note of Einstien's tribute to Gandhiji,[185] and dissociated himself from the views of an eminent Professor and economist, Brij Narain, that Gandhiji had done a 'disservice to the cause of Indian freedom.' He observed significantly :

'Professor Brij Narain's charges against Gandhiji are that by reviving the ancient Indian cult of ahimsa...Gandhiji rendered great disservice to the cause of Indian freedom ; and incidentally by thus basing his politics on an exclusively Hindu ideal, he kept the muslims away from the national movement. The second charge is that Gandhiji has turned the attention of the country to anti-diluvian economics the economics of village self-sufficiency.

As for the Professor's charges, they are not new. I do not agree with them as they have been stated, much less with the spirit behind them. I am no believer in non-violence. But I do not think that by teaching the unarmed Indian people the method of civil resistance, Gandhiji, has done a disservice to the country. On the contrary, I consider this to have been his *greatest service* to the Nation...

I do not say that Mahatmaji's economic views are *now entirely* acceptable to me, but I think that day has definitely been left behind when one merely created a few jokes at the spinning wheel and village self-sufficiency and called it a critique of Gandhism.' (emphasis ours)[186]

There was positive evidence in the terminology as well as the content of the above passage that hereafter J.P. leaned towards Gandhiji and his ideals, may be unconsciously still.

This trend coincided with his disappointment at the speech of Stalin, made before the Supreme Soviet on the occasion of the Twenty-seventh anniversary of the Russian Revolution wherein Stalin pleaded for avoiding war in future and described Britain, America and U.S.S.R. as the peace-loving countries. Reacting sharply to it, J. P. wrote :

All that Marx and Lenin taught about the nature and cause of war and the means of peace has been forgotten and the oppressed of the world betrayed.[187]

[185] *Ibid.*, p. 81.
[186] *Ibid.*, pp. 101-03.
[187] *Ibid.*, p. 112.

SEPARATION FROM THE CONGRESS

In 1945 J.P. was released from prison. Thereafter he engaged himself afresh in reviving the Congress Socialist Party. At the Kanpur Session of the Party in 1946 he, along with Narendra Deva, pleaded for postponing and delaying at that stage, any decision to secede from the Congress, with a hope that with Gandhiji's efforts the Congress might adopt some socialistic programmes and accommodate some of the socialist leaders in the party in some responsible positions. The socialists, however, decided eventually to boycott the Constituent Assembly as well as to give up the ministerial offices. J. P. was largely responsible for giving the lead in the matter of boycott, ignoring even a personal letter of Deva, wherein he reportedly 'had indicated his view in favour of participation.'[188]

NEW REALISATION

In 1946 he published an article entitled 'My Picture of Socialism,' wherein he declared that he still believed in Marxism, but, as there are rival thinkers within Marxian socialism itself such as the Stalinists and Trotskyists in Soviet Russia and the Communists and Royists in India, it was necessary that the 'Socialist Movement in India must evolve its own picture of socialism in the light of Marxian thought.'[189]

The article marked an important departure from what J. P. had advocated in his book *Why Socialism ?* or from his Speech at Madras, referred to earlier. He had maintained thus far that 'there has been one predominant school...founded by Marx...which was later on developed by Karl Marx's followers, like Lenin and so on.'[190] He maintained that 'there is only one type, one theory of socialism— Marxism.'[191] He did not consider that Gandhian ideas or Bhagavan Das's ideas provided in any way an alternative to socialism.

But he had now come to believe :

'No intelligent person today will doubt that the next stage in the evolution of human society is socialism. But will there be a like agreement on the question, what is socialism ? Different

---

[188] Sampurnanand, *Memories and Reflections*, p. 83.

[189] Reproduced in, Narayan, *Socialism, Sarvodaya and Democracy*, p. 41.

[190] Speech at Madras, reproduced in, File No. 36/3/34/Poll, p. 2.

[191] J. P. Narayan, *Why Socialism ?*, Banaras, All India Congress Socialist Party, 1936, p. 1.

114

theories of socialism and different pictures of a socialist society have been presented from time to time by socialist thinkers and workers.'[192]

J. P. had come to realise that even within Marxism there could be 'different' schools of socialism. Probably, this belief led him to evaluate all over the socialist postulates for Indian socialism.

HIS WRITINGS

The first work of J. P. appeared as *Why Socialism?* in 1936, containing the exposition of Marxian or 'Scientific' socialism. It was a powerful exhortation for accepting socialism as the goal by the Indian National Congress and also by the people in general. In 1946 Yusuf Meherally edited a collection of his speeches and writings under the title *Towards Struggle* with a short biographical sketch of J. P. This also contained his letters to the 'Freedom Fighters' written during the course of the 1942 Revolution.

His diary notes of 1944—the year of confinement in the Lahore Fort—appeared in 1959, under the title *Inside Lahore Fort.* This is a highly informative booklet and it also provides an insight into the gradual, even though unconscious, transformation of his ideas on Gandhian lines. In 1956 a collection of his speeches and articles appeared under the title *Socialism to Sarvodaya.* In December 1957 an ideological evolution of his thought appeared in the form of a long letter under the title *From Socialism to Sarvodaya.*[193] Another collection of his letters, speeches and writings appeared in April 1958 under the title *Towards a New Society.* In February 1959 a small pamphlet appeared under the title, *The Dual Revolution.* This contained his Gandhian approach that social revolution must be preceded by human revolution. One of his most thought-provoking works appeared under the title *A Plea For Reconstruction of Indian Polity.* This was about his essential ideas concerning the inadequacies of parliamentary democracy and a plea for the adoption of decentralised socio-political order in India. Another important collection of his articles and writings appeared as a *Picture of Sarvodaya Social Order* in February 1961. In the same year and in the same month, another important work advocating *Panchayati Raj*

[192] Narayan, *Socialism, Sarvodaya and Democracy,* p. 40.
[193] The same letter also appeared under the title, *The Evolution Towards Sarvodaya.*

for India appeared under the title, *Swaraj For the people.* In addition to these, he wrote a few pamphlets, such as *Political Trends,* (*1951*), *Sarvodaya Answer to Chinese Aggression* (*1963*), *The Challenges After Nehru* (1964), etc. In 1964 Bimal Prasad, an eminent scholar of J. P.'s ideology, produced a chronologically representative collection of his articles, speeches and writings under the title, *Socialism, Sarvodaya and Democracy.* It also contained by far one of the most evaluative introductions of J. P.'s ideology.

IDEOLOGICAL TRENDS

The evolution of J. P.'s socialist ideology can easily be divided into three broad phases : the Marxist phase between 1929 and 1946, the phase of democratic socialism between 1946 and 1954, and the Gandhian phase since then. The transformation from one phase into the other was gradual and evolutionary, leading one phase into the other. However, it appears, even within a single phase that his ideas remained evolving.

For almost the whole of the period between 1929 and 1946 J. P. was an ardent believer in Marxian socialism. But right from the beginning, at no stage probably, he was favourably disposed towards the Indian or the Soviet communists. The anti-nationalist stand of the Indian communists and the violent 'purges' in Russia shocked him deeply. On this issue the other socialists also were fully in agreement with him.

MARXIAN SOCIALISM

J. P. believed generally in the 'scientific socialism' of Marx and, to an extent, even in the Leninist elaboration of Marxism. He regarded socialism largely as an economic doctrine implying social or state ownership of the means of production and aiming at the eradication of inequality from society and concentration of wealth in fewer and fewer hands. The programmatic ideas included the abolition of private ownership and establishment of social ownership over the means of production. That involved the socialization of the key industries in society and also the elimination of the class of princes, landlords and other classes of exploiters. All these he considered to be necessary for 'the reorganization of the whole economic and social life of the country.'[194]

[191] Narayan, *Socialism, Sarvodaya and Democracy,* p. 4.

He did not consider then that Gandhism, or Bhagavan Das's ideas, or Manu's Scheme of Social Order, or political democracy, or Fascism, was in any way an alternative to 'scientific' socialism.[195]

BELIEF IN MATERIALISM

During this period he 'worshipped' at the shrine of the goddess of dialectical materialism. He agreed generally with the Marxian proposition that material forces affect individual and social institutions in large measures. He also conceded that, as a Marxist, he was an 'environmentalist.'[196] His line of argument, in opposition to Bhagavan Das's views, clearly, although indirectly, maintained the primacy of material forces in society. He observed:

'Social division (class) is an organic process of society. Marx showed that its primary source lay in the manner in which men earned their livelihood.'[197]

Dialectical materialism of Marx, he maintained, implied that the material forces primarily affected all ideological and social divisions including the institutional patterns of society. Pointing out the real difference between Marxism and Gandhism, J. P. pointed out that

......the real difference between Socialism and Gandhism is not in the 'materialism' of the one and the 'spiritualism' of the other. Those, as commonly used, are meaningless words. The starting point of Socialism is the inquiry into the causes of economic inequality; into the origin of princes, landlords, capitalists and paupers; into the secrets of human exploitation. [198]

The key to this enquiry, according to J. P. was in the Marxian theory of dialectical materialism which was also the basis of a socialist's enquiry into the causes of inequality. Gandhism does not attempt at any such enquiry.

THE PLACE OF INDIVIDUAL

With regard to the individual's place in society, J. P. held that the true end was the 'individual perfection.' But it could be brought

[195] *Ibid.*, pp. 69–126.
[196] Narayan, *The Dual Revolution*, p. 15.
[197] Narayan, *Why Socialism ?*, p. 118.
[198] *Ibid.*, p. 88.

about only through the 'utmost common good.'[199]   He thought that the environment and society by themselves do fundamentally mould the individual as well as social institutions.   He observed clearly that 'it is the social environment which shapes human behaviour.'[200] Naturally therefore, it was the society and the social environment, in which the individual lived, that determined the growth of individual and social life.   He worked on the hypothesis that if the behaviour of all the groups and classes has to be changed, the change is to be effected in the social organization itself.   He did not believe, at this stage, in the innate worth and the atomized entity of the individual and did not treat individual as an end in himself.   It was only later that he came to realise the importance of man as an individual, his inherent nature, and the need for his transformation as an ethical being, as a constituent unit of any social system.

Thus, in the first phase, it was the society, the social environment and the economic forces that were considered more important. A change in these, was supposed to bring about a better society, by itself.   He made no reference to the correctives of the individual as such, for obviously he considered the individual to be of little consequence in the context of the social whole.   The sociologist in J. P. also, probably, led him far on this track.[201]

PLEA FOR COMMUNITY-OWNERSHIP

Another interesting novelty in his thought, in the context of the orthodox socialist stand-point, was his advocacy for another type of industrial ownership in place of the ownership by the State or by the Producer's cooperative.   J. P.'s suggestion was for,

[199] *Ibid.*, p. 98.

[200] *Ibid.*, p. 97.

[201] He thought that society and social environment mattered most in bringing about socialism—which was nothing but 'social reconstruction. It was not a code of personal conduct.' Narayan, *Socialism, Sarvodaya and Democracy*, p. 3.

Also, in his unpublished dissertation entitled *Cultural Variation*, which he submitted for his Master's degree in Sociology at the University of Ohio in 1929, J. P. observed : the aim of sociology should be 'to make it possible for man to control his social environment, to direct his social destiny intelligently and rationally.' J. P. 's belief, therefore, in socialism might have been the outcome of this academic approach. Narayan, *Cultural Variation*, p. 2.

municipal or community ownership.' He observed

> I do not believe it is possible to find employment for many
> years to come for our surplus population, which would swell
> further at least by twenty per cent by the revolution in agricul-
> ture, in large industry alone ; secondly, because I desire to
> prevent the State from acquiring the sole monopoly in industry
> and employment. The state under socialism threatens as in
> Russia, far from withering away, to become an all powerful tyrant
> maintaining a stranglehold over the entire body of citizens.[202]

DEMOCRATIC SOCIALISM

J. P. realised increasingly that democracy or democratic method
was the *sine qua non* of socialism. He observed : There can be
no socialism without democracy. It is a common mistake these
days to think that there must be the dictatorship of the proletariat
in a socialist state. This is against the teachings of Marx. The
dictatorship of the proletariat has a place only in the transitional
period from capitalism to socialism. And in this period too it is
not inevitable in every case.'[203]

Thus he drifted away from the concept of proletariat
dictatorship also which was for long the gospel of the socialists and
his own. He now discribed his concept of socialism as 'an economic
and political democracy.'[204]

Continuing his theme, through another article entitled 'The
Transition to Socialism', J. P. described his ideal as 'democratic
socialism.'[205] The distinctive characteristic of this ideal was in its
technique of the socialistic transformation of society. He pointed out
'violent revolution and dictatorship, might conceivably lead to a
socialist democracy, but in the only country (U.S.S.R.) where it has
been tried, it has led to something very different, *i.e.* to a bureaucratic state, in which democracy does not exist. I should like to take
a lesson from history.'[206]

PRACTICAL NECESSITY OF STATE

J.P. appears not to have been worried about the ultimate shape

---

[202] Narayan, *Socialism, Sarvodaya and Democracy*, p. 46.
[203] *Ibid.*
[204] *Ibid.*, p. 48.
[205] *Ibid.*, pp. 49–56.
[206] *Ibid.*, p. 57.

of State under socialism. As the achievement of Independence itself was a remote possibility then the still more remote and hypothetical proposition was of the withering away of the state. As a Marxist, however, he confessed later that he had some appreciation of that theory. He was more concerned with the things as they were and the state as it existed during the transitional phase. In this regard, he maintained that 'No party in the world of today can build up socialism unless it has the machinery of the state in its hands.'[207] The state was to him a necessary tool and an instrument of power in society. The state also appeared to him as a coercive power. He explained :

> When the state is in your hands, you can legislate, you can use the whole magnificent apparatus of propaganda and education that, modern science has made available ; you can enforce your will. And if there is resistance, you can use the coercive arm of the state the police and the army to crush it. Behind every piece of legislation lies the state's power to persuade and, ultimately, to coerce.[208]

The programmatic picture of socialism also, which he visualised during this phase, underlined the progressive role and the continued necessity of the state. The state was to plan and regulate the whole economic life of the country.

METHODOLOGY OF TRANSFORMATION

With regard to the methodology of socialist transformation of society, J. P. had no doubt that resort to coercion could not be ruled out. Socialism could not be brought about by moral appeals and platitudes. He believed in the insurrectionary method, not excluding necessary violence.[209] He subscribed to the theory of the 'proletariat dictatorship, because, the owning classes by themselves could never be expected to sign their own death-warrant as a class. Hence, he believed in the concept of class-struggle—the class being conceived as a group of people depending on the particular mode of produc-

---

[207] Narayan, *Why Socialism ?*, p. 3.

[208] *Ibid.*

[209] Narayan, *Towards Struggle*, pp. 24–26. 'Also, Rammanohar Lohia said that none of the socialists, barring J. P., believed in the method of violence. He was not sure about J. P. 's position with regard to his attitude towards the method of violence ; this was revealed in an interview with Lohia.'

tion and the profit derived out of it.

J. P. also believed in the method of planning but he desired that there must be co-ordination between the centralisation on the one hand and the political freedom on the other.

J. P. however did not believe in the political democracy, as it existed then, and the whole apparatus of political system, parliamentary and constitutional processes, appeared to him to have been designed to protect and advance the interest of the ruling class. He was not shy of advocating a complete overthrow of the capitalist order of society. He believed that, without economic democracy, political democracy was meaningless. Adult franchise and representative systems based on private ownership of the means of production, within the capitalistic framework, could never serve the cause of the suffering masses. He, therefore, did not put great reliance on parliamentary system ; he had also no grounding in the processes of parliamentary democracy and its mechanism.

REDISCOVERING GANDHI

After the General Elections of 1952 in which the Socialist Party did not fare well, J. P. realised more and more the need for alliance and agreement between the like-minded parties so as to confront the Congress in future. In fulfilment of this desire he initiated the move, and succeeded in it, for the merger of the K. M. P. P. led by J. B. Kripalani with the Socialist Party. In 1952, shortly after the elections, the two parties merged together and formed the Praja Socialist Party. The merger was probably one of the most controversial of all the acts done by J. P. thus far, barring the United Front Policy of the 30s. But Asoka Mehta defended it not only as an act of expediency and political judgement but also as the perfect consumation of evolving ideals. He pointed out 'How complete the merger is and how pervasive its success is, is seen when we find Kripalaniji the doyen of the Gandhians talking to us in the syllables of socialism, and Jayaprakash, the Chief among the Socialists, talking to us in the idiom of Gandhism.'[210] Thus the merger, whatever be the

[210] *Report of the Special Convention of the Praja Socialist Party*, Betul, 1953, p. 75.

[211] In 1948, at the Nasik Conference of the Party itself he had indicated the need to understand Gandhian ideas, particularly his emphasis on the 'Ends and Means'.

political compulsions and considerations that might have prompted it, appears also to have been in line with the ideological trends in J. P.'s thinking since 1948 itself, if not earlier.[211]   In 1952, before the merger took place, J. P. explained to his party men that Marxism was itself a confluence of three streams of ideas : classical economics of Britain, revolutionary socialism of France and philosophy of Germany.   If that were so, he pleaded, 'Why should we not combine the Marxian thought with the thought and practice of Mahatma Gandhi and achieve a synthesis of our own.'[212]   Thus one can reasonably wonder if the 'merger' was not the direct outcome of this line of approach and thinking.   Of course, J. P. was not alone in the move for merger. Most of the pioneers within the party thought in a similar way.[213]

Within a year of the 'merger', another controversial move that involved J. P. was his response to the offer of Nehru to evolve some basis of cooperation between the Congress and the P. S. P. Following that gesture, J. P. formulated a 'Minimum Programme for National Reconstruction' on the basis of which, he showed his readiness to extend working cooperation to the Congress.   Even though the programmes were unacceptable to Nehru, the controversy did not subside without damaging the organizational strength and vigour of the party to a considerable extent.   It affected J. P. deeply.   It is from this time onward that J. P. realised the limits upto which the party could go along with him and he along with the party.   He talked in terms of stepping aside and to work even in a 'minority of one.'[214]

As the logical culmination of his ideological leanings towards Gandhism and *Sarvodaya*, J. P. attended the Bodh Gaya Sarvodaya Sammelan in 1954, and pledged his life for the cause of *Sarvodaya* and *Bhoodan*.   Thereafter began the phase of this '*Jeevandani*'—dedication of life to the cause of *Bhoodan* movement and *Sarvodaya*.

In his letter to Nehru, J. P. indicated his leanings towards Gandhiji and also towards Vinoba.   He pointed out :

[212] *Report of the Special Convention of the Socialist Party*, Pachmarhi, 1952, p. 34.

[213] Narendra Deva and Mukut Behari Lal, however, remained firm in their belief in Marxian socialism.

[214] *Report of the Special Convention of the Praja Socialist Party*, Betul, 1953, p. 74.

THE PIONEERS OF INDIAN SOCIALISM

> ...we have all been deeply influenced by Gandhiji. I do not mind saying that I have been rediscovering him lately and reunderstanding him...I do not find today Gandhiji's dynamism and incessant quest towards his ultimate values except in Vinoba, who has produced a remarkably Gandhian method for the solution of the country's biggest problem—the land problem.[215]

This was indicative of J. P.s strong affinity with Gandhism and even with Sarvodaya. He stood fully vindicated by 1953. As early as 1951, he had declared that *Sarvodaya* was no 'crankish' creed but 'outside the conventional socialist circles, it is the first attempt to picture concretely a new social order.'[216] In 1953, through another article, he made an open plea for Gandhism.

In the same year J. P. was invited to deliver the Presidential address at the First Asian Socialist Conference in Rangoon. He was again all for Gandhiji's and Vinoba's ideals. The address was dominantly theoretical and was an exposition of many vital philosophical propositions of socialism with regard to the changing conditions of Asia. He touched especially upon the ideological issue of 'amoralism *vis-a-vis* socialism.'[217]

In 1956 J. P. addressed the Second Asian Socialist Conference, held at Bombay, and suggested a new direction to the quest for socialism. This marked a newer understanding about socialism, and it was much more different from the orthodox Marxian ideology.

In 1957 J. P. addressed an open letter to a socialist comrade and traced the evolution of his ideology—from Non-cooperation Movement to communism, from communism to democratic socialism, from democratic socialism to Gandhism, and from Gandhism to *Sarvodaya*. He broke with the P. S. P. thereafter. What makes for the outsider a 'tortuous' reading of his life was explained by him, nevertheless, as the evolution of the same inner urge for freedom that had goaded him throughout his life. The ideological evolution took a straight linear direction. He observed in this connection :

> Freedom became one of the beacon-lights of my life and it has remained so ever since. Freedom with the passing of the years, transcended the mere freedom of man everywhere and

---

[215] Narayan, *Socialism, Sarvodaya and Democracy*, p. 80.
[216] *Ibid.*, p. 91.
[217] *Ibid.*, pp. 100–118.

from every sort of trammel—above all, it meant the freedom of the human personality, freedom of the mind, freedom of the spirit.[218]

Thus J. P. dissociated himself from party-politics and resolved to work for 'peoples' socialism', instead of 'state socialism.'[219]

In 1958 J. P. visited European countries and made close observation of the institutional patterns of European society. The experience of this journey was another factor that brought him 'Back to Mahatma Gandhi.'[220]

In his *A Plea For Reconstruction of Indian Polity*, J. P. showed his positive leanings towards the ideals of direct democracy, and pleaded for inculcating those virtues that could make it work. Having been fully aware of the failures of parliamentary democracy in the world, he appeared to be in search of a basic institutional pattern, on the model of the ancient Indian village order. In another pamphlet, *Swaraj For The People* he developed the theme further and urged for freedom from below and for establishing a *Panchayati Raj* without party-politics and elections. On both the pamphlets the stamp of Gandhiji was deeply imprinted. Also the ideals put forward by C. R. Das and Bhagavan Das in their booklet *The Outline Scheme of Swaraj for India* appealed to him considerably.[221]

For over the full decade following 1957 J. P. engaged himself in the Bhoodan movement and served the country in different spheres. One of the great champions of civil liberties in India today, he is also an advocate of international peace and amity. In an address to the United Nations Association of Coleford, England, he explained the philosophy of Bhoodan as that of 'world peace' and of 'creating the foundations of a peaceful life.'[222] In 1960, while inaugurating the War Resisters International Conference, he advocated the need for creating a non-violent 'social order' internally and a *Shanti Sena* for non-violent defence through martyrdom, externally.[223] He also emphasised the need for dual revolution—'social revolution' together with

---

[218] Narayan, *From Socialism to Sarvodaya*, pp. 9–10.

[219] *Ibid.*, p. 39.

[220] Narayan, *Socialism, Sarvodaya and Democracy*, p. 181.

[221] *The Outline Scheme of Swaraj for India* included, among other things, a strong plea for reviving the old order in which villages were the pivotal units of administration.

[222] J. P. Narayan, *The Dual Revolution*, Tanjore, A.B.S.S.S., 1959, p. 1.

[223] *Ibid.*, pp. 24–25.

'human revolution'—which alone could be the guarantee for peace.

J. P. has always lent his support for the cause of international peace and freedom of the people in the world. He has been one of the most ardent spokesmen for the cause of the Tibetan people. He has ceaselessly worked for peace both within and outside the country. His attempt in finding a peaceful solution to the Nagaland problem well recognised. He has also tried to foster a bond of amity between the people of India and Pakistan.

As an advocate of *Sarvodaya* and *Gramdan* today J. P. still maintains that his philosophy is the philosophy of Socialism. He pointed out that even gramdan is a unique form of socialism—'a form of socialism the like of which history had not seen before.'[224]

VI. Ram Manohar Lohia

Ram Manohar Lohia (born 1910 at Akbarpur in Uttar Pradesh) grew up in a family environment, in which the nationalist and Gandhian influences were rather strong from the beginning. He had his education at Akbarpur, Bombay, Varanasi, Calcutta and Berlin. Even as a student, he had a keen sense of individuality. He took part in the student movement of his time and came in contact with Subhas Chandra Bose and Jawaharlal Nehru.

The two greast influences on his life were exerted by Mahatma Gandhi and his father Hiralalji. It is from them that he imbibed the zeal for serving the cause of the down-trodden and the poor in society. The Gandhian method of civil disobedience and non-co-operation with evil and any unjust law or system greatly appealed to him. His language and philosophical bent of mind had the imprint of some German influences. His lofty sense of national-ism too was probably strengthened in the German environment.

Lohia had a great fascination for the study of economics, philosophy and history. In each of this field, the choice for Germany as his place of study had a great bearing. He came in contact with the Hegelians, the Marxists, the economists and some recognised socialists of the time. Among the socialists with whom he came to be particularly acquainted were Schumacher,[225] a German social democrat and Brailsford, a British socialist. It was in Germany that

---

[224] J. P. Narayan, *The Challenges after Nehru*, Thanjavur, Sarvodaya Prachuralaya, 1964, p. 15.

[225] He was a different person from the one who was Lohia's teacher.

his initial repulsion against violence began. It is said 'Having eye-witnessed the growth of militarism on the continent Lohia developed a strong aversion for violenee.'[226]

GERMAN INFLUENCES

His study in Germany, particularly the knowledge of German language bore impact on his language and expression which became sanskritised and, to an extent, also Germanised. His interest in the quest for philosophical truth and the ultimate reality remained enduring in him, and that might be a reason that in the socialist movement he consistently emphasised the importance of ideological clarity about the fundamentals.[227] He developed the faculty of original thinking and critical acumen for which the German philosophy and language were greatly helpful. It was in and through German language and philosophy that he inculcated deep interest in the Hegelian and Marxian ideas. Often he discussed Hegel and Marx in a *tete-a-tete* with his friends, whether in a class room or a restaurant.[228] As both Hegel and Marx belonged to Germany, probably, no other place would have better suited than Germany for such an intellectual discipline and also probably no other language suited then German and French. He had a working knowledge of French also. In his statement to a trial court in 1940 Lohia had conceded that he had considerable German influence on his mode of expression.

TRAIT OF ARDENT NATIONALISM

Thus Lohia distinguished himself as a profound scholar and thinker and manifested ardent sense of nationalism. One may wonder that the German ideal of lofty nationalism might also havs something to contribute to his already nationalistic bent of mind, cultivated in his family environment and during his student-days. His ideal of nationalism and love for freedom knew no compromise and his total ideology including socialism was conceived within the bounds of his patriotic sense of nationalism. He revealed that 'independence' was the most burning urge in him. At the Patna gathering of the Congress socialists in 1934, he made an unsuccessful attempt to get

[226] Bhargava, *op. cit.*, p. 40.
[227] Kelker, *op. cit.*, p. 6.
[228] R. Lohia, *Wheel of History*, Hyderabad, Navahind, 1963, pp. 1–5.

the world 'complete independence' inserted in the resolution concerning the objective of the C. S. P., which had been described simply as 'the establishment of socialist society.'[229] However, at the Bombay Conference of the C. S. P. he was successful in getting his suggestions accepted. In this connection he also revealed that the opposition at Patna was due to the 'Nasik group men' who had come out with a well-formulated draft of their own. From the beginning, therefore, Lohia showed his disability to reconcile fully with any scheme or programme over which he himself had not applied his mind fully. His concept of socialism was integral to his concept of 'independence' or nationalism; the latter could not be subordinated to the former.

ROLE WITHIN THE C. S. P.

His place among the founding fathers of the Congress Socialist Party is well recognised although his services were saldom put on records.[230] At the Bombay session of the C. S. P., he was chosen to the newly proposed official organ of the party entitled *Congress Socialist* from Calcutta. It is through the columns of this magazine that Lohia brought out many thought-provoking articles on the cultural problems. At this stage he criticised the constructive programmes of Gandhiji.

At the Lucknow Congress of 1936 a Foreign Affairs Department was proposed to be established in the AICC. Following it, Nehru, the President of the Congress, requested Lohia to take the charge of the Department. After some initial reluctance and persuasion by Narendra Deva he condescended to undertake the job. Thereafter, he shifted his headquarters from Calcutta to Allahabad. The office of the *Congress Socialist* was also shifted from Calcutta to Bombay and Lohia was relieved of the responsibility of its publication. The first publication he brought out through his new office was 'On the Struggle for Civil Liberties.' And a few more bulletins followed. It was during this time that he conceived the idea of a third camp for India in the context of the Soviet and

---

[229] Lohia revealed this in an interview ; subsequently this fact also appeared in, Kelker, *op. cit.*, p. 54, and Sharad, *op. cit.*, pp. 81–82.

[230] Lohia's own feeling was that too much emphasis had been laid on the 'Nasik group men', while the role of Narendra Deva, Sampurnanand and his own were not of less consequence in the formation of the C. S. P. This was revealed in an interview.

the American blocks.

Within the C. S. P., Lohia was among those who opposed J. P.'s initiative in launching the 'United Front' policy with the communists. He was also oppossed to any dogmatic approach towards Marxism. In 1938 at the Lahore session of the C. S. P., he was elected a member of the National Executive Committee of the Party.

Even before the Second World War had broken out, Lohia opposed any move to entangle India into the War. To him it appeared that both Germany and England were preparing for waging an imperialist war in their own interests and the poor in the world were to derive no benefit out of it. When the War eventually became a certainty, Lohia drew out a four-point programme : to oppose military recruitment; to organize movement in the princely states; to organize the porters against loading and unloading the War goods; and to refuse payment of the War taxes and contribution to the War loans.[231] It was in course of his opposition to any form of co-operation in the War that on May 24, 1939, he was arrested for the first time. He was, however, shortly released to be arrested again on June 7, 1940, and was convicted for a period of two years. In course of his statement before the trial court, he observed that all over the world there should be uniform rule of democracy and imperialism and capitalism should have no place.

ROLE IN THE 1942 REVOLUTION

During the 1942 Revolution, Lohia having been released earlier in December 1941, went underground and organized a secret mobile broadcasting centre from different parts of the country. He contacted J. P. in Nepal who had also escaped out of prison to lead the freedom struggle through underground means.[232]

At that time Lohia advocated insurrectionary methods and the methods of sabotage—the destruction of the means of communication etc. The whole story of the period was one of adventure and violent underground activities. Both Lohia and Patwardhan were recognised than as the followers of Gandhiji, and yet under the context of the situation, they justified their use of insurrectionary violence. However, they clearly distinguished between destructive violence in general

[231] *Ibid.*, p. 74.
[232] The two other socialist colleagues who were out for underground activities were Achyut Patwardhan and Aruna Asaf Ali.

and the violence launched by them. Lohia was eventually arrested in 1944 and released in 1946.

GOA AND NEPAL

Shortly after his release Lohia took up the cause of the Goan people under the colonial rule of the Portuguese then, and initiated agitation for civil liberties of the people. He went to Goa and twice he was imprisoned in 1946 by the Portuguese authorities, and was ordered to leave the Goan territory. He received big support from Mahatma Gandhi, who however, maintained that Lohia's politics might be different from his, but the cause he had espoused was ennobling and just.[233]

Lohia also devoted himself to the work of the reorganization of the C. S. P. He presided over the Kanpur session of the party in 1947. It was under his Presidentship that the prefix 'Congress' was dropped and the party came to be designated simply as the Socialist Party.

Lohia was also one of those who inspired the freedom movement of the Nepalese people against tha Rana regime and the British colonial hold over it. In 1946 he had advised some Nepalese people to initiate the process of their freedom, and in 1947 be came out with the suggestion for the formation of the Nepali Rashtriya Congress. In a press statement Lohia drew the attention of the people towards the conditions of the Nepalese whom he described to be a part of the British colonial rule, although it was from Nepal that the veteran gorakhas were recruited for the defence of the whole empire.

In his Presidential address to the Kanpur session of party, Lohia emphasised the need for fresh thinking on the fundamentals of socialist theory so as to strengthen the organization of the party. He particularly stressed the need for establishing 'peoples' *raj* where no distinction of caste, creed or colour will be allowed to exist [234], and also of achieving the 'objectives of establishing socialism and nationalism.'[235] He criticised both the Congress and the Communist Parties, the former for its 'undemocratic ways' and the latter for its non-Indian approach.

[233] Probably the reservation was on the score of insurrectionary method to which Lohia subscribed during the 1942 movement.
[234] Address cited in, *The Indian Annual Register*, 1947, I, p. 189.
[235] *Ibid.*, p. 190.

POST-INDEPENDENCE ROLE

In 1952 Lohia presided over the Pachmarhi session of the Socialist Party and in his Presidential address he laid down the 'Doctrinal Foundations' of Indian socialism. The address was markedly Gandhian in tone and temper, hence many decried it as completely 'un-Marxian.'[236]

After the merger of the Socialist Party and the K. M. P. P. a new Gandhian phase of the party began since 1952-53. Lohia, however, manifested disagreement with the way the 'Nehru-J. P. talk's began for cooperation between the P. S. P. and the Congress in 1953. He also criticised Asoka Mehta's thesis of the 'Political Compulsions of a Backward Economy' as full of 'faulty and mechanical reasoning.'[237] Lohia however showed his unwillingness to share the organizational responsibility at that stage and issued a warning that 'There are differing trends and opinions in our Party.'[238]

On the positive side, he suggested that 'a commission for the purpose of framing programme for the Party' should be appointed and hoped that 'It may be possible that when such a commission gets down to work what appear to be formidable theoretical differences may turn out to be very small differences in actual practice.'[239]

At the Allahabad session of the P. S. P., Lohia was elected its General Secretary in December 1953. Shortly after it he led the U. P. Irrigation *Satyagraha* for remission of enhanced rate in the State. He was arrested in the process under the U. P. Special Powers Act, 1932, against which he moved the courts, including the High Court, and recalled the ideals of Socrates, Thoreau and Gandhiji in defence of the right to peaceful civil disobedience. His stand was fully vindicated by the Allahabad High Court, and he was released from the prison along with a thousand other *Satyagrahis.*

BREAK WITH THE P. S. P.

But even before his trial ended, an incidence of police firing had taken place under the Socialist Government in Travancore-Cochin

[236] *Report of the Special Convention of the Socialist Party*, Pachmarhi, 1952, p. 30.
[237] *Report of the Special Convention of the Praja Socialist Party*, Betul, 1953, p. 43.
[238] *Ibid.*, p. 49.
[239] *Ibid.*

State. Lohia had sent a telegram from the prison itself to its Chief Minister, P. Thanu Pillai, to resign over the issue and save the face of the party. But he declined to do so, and the party also felt that Lohia's letter should not have been written without ascertaining the views of the National Executive. He thereafter refused to co-operate with the party and resigned the post of its General Secretary in September 1954. He also refused to serve on its National Executive Committee and on the Central Parliamentary Board.

SOCIALIST PARTY

By the end of 1955, he founded a separate Socialist Party comprising the dissidents from the P. S. P., and its inaugural session was held in Hyderabad on 28th December 1955.

The birth of the new Socialist Party, under Lohia's leadership, marked another phase of socialist movement in India and from its inception till the day of his death in 1967, Lohia remained the undisputed leader of the party. In 1956 he also started editing an English magazine entitled *Mankind* published from Hyderabad. After 1956 *Mankind* became the chief organ of his ideas. In 1963 Lohia was for the first time elected to the Lok Sabha and thereafter he remained its elected member all his life.

CRUSADER OF LIBERTY AND EQUALITY

The two important aspects of Lohia's life were his wide travels abroad and the number of arrests he courted in his life in varying conditions. With regard to arrests, one may wonder if even a veteran anarchist had courted as many arrests as Lohia did. Arrested for no less than twenty times in a period of thirty years by the British, Portugese, Nepalese and the Indian Governments, he developed a great distaste for jail-life. It was not the agony of jail-life but the tyrannical ways of the curtailment of liberty, especially civil liberty, that tormented him. His bitter reaction, at times, crossed the limits of his endurance. Lohia was pitched against injustices of all kinds, and in particular, the social and economic inequity or injustice was his main target. He consistently opposed the caste distinction and untouchability in society.

VISITS ABROAD

After his return from Germany, in 1933, Lohia visited Europe in 1949, He attended as a delegate from India, the Stockholm Convention for a Federal Government of the World. He travelled Germany, France, England, Israel and Egypt and touched at some western parts of Africa. After the World War II he attended the First Conference of the Socialists held in Frankfurt in 1951. Lohia was sent there as an observer from India. During his second journey he travelled Japan, Hongkong, Indonesia, Thailand, Malaya and Ceylon. It was during this journey that Lohia emphasised the need for calling a conference of the Asian socialists. To this end, he, along with a Japanese socialist, issued a joint communique.

In June 1953 he went to America and met many American socialists including Thomas Norman. He also met Einstein and the labour leader Walter Ruther. There he evinced great interest in the Negro problem and denounced the distrimination between the white and the black races.

In 1963 Lohia visited Byzantine, Athens, Rome, Cairo and Italy. In 1964 he visited America for the second time. While in America he resisted the discriminatory treatment meted out to the Negroes and coloured men like him. He gladly put himself under arrest, but desired that the cause of civil liberty must not suffer.

AMONG THE FOUNDERS OF THE ASIAN SOCIALIST CONFERENCE

Lohia's wide travel experiences had convinced him about the need for calling a conference of the Asian socialists as early as in 1951. In March 1952 the socialists of India, Burma and Indonesia met together to found the 'Asian Socialist Conference.' In an address to the preliminary committee, Lohia made exhaustive reference to the special conditions prevailing in Asia, with a particular reference to its religious outlook, utter poverty and agriculture-oriented economy. He maintained that under Asian conditions communism and capitalism were too inadequate to meet the needs and cope with the problems. In the First Asian Socialist Conference, however, Lohia did not participate, for reasons of his disappointment with the line of policy that the P. S. P. as a whole was pursuing. He had his reservations on that score. But later in 1954 he attended the meeting of the Bureau of the A. S. C. held at Kalaw in Burma, and exhorted it to pursue an independent line of policy with determination to oppose colonialism tooth and nail.

The Socialist Party that Lohia led since 1956 had appreciable success to its credit in the Fourth General Elections of 1967, and in two biggest states—U. P. and Bihar—it was returned as the second largest party. Lohia died in 1967 following an operation and it was an untimely unexpected death almost at the peak of his popularity.

LOHIA'S WRITINGS

Lohia's writings between 1934 and 1947 are available to day in the pages of the *Congress Socialist* and the bulletins published through the Foreign Affairs Department of the AICC. All his compiled works were published after Independence. He delivered a series of lectures in 1952 at Hyderabad, which were published in 1955 under the title the *Wheel of History*. This followed a number of compiled works, such as the *Will to Power, Fragments of A World Mind, Guiltymen of India's Partition, Marx, Gandhi and Socialism, Rs. 25,000/- A Day, The Caste System, India, China and Northern Frontiers, Interval During Politics, Language, Lohia and American Meet* and a number of pamphlets mostly published in Hindi.

ATTITUDE TOWARDS GANDHI AND MARX

Lohia along with his colleague, Achyut Patwardhan, has been described as representing the ideals of 'democratic socialism tempered by Gandhian concepts of decentralization and the use of non-violent civil disobedience techniques for nationalist and class struggle.'[240]

During the 1942 Revolution, however, Lohia justified the method of insurrectionary violence with a view to achieving independence under the special context existing then. Lohia however distinguished it from 'violence', in the ordinary sense of the term; yet Gandhiji did never justify the use of insurrectionary means in any way. In this respect Lohia could not follow Gandhiji, and he transcended the bounds of pure and complete non-violence as advocated by the latter.

In other matters, too, Lohia appeared to be a non-conformist Gandhian. He did not believe in God and soul, the central pillars of Gandhian thought. Lohia disputed Gandhiji's statement that the 1934 Bihar Earthquake was the result of sin of untouchability

[240] R. L. Park, and I. Tinker, *Leadership and Political Institution in ndia*, Madras, Oxford University Press, 1960, p. 189.

committed by the people of Bihar and the consequent wrath of God upon them. Thus even during the period under reference, although Lohia had great regard for Gandhiji and admiration for his ideals, he was, nevertheless, not a dogmatic follower, he had reservations on many points.[241]

Lohia, had come in contact with Marxian ideas while he was yet a research scholar in Germany. But he did not develop any dogmatic affinity with Marxism either. He pointed out that during the open Rebellion of 1942-43 against British rule, when socialists were in prison or being hunted and communists waged their 'Peoples' War' in companionship with foreign masters, the doctrine of Marxism appalled me with its wide range of contradictory applications. To recover its truths and demolish its untruths became my desire.[242] It is important to recall that it was the application of Marxism in India by the communists that appalled him against that theory. He also discovered some basic inadequacies in Marxism, which were formulated in his essay 'Economics After Marx'. Pointing out to one of its assertions that the proletariat revolution was first to occur in the most advanced industrial country, he observed :

> Where is the capitalist chain to break ? At its most developed link, says Marx; at its weakest link, says Trotsky; and, between these two with various other shades, communism will of course always be right. Lenin's explanation denies Marx as much as Trotsky's does. Lenin explains the Russian revolution by the active role of the Bolshevik Party......How this final activity of the class struggle flew out of its iron laws nobody has cared to explain on any scientific basis.[243]

Another inadequacy to which Lohia made a pointed reference concerned the Marxian concept of capitalist development. He felt that Marx conceived of labour as 'an abstract thing' while it was always related to the concrete world of place and time. He held that Marxian theory of capitalist development had been conceived on the basis of the 'internal' principle of labour and the contradiction generated 'between the value and the use value of labour—power, between the working class and the capitalist class of the selfsame structure.' He observed :

[241] This was observed in an interview.
[242] R. Lohia, *Marx, Gandhi and Socialism*, Hyderabad, Nava Hind, 1963, preface, p. 1.
[243] *Ibid.*, p. 9.

THE PIONEERS OF INDIAN SOCIALISM

Marx's capitalism was that of a self-moving West-European circle, no doubt causing great repercussions in the outside world, but the principle and laws of its own movement were exclusively internal.[241]

Lohia however regarded this as an unreal picture and expressed the view that in the 'free' Western countries, that is, in the ruling countries the capitalist development evolves differently from that of the subject and colonial countries. He observed in this connection :

In its place must arise a picture of two circles, one placed inside the other, the inner circle representing the free capitalist structures with their dynamic in the contradiction between capitalist profits and mechanized labour, the othe circle representing the colonial economy of the rest of the world with its dynamic between imperial exploitation and colonial labour : the rim of the inner circle possessing an enormously porous capacity to suck into itself the dynamic of the outer. This is the only way in which we can join up the capital labour dynamic with the empire-colony dynamic and arrive at a consistent understanding of the development of capitalism.[245]

Between imperial and colonial labour also, Lohia made a clear distinction and had a dig at it in strong words :

Labour has been either imperial or colonial, and there have been vast divergencies in their values. ...Human labour has shown a remarkable tenacity to live and work, and its requirements have varied from the minimum of 2 annas a day for colonial labour to that of Rs. 4 a day for imperial labour. This shows that requirements of labour are dictated, not by nature or physique, but by history.[246]

It is because of such inadequacies in Marxian thought that Lohia did not develop any dogmatic belief in it. He claimed, however, to have followed the basic tenets of Marxism. He pitched himself against capitalism, imperialism and colonialism and for this he derived considerable inspiration from Marxism.

As no systematic attempt was made by Lohia to formulate his ideas during the pre-Independence phase, like some of his other socialist colleagues, his ideas remained largely incipient and unfledged. It was only with the fullness of time, particularly after independence that his ideas, tempered by Gandhian ideals, look a shape.

[244] *Ibid.*, p. 16.
[245] *Ibid.*, pp. 16–17.
[246] *Ibid.*, pp. 17–18.

VII. Asoka Mehta

Asoka Mehta was born in 1911 and received his early education in Ahmedabad and Sholapur. His father Ranjit Ram Mehta, was an eminent educationist of his time and had great influence with the cultural circles of Gujarat. His grandfather was the Chief Engineer of the Ahmedabad Municipality and, thus he had the chance to live in the industrial and urbanised environment from his childhood. 'The most significant fact about his family is that it has no rural roots. His ancestors, for seven generations, never owned any land. Moreover birth and growth in industrial centres like Ahmedabad and Sholapur further urbanised his outlook.'[247]

Mehta's college education began at Bombay, and it was in that city that he came in contact with the nationalist and youth movements of his time. He took active part in the youth organizations in the city of Bombay. He graduated from Bombay University in 1931 and, owing to the tense political conditions in the country, could not pursue his college studies further. He took keen interest in the *Swadeshi* movement of the time and participated in the *satyagraha*, strikes and political agitations.

During the 1932 Civil Disobedience Movement he went underground for some time but was eventually arrested, and kept in the Nasik Central Jail for the first time, alongwith a number of socialistically inclined youths. He was, probably, the youngest among those who met together in the prison to conceive the idea of organizing a distinct socialist party within the Congress itself. There he met J. P. and received his 'first lesson' in Marxism. As Marxist literature was secretly smuggled into their prison cells, he took full opportunity of acquainting himself with its theoretical formulations.

Mehta came out of prison as a convinced socialist. He was, however, inclined more towards the European strands of socialist thought as represented through the concepts of social democracy and democratic socialism than towards Marxism. According to Hari Kishore Singh, he is a good example of the social democratic strand in Indian socialism, his political thinking having been influenced by European democratic socialism. He has never been enthusiastic about the importation of Russian techniques into India and

[247] Bhargava, *op. cit.*, p. 64.

has not been appreciably influenced by Marxism.[248] Mehta was also influenced by J. P. and worked in close comradeship with him. In 1936, when Lohia was relieved from the responsibility of the publication of the *Congress Socialist,* Mehta was saddled with the job and he edited the weekly till its close in 1939. The sheaves of this Weekly are the main source of his ideas during this period.

Mehta took part in the individual *Satyagraha* of 1941 and the Quit-India Movement of 1942 and, in the thick of the movement, courted imprisonment for a three-year-term for the second time. Although he did not participate in the underground activities, led by some of his colleagues, he justified it in strong terms. He observed :

> The essence of the underground lies in building up parallel authority...to deny and destroy the authority of the occupying enemy and to that end project its own power.[249]

It was not till 1946–47 that Mehta rose to prominence in the Party as well as in the labour movement. But as early as 1939 he had been entrusted with the work of organizing the labour bureau in Bombay. It was at this stage that he 'learnt his first lesson in trade union field.'[250] And since then he took great interest in the labour movement.

In 1947, when the Congress decided to dissociate itself from the AITUC, that had come to be dominated by the communists, Mehta strongly opposed that move. He pleaded with his socialist colleagues not to cooperate with the decision of the Congress to form a separate labour organization as the INTUC. But, when the Congress did act upon its decision, and, eventually, the INTUC was formed, he pursuaded his party men to form a separate labour-wing of the Socialist Party to be designated as Hind Mazdoor Sabha, in 1949.

The reason for seceding from the AITUC was that the Congress having withdrawn, the socialists alone were not in effective position to capture the organization by themselves. And the reason for not co-operating with the INTUC.—the newly formed labour-wing of the Congress, was that Mehta was not prepared to

[248] H. K. Singh, *op. cit.,* pp. 20–21.
[249] Asoka Mehta, 'The Underground', *Janata,* I, Feb. 10, 1946, p. 2.
[250] Bhargava, *op. cit.,* p. 66.

concede that arbitration alone was the 'sheet anchor of trade union-ism'—an ideal to which both the INTUC and the Congress were committed.[251] Mehta had been connected with different trade unions— in textiles, railways, engineering, post and telegraphs, etc.

In 1950 Mehta was elected to preside over the Eighth Annual Session of the Socialist Party. His presidential address touched upon many problems which highlighted the direction which the socialist thought and movement in India was to take. Therein he emphasised the need to clarify the fundamentals of socialism and warned that in the absence of clear objectives of socialism, 'the sense of betryal has gone so deep that such vision (socialism) stirs little enthusiasm, it is dismissed like the pot of gold at the foot of the rainbow.'[252] He also emphasised the need to develop pluralistic approach to varied problems, for he considered that 'life's lotus was many layered and every petal was precious.'[253] He cautioned against the trend of 'etatism', which the communistic way of approach was generating in society; that left no area of life private and free and thus 'robbed' man of his individuality. He maintained that the 'ultimate truth of life is not historical and sociological'; the ethical appeal was an eternal truth of life. And, therefore, socialism had partly socio-economic and partly ethical appeal.[254] Indeed there was a 'Wilsonian' touch of idealism in the address, but it was, at the same time, reflective of the fresh evaluation of socialist objectives that was taking place within the ranks of the Party, ever since 1947-48.

Mehta took leading part along with Jayaprakash Narayan in bringing about the merger of the Socialist Party with the K. M. P. P. He also undertook the onerous duty of organizing the newly created Praja Socialist Party. He had been the General Secretary of the Socialist Party since 1950 and held the position till 1953. Prior to it, he had been the Editor of the *Janata*—the official organ of the Socialist Party which was established in 1946.

In 1953 he cooperated fully in the move for organizing the

[251] Myron Weiner, *Party Politics in India*, London, Oxford University Press, 1957, p. 51.
[252] *The Eighth National Conference of the Socialist Party*, Madras, 1950, p. 28.
[253] *Ibid.*, p. 29.
[254] *Ibid.*, p. 32.

Asian Socialist Conference and lent valuable support to J. P. who led the delegation to the First Asian Socialist Conference in that year. In 1956 he led he P. S. P.'s delegation himself to the Second Asian Socialist Conference held in Bombay. There he was also chosen for the membership of the Bureau meeting of the A.S.C.

In 1958 Mehta had declined to accept the Chairmanship of the P. S. P. However, from 1959 to 1963, he remained the Chairman of the P. S. P. By this time Mehta had come to believe that co-operation, and not opposition to the Congress, was the crying need for the cause of socialism. In this hope, he accepted the Deputy Chairmanship of the Planning Commission, shortly before the death of Nehru, and soon after, he joined the Congress.

In his Presdential address to the Sixth National Conference of the P. S. P. in 1963, Mehta pointed out that 'Indian Economy has reverted to stagnation' and with the existing pace of economic development, the increased burden of defence must lead to inflationary pressure and the dilemma of destructive price-rise versus added taxes.' He further warned that 'whatever be one's social philosophy it is difficult to understand how one can tolerate inefficiency in the public sector and get-rich-quick habit in the organized private sector.'[255] The public apathy and the inability to 'articulate' what the people want might lead to fatal consequences. It was a pointed warning that the boosting up of national economy was a primary need to save the nation from stagnation and ruin. In the process the philosophical approach was necessarily sub-ordinated to the force of pragmatism.

Mehta was elected to the Lok Sabha for the first time in 1954 and again in 1957. In 1966 he was elected to the Rajya Sabha. Thus, he has had a long experience of a parliamentary career—being a member of one or the other chamber of the Parliament for a considerable period. During the long tenure of his membership, he proved himself to be a successful parliamentarain. He was appointed the Chairman of the Food Grains Enquiry Committee of the Government of India and the report that he submitted in the above capacity earned for him high praise. After the death of Nehru, he was made a Minister in the Union Government. He

---

[255] *Report of the Sixth National Conference of the Praja Socialist Party,* Bhopal, 1963, p. 44.

remained in office till 1968, and resigned on the issue of India's stand on Czechoslovakian episode.[256]

SOCIALISM : NO PLACE FOR ORTHODAY

Mehta has been one of the great exponents, probably next only to Nehru, of democratic planning in India. Ever since he put forward his views with regard to the 'politics of planned economy', he had emphasised the need to reshape and reorganize planning, in terms of its objectives as well as its priorities, so as to suit the Indian conditions. Even today, he believes that democratic method alone could be followed for planning in a democratic society. He has come to believe, even more strongly, whether planning succeeds or fails, it has got to go along democratic lines *i.e.* the parliamentary ways.[257] He is a convinced democrat, and, like Nehru, he believes that planning has necessarily to be subordinated to the democratic ways and methods ; dictatorial ways have to be discarded.

Mehta did not give any evidence of his belief in the concept of class-struggle and in the materialistic interpretation of history. but probably he was convinced as strongly as any other Marxist, that capitalism was inadequate and rotten to its core. He realised that socialism had become important 'because capitalism has run its course and fails to be a deliverer of our drudging millions. There are thus historico-social reasons for the sudden importance of socialism in our country.'[258]

Elaborating the socialists' opposition to capitalism, Mehta observed further :

> Our opposition to capitalism is not only on the ethical ground of equality. The present system of social organization lacks not only moral but economic health...Capitalism is both morally and economically prostrate. Our criticism is, therefore, not merely of distribution but also of production.[259]

He pointed out that, whatever concessions capitalist system might have granted to its workers in the beginning, the concessions were gradually lessened or withdrawn, both in England and in Germany,

---

[256] The Government of India did not outright condemn Soviet Russia's invasion on Czechoslovakia, Mehta took exception to it and resigned.

[257] He observed this in an interview in New Delhi on 2nd April, 1968.

[258] Asoka Mehta, 'Our Cavalier Critics', *Congress Socialist,* I New Series (28), July 4, 1936, pp. 11–12.

[259] *Ibid.,* p. 12.

right in its 'old age.'[260]

The way Mehta favourably depicted the upsurge of utopianism in his *Studies in Asian Socialism*, of course at a much later date, was suggestive that he had at no stage been an orthodox Marxist himself.

Mehta is recognised today as an economist, a great leader of the socialist movement, an acknowledged theoretician of democratic socialism, and also as an effective parliamentarian. He is many things—'a journalist, economist and dialectician rolled into one.'[261]

THE CONGRESS SOCIALIST PARTY : ORIGINS AND IDEOLOGY

Apart from the pioneers, whose socialistic account of life and thoughts, we have traced above, there have been many more prominent figures in the C. S. P., such as Yusuf Meherally, M. R. Masani, A. Patwardhan, Kamladevi Chattopadhyaya, P. Tricumdas, Sri Prakasa, S. M. Joshi and N. G. Goray. Among them, the latter two have been called upon to play even much more important roles in the socialist movement of the country after independence ; Joshi was the chairman of the erstwhile SSP and Goray was the Chairman of the erstwhile PSP—the two leading proliferations of CSP. It is curious, however, that barring Meherally who died in 1949, all others either lost faith in socialism or simply inactivated themselves, shortly after independence. Patwardhan adopted spiritual lines, Masani led for long the Swatantra Party as its General Secretary—the only professedly un-socialistic party in India today, Kamladevi devoted herself to the welfare work and social service, while Tricumdas, and Sri Prakasa (now dead) simply inactivated themselves. It is important to note, however, that the experiences of these men convinced them that the ideals of political democracy, individual freedom and ethical pursuits of life demanded radical modifications in the orthodox concept of socialism.

They were conscious of evolving socialism in India as a synthesis of the Eastern (*i.e.* Indian) and Western ideals. All of them reacted sharply against the communistic ways and methods. Masani's book *Socialism Reconsidered* (1936) may be taken today as one of the earliet mile-stones on the track of reversion from Marxism. It

---

[260] *Ibid.*

[261] L. N. Sarin, *Studies of Indian Leaders*, Delhi, Atma Ram & Sons, 1963, p. 13.

culminated later, although for different reasons, in Patwardhan's disillusionment and his plunging into the exploration of shrouded and mysterious regions'. The trend reached its climax when J. P., in the words of Asoka Mehta, returned 'after a prolonged detour of communism, Marxism, Democratic socialism, to the utopian Gandhism',[262] and we may add, to *Sarvodaya.*

The C. S. P. was formed in the year 1934. The immediate factors that led to the origin of the C. S. P. were the prison confinement of a number of youthful and socialistically inclined radical leaders in the four walls of the Nasik Central Jail, where they found time to meet together and discuss their socialist programmes; and, they studied secretly Marxist literature in their cells. The failure of the 1930 and 1932 Civil Disobedience Movements convinced them of the futility of the Gandhian method of struggle. The failure of the Gandhi-Irwin Pact of 1931 and two successive Round Table Conferences generated in them a firm conviction that radical method of struggle alone could be effective. The decision of some congressmen to revive the old Swaraj Party greatly disappointed these radical youths. In the wake of it, the decision of Mahatma Gandhi to retire from the Congress was interpreted by some of them as 'the proof of the failure of non-violent methods to achieve national independence.' Further, during this period the communists had been isolated owing to their anti-nationalist stand. According to M. R. Masani, it was to fill up the gap left by the failure of the Communist Party that the Congress Socialist Party was brought into being.[263]

There had been much deeper and wider reasons also that led to the formation of the C. S. P. The failure of the parliamentary institutions, the growth of fascist menace in the world, the dangers involved in capitalism and imperialism, etc., also prompted the radical leaders to organise a separate party. In this connection an assessment presented by Narendra Deva may be taken to be more authentic. He pointed out :

> The Party has come into existence as a result of a group of Congressmen in the course of the struggle. They came under the impact of the socialist thought of the world. They saw that a crisis had come over democracy in the West and that parliamentary institutions were crumbling on all sides. They

[262] H. K. Singh, *op. cit.,* p. 1.
[263] *All-India Congress Socialist Party* (Report), 1937, p. 3.

also saw that the fascist menace was growing apace, that capitalism was in a decadent condition and had entered its last stage of imperalism. They saw clearly that the choice before the world now lay between fascism and socialism and that capitalist democracy seemed to have no future before it. They found the world in the midst of grave economic crisis which did not seem to end. They found that it was Russia alone which had made substantial advancement towards socialism and that in the midst of the surrounding gloom it was the only hope of the poor the oppressed and the downtrodden for whom it was a great inspiration today because it is a precursor of a new era for the masses of humanity. Having studied the history of revolutions in other countries they came to the conclusion that the programme of the Congress should be fundamentally altered in order to achieve complete independence. The dire necessity of the anti-imperialist struggle led to their conversion and they quite rightly desired to develop the Congress platform for an anti-imperialist struggle.[264]

The ideology of the party was chiefly indicated in the Thesis presented and adopted at its Meerut and Faizpur sessions. The Meerut Thesis described its ideology as 'Marxian Socialism.'[265] This indicated its positive programme to launch an anti-imperialist struggle and struggle for national independence. Independence and socialism were integrally conceived as a single pursuit. The Faizpur Thesis declared that the Congress was to be developed and broadened into a a powerful anti-imperialist front to lead the freedom movement in India as a 'multi-class struggle of the peasantry and the working and middle classes.'[266] At its Lahore session, the Party strongly advocated the need for escalating nationalist struggle to princely states.

It is regrettable that during 1934–38, the active years of the Party, 'Marxian Socialism' was not elaborated much so as to throw adequate light on specific ideological issues such as materialism and spiritualism, the place of individual in society, the nature of state, or the methods of attaining socialist order of society—the issues that we have choosen for our study in the chapters that follow.

Among the pioneers of the party at least three distinct ideological strands were clearly discernible, the Gandhian strand represented, to an extent, by Rammanohar Lohia and Achyut Patwardhan, the social democratic strand represented largely by

---

[264] Deva, *Socialism and National Revolution, op. cit.,* pp. 74–75.
[265] *All-India Congress Socialist Party,* (Report), p. 28.
[266] *Ibid.,* pp. 24–25.

M. R. Masani and Asoka Mehta, and the Marxian strand represented largely by Narendra Deva and Jayaprakash Narayan.[267] Among these three strands, it has been rightly pointed out that 'there was no clearly defined ideology, but an uneasy compromise between the Marxists and the non-Marxists.'[268] We have indicated further, that among the pioneers, probably, there was not a single thinker who could be said to be unreservedly Marxian or unreservedly Gandhian.

The 'reservations' with regard to Marxian and Gandian ideologies, were so much bolstered up later as to lead to several proliferations of the organisational and ideological wings of the C. S. P. The ideological fluidity of the C. S. P. was its greatest handicap and unfortunate though it was, in the context of India, it was some what understandable. It was realised more and more, when the party came to be reorganised in 1947, that the ideological quest was of primary importance. It is only since then that the fundamental issues of Indian socialism came to be discussed and analysed through the party-platforms and individual writings. To these we shall now turn.

---

[267] Nehru, who was not in the party, reflected a synthetic strand of British and Marxian socialism.

[268] Quoted in, *Park and Tinker, op. cit.*, p. 189.

4

INDIAN SOCIALISM :
THE PHILOSOPHICAL FOUNDATIONS

IMPORTANCE OF THE POST-INDEPENDENCE PHASE

In the evolution of the socialist ideology in India, the post-Independence period was of paramount importance. Till then it appears that the fundamental philosophical propositions of Indian socialism had not been discovered. Marxian socialism alone was conceived as the real socialism. The impact of British ideology on the Indian trade union movement, which was strong between 1920 and 1927, and the impact of Gandhiji on the Indian National Congress, which was strong between 1920 and 1932, remained sublime and under surface, during the rest of the pre-Independence period. In contradistinction to these, the ideology of socialism represented by the left-wing of the Congress, i. e. the C. S. P., was equated with almost all that the Soviet communism implied. In 1952 J. P. made a clear confession in this regard :

> 'Let us trace back the evolution of the Party's ideology when in 1934 the Party was founded, we called ourselves a Marxist Party. What did we understand by Marxism then ... Those were the days when all socialists drew inspiration from the Russian Revolution and the efforts of the Bolshevik a Party to build socialism. Generally speaking, Marxism was till then very largely identified, atleast for us with all that Russia stood for.'[1]

Hence, the fundamental approaches in Indian socialism during the three colonial decades before Independence, were not much different from those which were generally implied under Soviet communism. Although many ideological strands combined within the National Congress and even within the C. S. P., such as,

[1] *Report of the Special Convention of the Socialist Party*, Pachmarhi, 1952, p. 28.

Gandhism, British socialism, Marxism, it is important to bear in mind that none of those ideologies was wholly acceptable to the Indian socialists without considerable modification. Marxism particularly was understood by them in different light than in which it was presented by the Soviet communists. We have indicated already that even the greatest among the Indian Marxists—Deva and J. P., had their Independent interpretations about Marxism; on some points they had serious reservations. And one of the greatest among the Gandhians—Lohia was at best a 'non-conformist' Gandhian. The British ideologies of constitutionalism, liberalism, democratic socialism, etc., had also been diluted to suit the Indian conditions. Therefore when it is suggested that during the colonial or pre-Independence period Marxism became the dominant ideology of the Indian socialists, it does not mean that Marxism, in all its bearings, was acceptable, and, farless, that it alone was acceptable by all socialists within the Congress or the C. S. P. Marxism, nevertheless, was the most important single ideology of Deva, J. P., and the C. S. P. as a whole. Even though Marxism was only vaguely understood and variedly interpreted, there was a general feeling then that it alone constituted the main stream of socialism.[2]

DRIVE TOWARDS GANDHISM

After Independence, there was a greater and calculated tilt towards Gandhism, even though this change was considerably resented by some partymen from among the rank and file of the Socialist Party.[3]

At the Kanpur session of the party, in place of Marxian socialism, democratic socialism came to be described as the professed ideology of the Socialist Party. And since then there has been a consistent leanings towards Gandhism. In his Presidential Address to the Special Convention of the Party in 1952, Rammanohar Lohia pleaded that as both capitalism and communism were closed systems now, Gandhism alone could provided the newer basis for Indian socialism. Again to this Address also there was considerable opposition. J. P. had to come out with a spirited defence of Lohia's address, and

[2] M. R. Dandavate, *Evolution of Socialist Policies and Perspectives*, Bombay, Lokamitra Publications, 1964, p. 4.

[3] See *Report of the Sixth Annual Conference of the Socialist Party*, pp. 8–10.

he justified the need for a synthesis between Marxism and Gandhism in the following words :

> Let us not forget that Marxist philosophy is incomplete, it will remain incomplete, for scientific thought ever grows and with every addition it becomes richer in content. Lenin had once said that Marxism is a confluence of three streams of ideas : Marx took classical economics from England, revolutionary socialism from France and philosophy from Germany and achieved synthesis of his own. Out of this synthesis he later developed his theories, which came to be known as fundamentals of Marxism, dialectical materialism, class struggle, and surplus value. As Marx had to achieve a synthesis, so have the Indian Socialists. Why should we not combine the Marxian thought with the thought and practice of Mahatma Gandhi and achieve a synthesis of our own.[4]

The above observation was a pointed evidence of how a new synthetic ideology was being gradually, but calculatedly, evolved in India, and the Gandhian ideology, which had so far been confuted and coffed at, had come to be increasingly incorporated into the Indian socialism. With this synthesis Indian socialism came to rediscover its new grounds and a new vista was made open before it with regard to socialist methodology and also, to an extent, its objectives. It is this turning-point in the ideological evolution of Indian socialism that entails a study of its fundamentals and philosophical propositions as they were evolved in the post-Independence period.

MATERIALISM AND SPIRITUALISM

One of the major philosophical premises on which Marxian socialism was construed was the theory of 'dialectical materialism.' It was said to imply the primacy of 'matter' over 'mind' (or spirit), in the context of Hegelian dialectics which implied the priority of 'mind' over 'matter'.[5] But, although dialectical materialism of Marx was a basic philosophical proposition, it was subjected to various interpretations including that it was a theory for the justification of

---

[4] *Report of the Special Convention of the Socialist Party,* Pachmarhi, 1952, p. 34.

[5] One of the authentic accounts of Marxian theory of dialectical materialism and its difference with Hegelian proposition is presented in G. Plekhanov's *Fundamental Problems of Marxism,* Calcutta, Saraswaty Library, 1944, p. 119.

economic or material needs of life exclusively. What subjected Marxian concept of dialectical materialism to be, broadly, conceived as out and out materialism, devoid of any spiritual or religious or ethical content, was due, probably, to many reasons. The first reason, according to George H. Sabine, was that the sources of the study of dialectical materialism were scanty and 'polemic', and there was no 'systematic exposition of it.' The second, and the more easily conceivable reason, however, could be attributed to Marx's criticism of religion. In India particularly, with its deep seated religious and theological background, the second reason was more sensitively communicative. It was little realised that even on religion, probably, Marx did not say anything new; he only followed the logical conclusions of the Hegelian proposition and the 'revolutionary' quality of Hegelianism itself. Again in the words of Sabine :

> The Hegelian philosophy, properly understood, Marx regarded as revolutionary in its implications, in spite of the reactionary uses to which conservative Hegelians put it...The revolutionary quality of Hegelianism is most apparent in its criticism of religion. The dialectic shows that all supposed absolute truths and transcendent relegious values are in fact relative...A radical use of critical Hegelianism shows the true nature of religion as a merely illusory satisfaction and hence as 'the opium of the people.'[6]

The third and the foremost reason was probably digged out from Marx's own writings. Marx applied the dialectical materialism to the study of human history, with reference to the role that the productive forces play into it. It has often been termed as 'historical materialism. It is from this aspect of dialectical materialism, i.e. the concept of historical materialism that both Lenin and Stalin derived their materialistic conception of history. Marx observed :

> In the social production which men carry on they enter into definite relations that are indispensable and independent of their will ; these relations of production correspond to a definite stage of development of their material powers of production. The sum total of these relations of production constitute the economic structure of society—the real foundation, on which rise legal and political superstructures and to which correspond definite forms of social consciousness. The mode of production in material life determines the general character of the social, political, and spiritual processes of life. It is not the cons-

[6] *Ibid.*, p. 633.

ciousness of men that determines their existence, but, on the contrary, their social existence determines their consciousness.[7]

From this fundamental proposition both Lenin and Stalin derived the lesson that the modes of production, at a given stage of society, determine the social, moral and political patterns of society. Hence the economic factors, *i.e.* the material forces, play the predominant part or the primary part, and the other factors are by themselves influenced by it. Lenin and Stalin were the chief theoreticians of the ideology of Soviet communism, which in · turn, during three colonial decades before Independence, exerted considerable influence on Indian socialists.

Lenin emphasised that Marxian concept of materialism did not imply the duality of matter and mind. There were no such things as 'knowable' and 'unknowable' as two separate compartments. There was only one thing, and one thing alone, as the primary substance ; call it by whatever name, but that was a perceivable thing and not an abstract fiction or imagination. That is, in Marxian concept of materialism there was as much non-duality in terms of MATTER as there was non-duality in Hegel in terms of the abstract IDEA. According to Lenin, Marx did not believe in the mataphysical expression 'thing-in-themselves.'[8] Lenin explained that materialism was the recognition of 'objects in themselves' or outside the mind. All ideas and sensations were the 'copies or images' of the external objects.[9]

It is such an understanding about materialism, that is, objects as they are, which formed the core of the socialists' thinking in India during the colonial period.

As, during this period, socialism meant only what Russia stood for, a natural inference was drawn that materialism was injected in socialism. Indeed, in a way, Marxism was 'materialism' just in the sense in which Hegelianism was 'idealism.' But, in senses beyond it, probably, the imputation of economic content alone in Marxism was not Marx's own creation, but the outcome of its pragmatic application in Soviet Russia.[10]

[7] Quoted in, *ibid.*, p. 642.

[8] V. I. Lenin, *Materialism And Empirio-Criticism*, Moscow, Foreign Language Publishing House, 1952, p. 14.

[9] *Ibid.*, p. 17.

[10] Eugene Kamenka maintains that the vision of Communism was 'not a vision of economic plenty or social security. Engels may have seen Com-

PHILOSOPHICAL USE OF THE TERM 'MATERIALISM'

Some of the pioneers of the socialist thinking in India were of course conscious of the philosophical context in which Marx had used the expression matter or materialist. Narendra Deva, for example, observed :

> The 'materialistic conception of history' which is a very important contribution of Marx has been misunderstood. Owing to the use of the word 'materialistic' in the expression it has often been thought that scientific socialism as propounded by Marx must be a materialistic doctrine. People say that Marx has denied the existence of mind, that he had no respect for spiritual values and that he did not recognize the force of ideas. It is said that Marx recognised only the supremacy of matter and regarded it as the only factor in the evolution of history. All these statements are incorrect...All that Marx means to say is that an idea can influence the course of history only when it realises itself in fact and thus becomes a thing. He has nowhere considered the question of the relative importance of mind and matter. Both are equally important. Man cannot create anything independently of the objective situation nor can a given objective situation by itself produce a result desired by man without his active participation. He only used the expression to distinguish his method from the idealism of Hegel who denied the reality of the world of experience and only recognised one Absolute Idea.'[11]

It was contended in the above observation that Marx did not deny the importance of spiritual and ethical values of life. But as these attributes in India were loosely equated with religious approach to life, which Marx professedly denied, Marxism was interpreted to imply negation of spiritual and ethical values.

A similar evaluation of Marx's materialism was made by Jawaharlal Nehru also :

> It was called 'materialist' because it was not 'idealist', a word which was used a great deal in a special sense by philosophers in Marx's day. The idea of evolution was becoming popular at the time...Some philosophers had tried to explain human

munism that way ; Marx did not.' Eugene Kamenka, *The Ethical Foundation of Marxism*, London Routledge and Kegan Paul, 1962, p. viii.

[11] Deva, *Socialism and National Revolution*, pp. 20–21.

Also, a similar explanation was given by Shyam Sunder—a pseudonym —in his article 'Socialism And Materialism', *The Congress Socialist*, II (38), Sept. 25, 1937, p. 12.

progress by vague idealistic notions of the progress...He proceeded therefore in a scientific way, examining facts. Hence the word 'materialist.'[12]

This was a further evidence that some of the Indian socialists realised that Marx put forward his theory of progress through matter, only in the context of reasonings like 'progress of mind.' Therefore, materialism was basically a philosophical expression.

THE COMMON UNDERSTANDING ABOUT 'MATERIALISM'

However, it is curious, that Indian socialists generally did not keep the philosophical context continually in mind, and the expression was used in a loose sense. The reason was that Soviet communism generally indicated its concern for economic programmes—economic equality, nationalisation of the means of production, privileges of the working classes, etc.—and these were on the whole accepted as the real socialism. We have shown earlier that even Nehru, Deva and J. P. conceived socialism, during the 30s, generally as economic doctrine, concerned largely with the socialization of the means of production and the eradication of poverty from society. This led to a feeling that socialism was a theory of material and economic aspirations of life exclusively; hence it was only a 'materialist' theory. Of course it is not suggested that the impression was wholly unjustified. What is being emphasised is that the term had come to be used differently from its original context. Marx, indeed, had emphasised the importance of empirical objectives and external environment, in the words of Deva, 'in things' rather than 'ideas'. Throughout the pre-Independence period, on the whole, Indian socialists espoused the cause of material needs and economic interests of the 'have-nots'.

KNOWLEDGE ABOUT INDIAN PHILOSOPHY OF MATERIALISM

This may be of interest to recall that Nehru and Sampurnanand manifested some knowledge about the materialist philosophy of India of the past. However, it is doubtful, if their socialist ideas were influenced by that knowledge in any noticeable way. The type of materialism with which they were concerned was the modern materialist philosophy, particularly as it manifested in the writings of Marx and Marxist literature.

[12] Nehru, *Glimpses of the World History*, p. 546.

Nehru regretted that almost the whole literature on materialism of the ancient Indian philosophy was lost to India and the world. 'Among the books that have been lost is the entire literature on materialism which followed the period of the early *Upanisads.* The only references to this, now found, are in criticisms of it.'[13] He, further, revealed that Kautilya's *Arthashastra* recognised the philosophy of materialism as one of the major philosophies of India.

While elaborating the content of the ancient materialist philosophy of India Nehru wrote :

> The materialists attacked authority and all vested interests in thought, religion and theology. They denounced the Vedas and priestcraft and traditional beliefs, and proclaimed that belief must be free and must not depend on pre-suppositions or merely on the authority of the past. They inveighed against all forms of magic and superstition. Their general spirit was comparable in many ways to the modern materialistic approach ; it wanted to rid itself of the chains and burden of the past, of speculation about matters which could not be perceived, of worship of imaginary gods. Only that could be presumed to exist which could be directly perceived.[14]

Sampurnanand also gave evidence of some knowledge about the ancient philosopher—Charvak, and considered many imputations to his materialist philosophy wrong and misleading.[15]

The Indian socialists, on the whole, however, appeared to be unconscious of the ancient materialist philosophical traditions. Both their affinity with and repulsion against materialism were generated by their understanding of Marxism.

EMPHASIS ON SPIRITUALISM

While the socialists in India, on the whole, worked for the material well-being and emphasised the importance of economic factors in society, the Indian writers like Bhagavan Das and Mahatma Gandhi consistently emphasised the spiritual and ethical objectives of human life. Even religion and belief in God, they maintained, were among the basic human urges. As both Gandhism and

[13] Nehru, *Discovery of India*, p. 86.

[14] *Ibid.*, It would be interesting to compare the above evaluation of materialism with the present meaning of the that term.

[15] Sampurnanand, *Samajvad*, p. 114.

Marxism germinated in the Indian soil in an almost arithmetically similar period of time,[16] the former emphasising the 'spiritual' and the latter emphasising the 'material' objectives in life, there was a natural conflict between the two ideologies which continued during the whole of the pre-Independence period. Naturally, therefore, the issue of materialism *vs* spiritualism became an important theme of discussion amongst the socialist and the non-socialists alike. This highlighted the element of contradiction between the 'Western' and the 'Eastern' brands of socialism, represented respectively by Marxism and Gandhism. However, it was tried to be resolved in the post-Independence period : a synthesis of the two opposite ideologies. This synthesis today has become one of the distinctive characteristics of Indian socialism.

SOCIALISTS' CONCERN FOR THE MATERIAL WELL-BEING

The socialists in India, who believed in the theory of dialectical materialism, were reluctant to accept the proposition that socialism implied anything else than the reconstruction of a socioeconomic order based on social and economic equality and social justice. They did not subscribe then to the view that socialism could possibly strive for 'spiritual' or 'social regeneration' as well. The belief that socialism could be used for ethical and spiritual regeneration grew, especially in the post-Independence period, as a result of serious revaluation of the objectives and the content of modern socialism.

In none of the programmes adopted by the C. S. P. or envisaged by the individual socialists, there was any reference to social and spiritual regeneration. In the post-Independence period, however, there was a significant change.

In the pre-Independence period, Jawaharlal Nehru had consistently maintained that socialism was chiefly an economic doctrine. He said : 'Socialism as every school boy ought to know is, an

[16] The Bolshevik Revolution took place in Russia in 1917 and in the same year Gandhiji dawned on the Indian political horizon with a glare of success in Champaran. By 1920, news and inspiration from the Bolshevik Revolution began to reach India by the same year Gandhiji established his firm hold over the Congress. Between 1934 and 1947 the C. S. P. advocated the Marxian brand of socialism and, again, it was the exact period of Gandhiji's life in which he propounded the theory of 'trusteeship' as an alternative to socialism.

economic theory.'[17] He had also maintained that 'when I use this word, I do so not in a vague humanitarian way but in the scientific, economic sense.'[18] He had conceded that his interest in socialism was primarily due to his faith that the poverty and socio-economic inequalities in society could not be eradicated without it. Similarly Marxist like J. P. maintained :

> One of the greatest contributions of Socialism to humanity lies in the fact that it brings social progress under man's conscious control and direction. So far, with individualism and selfishness holding the centre of the stage, society has progressed blindly...
>
> Socialism holds the noblest prospects for the future of mankind ; and it is collective planning of the future that so unquestionably establishes its superiority over the present disordered social 'order'...Socialism opens a new page in history—new alike from the viewpoint of material progress as from that of moral and intellectual advance...
>
> An essential part of any scheme of planned social progress must be a planned economy. The economic organization of a country is the key to its entire life. Therefore, control over the economic organization and its conscious direction in the interests of the commonweal are a basic requirement.[19]

Thus the view that 'economic organization' and material well-being are primary and the rest, including 'moral and intellectual advancement', follows and flows from them was one that prevailed among the large section of Indian socialists. Of course, during the hectic period of the colonial decades, no serious thought could be given to the full content and objectives of socialism.

The term materialism has had two levels of approach : one—the philosophical level as to what is primary, the 'matter' as an element or the 'idea' as a being ; and the second—the economic level as to what is primary, the material and economic forces of society or the spiritual and the innate nature of men ? In the pre-Independence period the socialists in India, with a few exceptions were in favour of the first poser on both the levels. This position was gradually reversed after Independence.

[17] Jawaharlal Nehru, 'The Congress and Socialism', a penpicture appearing in, *The Indian Annual Register*, 1936, II, p. 344.

[18] *Nehru on Socialism, op. cit.*, pp. 66–67.

[19] Narayan, *Socialism, Sarvodaya and Democracy*, pp. 18–19.

J. P. DISTRUSTS MATERIALISM

The rethinking and revaluation that took place, in the post-Independence period, revived a big interest in the fundamental issue of materialism *vs* spiritualism. Gandhian ideas now came to dominate the socialists' ideology both in terms of methodology and objectives. Hence spiritual values, which formed the core of the Gandhian thought, came to be assessed by the socialists afresh.

Ever since the Nasik Conference of the C. S. P. in 1948, J. P. came much closer to Gandhiji and pleaded for introducing 'ethics in politics'. He even desired to attempt at the 'spiritual regeneration' of society. By 1952, having come close, ever to Gandhism, J. P. observed :

> For many years I have worshipped at the shrine of the Goddess of Dialectical Materialism, which seemed to me intellectually more satisfying then any other philosophy. But while the main quest of philosophy remains unsatisfied, it has become patent to me, that materialism of any sort robs man of the means to become truly human. In a material civilization man has no rational incentive to be good. It may be that in the kingdom of dialectical materialism fear makes men conform and the Party takes the place of God. But when that God himself turns vicious, to be vicious becomes a universal code.[20]

With this new realisation he posed before the socialists that 'no other question is more relevant today', than the issue of materialism and spiritualism alone provided the incentive to goodness. In course of his ideological journey from Marxism to Gandhism and *Sarvodaya*, J. P. realised that if the materialistic view were to be accepted 'the individual asks today, why he should be good. There is no God, no soul, no morality, no life hereafter, no cycle of birth and death. He is merely an organization of matter, fortuitously brought into being and destined soon to dissolve into the infinite ocean of matter.'[21] Thus, J. P. not only denounced the materialist philosophy but also asserted positively that incentive to goodness could come only from a deeper belief in the spiritual make of man. This belief naturally demanded transcendence of materialism.

[20] J. P. Narayan, *A Picture of Sarvodaya Social Order*, Tanjore, A Sarvodaya Publication, 1961, p. 18.
[21] *Ibid.*, p. 17.

PATWARDHAN'S NEW EXPLORATION

It was almost with a similar realisation that Achyut Patwardhan, broke his ties with the Socialist Party in 1950. In his parting letter to the General Secretary, couched in the typical Gandhian phraseology, he wrote:

'The inevitable result of this quest for political power is the growing vogue of ruthlessness in our public life ..Practice between parties and even within each party has reflected the decay of social standards and this tendency has debased our public life. On the one hand, it has led to the glorification of the state as the new Church Militant, it has on the other hand led to a total lack of brotherliness and tolerance between persons...There must be another approach to social regeneration...I must confess, that there is no ready made alternative of this type to which one could subscribe en masse. *It is an exploration in a region of human behaviour which is still shrouded in uncertainty.* Yet any new movement must begin in the first instance as the adventure of a single perplexed mind....'[22]

Needless to say that the 'spiritual regeneration' and the 'social regeneration' to which both J. P. and Patwardhan referred now were the result of a deeper realisation of values beyond the frontiers of materialism.

DEVA'S APPRECIATION OF GANDHISM

Concern for the ethical values and goodness brought home to the Indian socialists the lesson of utter futility in giving priority to material values over the ethical ones. While paying a tribute to Gandhiji, on his death in 1948, the elder socialist—Narendra Deva—observed : 'The path of life is in peace, in religion, in the sustenance of the social and spiritual values of life ; not in tyranny and bad conduct, not in hatred and enmity.'[23] Proceeding further, he exhorted the people to follow the path of Gandhiji and, if need be, even to give up party-politics with a view to starting a living cultural revolution through which Gandhian ideas could be spread all over the country.[24] Such an appeal, coming from no less a Marxist than Deva himself, was a pointer that the Gandhian ideas, symbolising the spiritual values, had come to be woven into the web of Indian socialism.

[22] *Report of the Eighth National Conference*, Madras, 1950, p. 7.
[23] Deva, *Rastriyata Aur Samajvad*, pp. 729–30.
[24] *Ibid.*, p. 731.

LOHIA'S EMPHASIS ON SYNTHESIS

About the same time, Rammanohar Lohia, in his own way, emphasised that for Indian socialism both capitalism and communism were equally closed systems, and the need of the time was to take inspiration from Gandhian ideas so as to evolve a synthetic ideology of its own. In so doing, Lohia was conscious that materialism alone could not do, but a striking balance between materialism and spiritualism was the need of the hour. He observed in 1952 :

> It may be doubtful whether the material and the spiritual, the lovely and the good, in fact, the beautiful and the true can even come to terms except by a trick of definition in which the one is absorbed by the other. Furthermore, the possibility of a continuing equilibrium in view of the dynamism and the demonism of the material may also be denied.[25]

Lohia regretted that Gandhian ideas were not followed truly but only ceremonially. Further, he pleaded :

> ...if an effort is made to build Gandhiji's postulates into economic and administrative systems and work them out, it would be possible for India to help in the creation of a new civilization. This is the specific job of socialism all over the word and especially of socialism in India.[26]

And, in a similar vein, he observed, like J. P., that, unless Gandhian or spiritual values were redeemed, the systems that have so far been practised —socialism being no exception—would make it unnecessary for the individual 'to be good.'[27] With that end in view, he observed :

> If there is any lesson to be learnt from Mahatma Gandhi's life and action, every one of us should strive to bring out the latent qualities of satyagraha and sagehood as well as sainthood. Let us not be frightened of sainthood. No to wish to deny the flesh is almost always to deny the saint altogether, and that is bad.[28]

The blending of the material and spiritual desires in man appeared to have been at the core of Lohia's thinking, particularly, since the death of Gandhiji.

What was important, according to him, was not to kill the

[25] Lohia, *Marx, Gandhi and Socialism*, p. 134.
[26] *Ibid.*, p. 136.
[27] *Ibid.*
[28] *Ibid.*, p. 137.

'bull' of materialism but 'to hold it by the horns.'[29]   Although Lohia appeared to have avoided falling into the trap of the riddle of 'materiality' *vs* 'spirituality', as he called it, he clearly realised that socialism could not be built on, purely materialistic foundations.[30]

MEHTA'S EMPHASIS ON ETHICAL APPROACH

Asoka Mehta appears to have been one among those few socialists in India who, at no stage, developed any affinity with the Marxian theory of dialectical materialism. He frankly conceded that he had no interest in the philosophical aspect of socialism. But the way he evaded the issue as well as the way he indicated the different sorts of appeal, which incline men towards socialism, were enough to indicate that he did not consider socialism to be exclusively a theory with economic concern. He realised that the 'ethical appeal is strong'[31] and that, from certain angles, 'the temple of free society demands...the bricks of new individuals.'[32]   Even Marx according to him, realised that the 'root' of the tree of life was man himself.[33] Mehta felt that in no sphere of life the generally accepted notions of materialism could provide the whole answer. He said that socialism had partly a socio-economic appeal and partly an ethical. The ultimate truth of life was not historical or sociological.[34] Therefore, it appeared to him that materialist philosophy alone could not be an adequate and comprehensive basis of socialism today. And, in that context, he showed his unmistakable appreciation of Gandhian ideas including those of Vinoba. He observed :

> To philosophic anarchy that is the ultimate objective of all socialists, utopian as well as scientific, Gandhi and Vinoba offer a constantly foliating approach.[35]

Thus, all the leading socialists like Deva, J. P., Lohia, and Mehta, to name but a few, advocated the need to assimilate the Gandhian or the spiritual values in socialism in varying degrees and propor-

[29] *Ibid.*, p. 204.
[30] *Ibid.*, pp. 198–206.
[31] Asoka Mehta, *Democratic Socialism*, p. 3.
[32] *Ibid.*, p. 4.
[33] *Ibid.*, p. 5.
[34] *Report of the Sixth Annual Conference of the Socialist Party*, Nasik, 1948, p. 32.
[35] Asoka Mehta, *Studies of Asian Socialism*, p. 94.

tions which had been, during the pre-Independence period, largely under-rated or even ignored.

THE GANDHIAN IMPACT THROUGH THE K.M.P.P.

The trend to incorporate the spiritual objectives in socialism since 1948 appeared to have become more dominant by 1953 and the years following it. The K. M. P. P. and the Forward Block, having merged themselves with the S. P. in 1953, strengthened the trend of blending Gandhism with socialism and spiritualism with materialism. In J. P.'s evaluation : 'The K. M. P. P. was Gandhian, at least its outstanding leaders such as Acharya J. B. Kripalani, Dr. P. C. Ghosh, Shri Kelappan were and are ideologically devout Gandhians... Netaji had rejected Marxian materialism and stood for the spiritual values of life, which he wanted to make the foundation of the new social order.'[36]

The origin of the Bhoodan Movement further created a spiritual climate and the socialists in India, particularly J. P., derived great inspiration from it.

P. S. P. WEDDED TO SPIRITUAL OBJECTIVES

In 1955 the Policy Statement of the P. S. P. also declared its objectives 'to build up a new social order, it is our solemn duty to vitalise what is essentially humanistic in our cultural and traditions to be helpful in the transformation of social life.'[37] The Policy Statement further declared : 'For Indian socialists the socialist movement has never been purely an economic movement. It has also been an ethical and cultural movement.'[38]

Thus the issue of spiritual and ethical values consistently emphasised by the Indian socialists, came to be incorporated into the above Policy Statement itself. It was indicative of the transformation of the ideology of the P. S. P. In no uncertain terms now it had been declared that the P. S. P., as a whole, stood for both economic and spiritual objectives of life and it was not exclusively an economic movement.

---

[36] J. P. Narayan, 'A Plea for Gandhism', reproduced in, Narayan, Socialism, Sarvodaya and Democracy, p. 119.

[37] Policy Statement, 1955, p. 2.

[38] Ibid., p. 4.

EVOLUTION OF THE 'BASIC APPROACH' IN NEHRU

Jawaharlal Nehru and Sampurnanand, greatly emphasised the spiritual values as the basic ingredients of Indian socialism. Both were greatly affected by Gandhiji's warning that

> ...in so far as we have made the modern materialistic craze our goal, so far we are going down-hill in the path of progress. I hold that economic progress in the sense I have put it is antagonistic to real progress...That you cannot serve God and Mammon is an economic truth of the highest value. We have to make our choice. Western nations are today groaning under the heel of the monster god of materialism. Their moral growth has become stunted.[39]

The moral of the above observation had consistently been impressed on the Congressmen and the people in general. Jawaharlal Nehru appeared, at no stage, to have forgotten this lesson. In his conversation with Tibor Mende and R. K. Karanjia, he conceded frankly that Gandhiji did 'spiritualise' him.[40] We have indicated earlier the spiritualistic and philosophical bent of mind of Nehru and the riddle he had to confront in regard to the Marxian and metaphysical approaches to the problems of human life right from the beginning and, more particularly, since 1945. It appears that at no stage, despite his socialist ideas, he subscribed wholly to the materialistic concept of life and society, not as only the result of Gandhian impact on him but also due to the impact of Indian culture and philosophical traditions on him. The philosophical bent of mind grew in him more and more, as he drew close towards the evening of his life. He explained this change in him clearly.

> ...Yes, I have changed. The emphasis on ethical and spiritual solutions is not unconscious. It is deliberate, quite deliberate. There are good reasons for it. First of all, apart from material development that is imperative, I believe that the human mind is hungry for something deeper in terms of moral and spiritual development without which all the material advance may not be worth while.[41]

In the post-Independence period, Nehru came also to drive increasing inspiration from the teachings of the Buddha, Gandhi, Vivekananda,

[39] Gandhiji's Address at Allahabad University on 22nd Dec. 1916, quoted in, M. K. Gandhi, *Economic and Industrial Life and Relations*, II, pp. 6-7.

[40] Tibor Mende, *op. cit.*, p. 27.

[41] Karanjia, *op. cit.*, p. 32.

and even Vinoba. He realised now, more than ever, the need for synthesis between 'science and spirituality'. In fact, this trend had been noticeable in him since the beginning and, more particularly, since 1945. By now he leaned heavily towards the vedantic ideals of life towards which his colleague Sampurnanand had been drawing the attention of the socialists for long. Nehru developed this line of thinking in his widely noticed article 'Basic Approach'. Making a direct reference to the altruistic element in life, Nehru wrote :

> In our efforts to ensure the material prosperity of the country, we have not paid any attention to the spiritual element in human nature. Therefore in order to give the individual and the nation a sense of purpose, something to live for and, if necessary, to die for, we have to revive some philosophy of life and give, in the wider sense of the word a spiritual background to our thinking.[42]

Nehru had thus come to realise that more satisfaction of the material needs of life could not solve the problems of life as a whole; hence he was now more and more inclined to accept the spiritual and ethical side of life, which the socialists generally had ignored during pre-Independence period. He became aware of 'something' he could not define, and the economic side of life as the sole aspect appeared to him to be absurd.

SAMPURNANAND'S PLEA FOR VEDANTIC FOUNDATION

In Sampurnanand's thinking the spiritual and the philosophical outlook was probably most pronounced. Ever since he felt the impact of Marxist ideas and became a founder-leader of the C. S. P., he had been 'dubbed' as a 'Vedantic Samajvadi'. Indeed, the Vedantic approach was not just skin-deep in him; it grew stronger and stronger till he found in the Vedanta itself the philosophical foundation of Indian socialism.[43] He considered any other basis, such as Marxism, inadequate and angular. He observed :

> 'In Indian thought, the substratum of the universe is pure consciousness. As the result of a process somewhat dialectical in nature, it became conscious, conscious of itself in the absence of any other object. Later, it evolved into the diversity that is the universe as we know it ...What is called Brahma in the

[42] J. Nehru, 'Basic Approach', *AICC Economic Review*, 10(8/9), Aug. 15, 1958, pp. 3–4, also, reproduced in, Sampurnanand, *Indian Socialism*, p. 73.

[43] Sampurnanand, *Indian Socialism*, p. x.

state of pure consciousness is known as *Paramatma*, the Universal Ego, when it becomes self-conscious. The individual ego is, of course, only a manifestation of the Universal Ego on the body-plane and possesses all the attributes of the latter, though in a more or less latent condition.'[44]

Further, he observed :

'The removal of nescience and the re-establishment in the fullness of one's own nature is the real goal of all life. This, the final objective, is consciously pursued by only a few, but, unconsciously, all living things are incessantly striving after it. It is called *moksha*.'[45]

INDIVIDUAL—THE INNATE SPIRITUAL ENTITY

To Sampurnanand it appeared that Indian socialism and Marxism differed fundamentally on the issue of 'materialism and spiritualism'. Not that man, according to Marx, was moved only by economic forces, and not by moral values were the outcome of external environment, the Indian philosophers regarded it as the outcome of man's own innate nature. In his own words :

No Marxist believes that man is moved only by economic forces and not motivated by moral considerations. The difference between our position and that of Marx is that we believe certain moral values to be a direct and inevitable manifestation of man's innate and inalienable nature ; Marx would have it that they are all products of the environment, created by the inter-play of productive forces. The aim of the reformer and the revolutionary will not be merely a dialectical study of the environment with a view to helping the forces tending to acquire preponderance as a historical necessity, but to study the innate nature of man and the tendencies that result from it and help to create an environment that will be most conducive to their satisfaction.[46]

The *moksha* i.e. the final salvation of life, according to Sampurnanand, cannot be achieved by any sort of social-order, howsoever constituted it might be. For it every individual 'will have to tread the path of spiritual discipline by himself.'[47] But, since man lives in society, the society can remove the hindrances to such

[44] *Ibid.*, p. 5.
[45] *Ibid.*, p. 7.
[46] *Ibid.*, pp. 8–9.
[47] Sampurnanand, *Indian Socialism*, p. 9.

'spiritual living by minimising the conflicts' and 'maximising ...
particularities for the exercise of moral virtues.'[48] The central point
in planning the social order, therefore, could be nothing else than the
individual himself. Thus to him it appeared that religion may not
have any significance in Marxism but, in Indian socialism, it did
matter substantially, whether or not one believed in God or religion
in its day-to-day meaning. He dwelt upon this need with calculated
emphasis :

> There can be no place for religion in Marxism. No communist
> can honestly believe in any form of worship. If consciousness
> is an accidental product of evolution, there can be no God and
> and no rational justification for religious faith or practice. In
> the scheme of things which I have outlined ... there is a distinct
> place for a *Paramatma*, and believes in survival of the Ego after
> death, there is certainly room for religion. This is all that I
> need say in this connection. Any elaboration of this point is
> not germane to our purpose. A man may or may not believe
> in God, as the term is commonly understood, but if this know-
> ledge is tempered with reverence, if he has an aesthetic app-
> reciation of a Something that pulsates through, and lends signi-
> ficance to, all that exists, if he instinctively feels a kinship with
> all life, he is truly religious.[49]

This may be mentioned here that since planning for individual and
his final salvation alone is the *raison d'etre* of a given social order,
socialism should be adjudged on the basis of this sole criterion.
Sampurnanand, like Bhagavan Das and Mahtma Gandhi, always
conceived life in a broader and deeper perspective; he could not agree
that a social order, planned for achieving material objective alone,
could ever lead a man to final salvation. He emphasised the need
for spirituo-material planning for achieving the full objectives of
socialism. He stressed the need of synthesis between materialism
and spiritualism.

NEW SPIRITUAL EXPLORATION

The Congress as a whole also, in its resolution on 'Democracy
and Socialism', clearly declared that 'mere material prosperity alone
will not make human life rich and meaningful. Therefore, alongwith
economic development ethical and spiritual values will have to be

[48] *Ibid.*
[49] *Ibid.*, pp. 10–11.

fostered.'[50]   In fact, the Congress had been emphasising the spiritual and ethical values of life right from the beginning, especially after the advent of Gandhiji on the Indian political scene.

The content of spiritualism in socialism has now progressively increased. With J. P. having turned over to *Sarvodaya*, and Vinoba, having given a lead in the transformation of the country on peaceful Gandhian lines, the climate appears to have been charged with spiritualistic fervour. Both are certain today that, eventually, socialism and Marxism 'will merge into *Sarvodaya*.'[51]

RE-LEARNING THE LESSONS OF INDIGENOUS APPROACHES

It may also be recalled here that the thinkers like Gandhiji and Bhagavan Das as well as Aurobindo and Sampurnanand believed in the supernatural and metaphysical reality of God or Spirit. They did much in drawing the socialists' attention towards the need for evolving a synthesis between the material and spiritual objectives of life.[52]   An important implication of their approach, naturally, has been that man was not the product of matter or external environ-ment but a product of 'Pure Consciousness'; he fulfils the very nature which is the cause of his 'Being'. Pure Consciousness, *i.e*, 'God' in more understandable term, manifests itself into the form of both spirit and matter, the sentient and the insentient. According to Sampurnanand 'we do not say that anything is non-conscious at any time. Insentience, non-consciousness, simply implies that cons-ciousness has withdrawn itself, to some extent, behind the veil of nescience.'[53]

Even though a few socialists could rise to such metaphysical heights and many did not believe in the metaphysical way of think-ing, nevertheless, there was a general feeling that man was not the product of environment, but was a part of the 'Spiritual' entity, and a fulfilment of his own innate 'Nature'.

[50] Resolution on 'Democracy and Socialism', *Congress Bulletin*, 12–1 & 2, Dec. 1963, Jan-Feb. 1964, p. 176.

[51] Narayan, *Evolution Towards Sarvodaya*, p. 1.

[52] For Gandhiji's metaphysical ideas, see V. P. Varma, *The Political Philosophy of Mahatma Gandhi*, pp. 37–49.

Also, Bhagavan Das, *Ancient Vs. Modern Socialism*, pp. 23–25.

Also, Sampurnanand, *Indian Socialism*, pp. 1–11.

[53] Sampurnanand, *op. cit.*, p. 5.

164

APPRAISAL OF THE TREND

The spiritual and ethical values of life in Indian socialism has of late been widely acknowledged. Gyanchand—an eminent economist says :

'At first socialism was viewed with distrust because of its imputed materialistic or at least non-spiritual philosophy. But now that socialism, as a description for the prevailing social approach, is more commonly accepted, there is a widely shared feeling that socialism suited to the specific needs of our people should be in accordance with the age-old deep currents of their common life and true to the urges of their inmost spirit.'[54]

According to Rohit Dave—an eminent socialist theoretician, any close study of human nature will lead one to the conclusion that

...man is a bundle of selfish and altruistic impulses. He wants to minister to his own material and spiritual needs....[55]

Thus Indian socialism was not only an advance upon the Marxian theory but also on *Sarvodaya*. 'The Sarvodaya philosophy concentrates its whole attention on the altruistic impulses in man and refuses to recognise his selfish impulses', but this is only as incomplete as the Marxian emphasis on material forces alone. Indian socialism was in favour of a middle position.

[54] Gyan Chand, *Socialist Transformation of Indian Economy*, Bombay, Allied Publishers, 1965, p. 17.
[55] Rohit Dave, *Socialism an Approach*, Bombay, A. S. Y. S. Publication, 1957, pp. 9-10.

5

INDIAN SOCIALISM : THE POLITICAL THEORY

Individual and Society

The analysis of the nature of the individual in society has a fundamental and vital bearing on the modern socialist thought. As socialism in India, during the initial years of its post-Independence phase, took new turn and gave fresh thought on many of its basic tenets, the place of man in society and the nature of individual also came to be seriously considered.

NATURE OF MAN

The concept of human nature, that is the nature of individual, takes one back to the issue whether man be considered a heap of matter, biologically evolved into a conscious being, or as an essence of the Divine Spirit, manifested in the physical shape of an individual being. On the acceptance of this or that poser, depend many fundamental stipulations of socialism. As indicated earlier, J. P. realised that man was not just a heap of matter, and materialism did not provide any incentive for goodness. In the same context he also explained that if we adopt 'Non-materialism' (*i.e.* spiritualism), as our approach

> '(it) elevates the individual to a moral plane, and urges him, without reference to any objective outside of himself, to endeavour to realise his own true nature and fulfil the purpose of his being. This endeavour becomes the powerful motive force that drives him in its natural course to the good and the true. It will be seen as an important corollary of this that only when materialism is transcended does individual man come into his own and become an end in himself.'[1]

---

[1] Narayan, *Socialism, Sarvodaya and Democracy*, p. 99.

INDIVIDUAL : THE SPARK OF THE INFINITE

It was curiously a similar realisation as that of Sampurnanand's, to which we have already referred in the previous chapter—
that if consciousness was an accidental product of evolution, there
could be no God and no rational justification for religious faith or
practice. In subscribing to this view he was only advocating the
Vedantic proposition, that 'man is...only a spark of the infinite.'
Thus, from that point of view, he maintained that 'the focul point
of all planning and organization was the individual himself.'[2]

> A theory of social organisation, if it is to be of practical
> application, must accommodate itself to the needs and the
> characteristics of mankind : it cannot function as a bed of
> Procrustes to which men must adapt themselves or be crushed
> out of existence.[3]

He preceeded further to explain that of the four fundamental goals
of man—*Kama, Artha, Dharma* and *Moksha*—The first three are
capable of attainment through physical, mental and ethical conduct
but the fourth and the last—*Moksha* is incapable of direct approach
by any sort of effort. With respect to *Moksha*, society or outer
efforts could do little. He explained :

> ...all that the best organized society can do is to create an
> atmosphere of reverence for that conscious source of all Being,
> that Power that manifests itself in and through us and inspires
> all that exist and makes the universe an integrated whole
> rather than an amorphous mass of blind phenomena and of
> conscious units that sparkle for a moment and then are no
> more. The removal of hindrances to spiritual advancement
> is another important function of social organisation.[4]

Thus, Sampurnanand emphasised the necessity of individual's
own efforts, even in the best organised social order, because the
purpose of life was one of salvation (Moksha), and the same could
not be had through social or outer efforts, but only through individual's own efforts and experiences. Any social organisation thus
becomes only a means to an end, the end always being the individual
himself, to be precise, his salvation. At best the function of society
is to create proper environment for spiritual development. Hence
socialism, being only a theory and practice of social re-construction,

[2] Sampurnanand, *Indian Socialism*, p. 10.
[3] *Ibid.*, p. 12.
[4] *Ibid.*

it appeared to him, as only a means to an end.

We have seen earlier, that towards the close of his life, Jawaharlal Nehru also, who denied being religious, conceded to the Vedantic point of view with regard to the nature of man. The Vedanta provided him the philosophy of the life-force as the inner base of every-thing that exists. Referring the same, he wrote :

> The old Hindu idea that there is a divine essence in the world and every individual posseses something of it and can develop it, appeals to me in terms of a life force. I do not happen to be a religious man, but I do believe in something—call it religion or anything you like, which raises man above his normal level and gives the human personality a new dimension of spiritual quality and moral depth.[5]

NEHRU'S FIRM FAITH IN INDIVIDUAL AND INDIVIDUALITY

The socialist ideas of Nehru cannot be understood save in the context of his deep belief in man and in the dignity of human existence. It was not manly for him to reconcile one's self with injustice that endangered human dignity ; ideas and institutions which supported such injustice must be changed and it does not behave the dignity of man to submit to such wrongs.

> As I see round I see the crumbling ruins of a proud civilisa- tion strewn like a vast heap of futility. And yet, I shall not commit the grievous sin of losing faith in man...God we may deny, but what hope is there for if we deny man and thus reduce everything to futility ?[6]

Thus, Nehru affirmed his full faith in man. It was from that fundamental belief in man that he derived strong individualistic trends in thought. The manner in which he reacted to the alleged charges of 'familial influences' on him during his family's visit to Russia, to which we have already referred, may also be an evidence of his sense of 'self-possessedness' and ardent sense of individuality. He observed :

> We (Indians) have been terribly individualistic, almost to the extent of anarchy, each going his own way...In fact Hindu society is anarchistic. It is a curious combination of extreme social discipline and anarchism in thought.[7]

---

[5] Karanjia, op. cit., p. 33.

[6] Nehru, Discovery of India, p. 479.

[7] Mende, op. cit., p. 30.

It appears thus that the foundation of socialist thinking in Nehru's thought had been laid on the rock-belief that man and his individuality must not be surrendered to any scheme of social order.

Apart from the indigenous strand of thought, which reached its climax in Gandhism—emphasising consistently the individuality of man and his worth and dignity—the fact that among the recognised Indian socialists Nehru, Sampurnanand and J. P. asserted the spiritual 'at-one-ment' of man with the higher Divine Essence led to a change in the socialists' approach towards man and society. It got a new turn, or atleast, a shift in emphasis.

INDIVIDUAL : THE CORNER-STONE OF DEMOCRATIC SOCIALISM

The fact that 'democratic socialism' became the ideal of the Socialist Party since 1947 was a direct consequence of the realisation that individual was, from a deeper point of view, an end in himself. His freedom and individuality mattered more than anything else in the ultimate analysis of any social order or philosophy, and, towards this, the contributions of Deva, Lohia and Mehta were also considerable. Narendra Deva pointed out that freedom was the very nature of man. It is difficult to suppress one's individuality and freedom. He observed :

> New trends are bound to arise which will approximate more and more to democratic socialism. This is because ultimately man will affirm his essence and, if freedom and democratic sentiment are not his essence, what else it can be ? He will not always tolerate authoritarian rule, nor will he put up with the measures which tend to suppress him. It is man's nature to seek self-realisation by expanding his self.[8]

Thus, Deva believed in the potentiality of the individuals' 'self', which sought to expand itself in society. No social order could justifiably suppress it. Probably, his studies of Buddhism also, in the post-Independence period, impressed upon him the truth of the cycle of life and death, from which man could emancipate himself only by following a certain code of conduct of life. It is true that Deva did not express himself categorically in favour of the theory of reincarnation, but his uncertain and vague position on his point was itself indicative of his foliating attitude in this period.[9]

[8] Chairman's Address, *Report of the Second National Conference of the Praja Socialist Party*, Gaya, 1955, pp. 118–19.
[9] Kelker, *op. cit.*, p. 266.

EMPHASIS ON INDIVIDUAL AS BOTH END AND MEANS

Rammanohar Lohia realised the futility of both capitalistic or communistic theories, because they were the outcome of a fundamentally ignorant and erroneous concept of human nature and a denial of the innate worth of the individual. Commending Gandhiji's ideas as the basis of modern socialism, Lohia observed :

> In the modern world, organization has become so embracing and powerful that the individual is completely subservient to it. No matter where the origins of modern civilization lay it is today the civilization of the collective, where the individual is only a number in the mass and his effectiveness exists in so far as he is a part of the mass...

> And in the context of this modern civilization Mahatma Gandhi came along and said that even if you do not have an organization to support you, even if you do not have arms to wield, you have got something inside you which enables you to resist oppression and injustice and also to bear suffering manfully. It was this strange and powerful quality of Gandhiji's actions in his last thirty years that fascinated the attention of modern man and made him believe that the future might still contain the ingredients of a new world.[10]

It need not be emphasised here that the reference to 'something inside you' which was the core of Gandhian thought, appeared to Lohia as a sure and ultimate guarantee against tyranny and oppression. Lohia, further explained :

> Man has been variously defined...Man has often been called a thinking animal. It is left to him to doubt whether he really thinks, a good evidence of his capacity to think, and, if so, how far his conscious thinking affects his activities, his memory and associations. He has also been defined as a tool making element, a definition better than most. *But there is another special quality of man and that is his awareness of himself* and his...relationships. Whether these relationships are with God, or with others and a nameless whole, is a secondary question ; what matters is the awareness and quality of those relationships.[11]

In the above observation Lohia, like Nehru, denied his attachment with God or religion and yet recognised the compelling 'special

[10] Lohia, *Marx, Gandhi and Socialism*, pp. 121–22.
[11] R. Lohia, *Wheel of History*, Hyderabad, Navahind Prakashan, 1963, pp. 2–3.

quality' of man, which made man appear different from being just a 'tool' or heap of matter. He considered man to have been the central point in Gandhian thinking. Countering the charge that Gandhiji had over-emphasised the importance of the individual, he observed :

> It may well be that Mahatma Gandhi tended to over-empha-
> size the individual and under-emphasize the environment. Let
> it also be realised that socialism has tended to over-emphasize
> the environment and under-emphasize the individual.[12]

Thus Gandhiji's emphasis on individual, Lohia maintained, might have been directed against the socialists' too much emphasis on environment. For Lohia the individual was both his own end and means.

Lohia emphasised greatly the need for a blended emphasis on the 'individual' and the 'social' aspects of life. He made a pointed reference to this in his presidential Address to the Special Convention of the Socialist Party at Pachmarhi in 1952 :

> The opposition between the individual and the social is resolved
> as soon as the two-fold character of the moment is borne in
> mind. For the moment as the link with the past and an
> expression of the future, the individual is the product of
> environment and the instrument of its change. For the moment
> as an expression of the present, he is the executor of his human
> destiny and the moulder of environment. The individual is
> both an end and a means : as an end, he is the unfolder of
> love unto all, as a means, he is the tool of revolutionary anger
> against tyranny. All problems of the individual and the
> social, of ends and means, fall in their true perspective.[13]

Lohia realised that in socialism today exclusive emphasis either on 'individual' or 'social' was not correct ; only a blended emphasis on both could be the real basis for Indian socialism.

'ROOT WAS MAN'

Asoka Mehta, taking inspiration from that aspect of Marx in which he described that the 'root was man', considered that socia- list approach to the problems of man and society could not be complete unless an attempt was made to understand the nature of man and manifold aspects of life. Mehta is greatly alive today to

---

[12] Lohia, *Marx, Gandhi and Socialism*, p. 137.
[13] *Ibid.*, p. 375.

the importance of individual, and, perhaps, he is one of the strongest critics of the totalitarian ways of the Soviet communists. He felt that in any social set-up the individual has to be accepted as the central object.[14]

In the Presidential Address to the Madras session of the Socialist Party, Mehta made a pointed reference to the danger of 'unbalance' between man and nature. 'The individual becomes an isolate' and he warned that the danger must be warded off; there should be no such 'indifference' towards the individual that 'freezes' him.[15]

The trend towards the realisation of the importance of man and individual in socialism came also to be reflected in the ideologies of the Indian National Congress and the Socialist Parties.

In fact, the trend towards the recognition of individual's status and dignity in the Congress can be traced back to its very origin. For, liberalism was the basic factor in the composition of the Congress since the beginning. In vague socialistic sense, we can trace this trend in the Karachi Resolution on Fundamental Rights itself, wherein individual's freedom of association, speech, language, culture, religion, equality, including the 'freedom of conscience', etc., were to be guaranteed after the achievement of Swaraj. To an extent, the same assurances were incorporated in the Constitution of the Republic of India after Independence, as it was largely drafted at the instance of the Congress leaders. In the report on Fundamental Rights submitted to the Constituent Assembly it was clearly accepted that: 'All persons are equally entitled to freedom of conscience, and the right freely to profess, practice and propagate religion, subject to public order, morality or health.'[16] It may be suggested here that recognition of the right to freedom of conscience implied fundamentally a recognition of the spiritual entity of the individual.

It is true that even in the Constitution of the U. S. S. R. certain Fundamental Rights are granted including religious freedom and the freedom of conscience: but the basic difference appeared to be, in what Vyshinsky pointed out, that in the Soviet Constitu-

---

[14] In an interview with the writer on April 2, 1968, in New Delhi.

[15] Presidential Address of Asoka Mehta to *The Eighth National Conference of the Socialist Party*, Madras, 1950, p. 8.

[16] Mitra, *op. cit.*, Jan-June 1947, I, p. 325.

tion 'The right to work is the foundation whereon the Soviet citizens' right and freedoms rest.'[17] Whereas, it may be suggested, in the Indian Constitution no such condition-precedent was attached to the enjoyment of such a previlege. In other words. while in the Soviet Constitution fundamental rights flowed from the logic of work: in the Indian Constitution they flowed from the logic of individuality itself. Hence, the freedom of 'conscience' has more meaningful connotation in the Indian Constitution.

In fact the whole superstructure of the Congress ideology had been built somewhat on the Gandhian foundation—presuming primacy and the essential goodness of man. Individual was considered entitled to dignity of status and individuality. He was the cornerstone of Gandhiji's concept of Swaraj.[18] Explaining the difference between 'his' concept of socialism and socialism in general, Gandhiji observed: 'I want freedom for full expression of my personality, under the other socialism, there is no individual freedom. You own nothing, not even body.'[19] He claimed that under 'his' socialism i.e. 'Sarvodaya' every individual was to flourish irrespective of any distinction of caste, creed, sex and colour.

BELIEF IN THE SOCIABILITY OF MAN

The *Policy Statement* of the P. S. P., of course, nowhere indicated that individual could be treated as an end in himself. Its whole burden of thought was to prove its positive hostility or opposition to individualistic conception of society. Yet, it declared significantly that society 'does not exist apart from the individuals who constitute it.'[20] It did imply, therefore, that the unit of society was the individual himself. Its opposition to 'individualism' was only, to the extent it implied that 'each individual is an independent whole with private pains, pleasures and interests and explains existing social arrangements as contractual obligations to which each individual commits himself out of his own interest.'[21] Hence what the P. S. P. was opposed to was not the individual but the narrow

---

[17] A. Y. Vyshinsky, *The Law of the Soviet State*, New York, Macmillan Co., 1954, p. 563.

[18] Gandhi, *Economic and Industrial Life and Relations*, I, pp. xx–xxv.

[19] *Ibid.*, p. xxxv.

[20] *Policy Statement*, 1955, p. 63.

[21] *Ibid.*, p. 62.

and self-seeking egoistic concept of individualism.

There was a clear ambiguity as to whether or not the individual had some intrinsic worth of his own, whose object was not outside his ownself, although it found full expression in the individual writings and speeches of some of the pioneers, referred to above. On this point it appears, there was some sort of a gap or discrepancy between the individual writings of the socialists and the collective thinking of the P. S. P.

Yet, it was not without significance that the *Policy Statement* refused to accept that man was essentially bad and egoistic. It believed fully in the sociability of man. It was enough of a ground to build upon it any sound superstructure of a social order in which the individual was not to be subordinated or negated altogether. The *Policy Statement* declared :

> Man is essentially a social being, possessed of social impulses and pervaded by society. Society is an element of life...
> Pure 'egoism' is an absolute abstraction of intellect. Man is also moved by social impulses...so it is not human nature but the social system which is to be blamed for the dominance of selfishness, in our behaviour.[22]

The P. S. P.'s realisation that man was a social being and amenable to social impulses was, of great significance. Without such an approach the methodology of socialist transformation of society could not be conclusively arrived at. Whether or not individual was amenable to social impulses by nature was a fact on which could depend the justification or otherwise of the socialists' method of class-struggle and revolution as also the Gandhian method of non-violence and moral appeals.

On the whole, it appears that two important factors moulded the approach of the socialists and their parties on the issue of individual and his place in society. These were first, the impact of the indigenous thought on Indian socialists and, second, the adverse impact generated by the violent purges and other excesses committed under Soviet communism.

THE INDIGENOUS IMPACT

The indigenous thought—a glimpse of which has been provided earlier—manifested a fundamental affinity with the Indian philosophy

[22] *Ibid.*, p. 63.

and culture.   There has been a fundamental spiritual and moral note in Hindu philosophy.

This was also one of the basic propositions of the philosophy of *Vedanta* that man was only a part of the *Paramatma* (Pure Consciousness), hence entitled to recognition as a sacred entity by himself. As the philosophy of *Vedanta* came to be commended, by both Sampurnanand and Jawaharlal Nehru, the indigenous thought appeared to have had not only limited appeal for thinkers like Gandhiji and Vivekananda but also pervasive appeal for the socialists. The indigenous thought appears to have greatly impressed upon the socialists the 'spiritual' and the 'sacred' character of individual's personality, and once that belief was injected in Indian socialism, any opposition to individual, except of course in the perverted sense of an individualistic society, was out of the question. What was now impressed upon the socialists was the need for a synthesis between the individual and society.

REACTION AGAINST BOLSHEVIK 'PURGES'

The other factor that appears to have led to sympathetic and considerate attitude towards the individual was the outcome of a reaction against the oppressive and violent manner in which the dissenting voices in the Soviet Uuion had been sought to be subdued. In India the 'purges' appeared to have shaken the conscience of even the professedly devout Marxists.   On no single point one gathers the impression as much unanimity amongst all shades of socialist thinkers in India, as on the issue of purges and regimentation in Soviet society.   All socialists decried it with one voice.   The records we have covered, as well as not covered thus far, are full on the issue of its condemnation.   We might recall that Nehru, Deva, Sampurnanand, J. P., Lohia, Mehta and not to mention many others like Patwardhan and Masani, denounced the communists' ways.   That was largely due to the violent and the tyrannical methods of authoritarianism, perpetuated within the iron-curtain of the Soviet society.   Bolshevism got a very bad image into their mental vision, and the inner repulsion against violence, that germinated in the minds of the Indian socialists, threw them back to enclasp the individual.

Asoka Mehta reacted sharply against the concept of a 'mass man', which he considered to be the direct outcome of the authoritarian rule and the communist' line of thinking. He observed :

> The Communists leave no area of life and thought private, that is free. The all-embracing control robs man of his individuality and subordinates him to a collectivity. Instead of freeing man and endowing him with responsibility the Communists enhance his dependence and emphasise conformity... In the place of free and human being a new and a terrible mass-man...has emerged.

> The mass-man is taught to believe in the sacrifice of the individual to the collective, the substitutability of one individual by another, the non-validity of individual morality with respect to the collective, the necessity and inflexibility of hierarchical discipline and the inevitability and the strange beauty of violence...The mass-man functions not on the human, but zoological level.[23]

Such debasement of the position and the status of individual, Mehta considered, was ruinous for socialism, and cautioned that 'tyranny and totalitarianism may frighten or fascinate man for a while, but the spirit of man is ultimately dauntless.'[24] Both the language and the manner of expression are suggestive of the depth of his feeling on the issue.

The importance of individual and his status in Indian socialist thought, in the period under review, should not, however, he considered a novelty altogether. In fact, the socialists in India realised this from the beginning. J. P. observed in *Why Socialism ?* itself :

> 'Individualism has been the prominent *motif* in our culture only in the sense that perfection of the individual has been its ideal ; and if individual perfection is the goal, the socialist has not the least difficulty in showing that such perfection can come about only by aiming at the utmost common good.'[25]

There has been yet another point of view from which individualism and socialism have not been considered antagonistic theories. If anything, this has been said that 'the aims of the socialists and the individualists do not in the long run differ.'[26] Socialism was in a

[23] *Presidential Address of Asoka Mehta to the Eighth National Conference of the Socialist Party*, pp. 10–11.

[24] *Ibid.*, p. 11.

[25] Narayan, *Socialism, Sarvodaya and Democracy*, pp. 15–16.

[26] C. E. M. Joad, *Introduction to Modern Political Theory*, Oxford, The Clarendon Press, 1959, p. 51.

way an advance upon the theory of individualism which was found
wanting in adequately ensuring equity among the different classes in
a technology-oriented civilisation.

NEED OF DISCREET BALANCE

An important aspect of socialist thinking in India has been, at
least in the post-Independence phase, to highlight not the elements of
antagonism between socialism and individualism, but to emphasise
the need of a discreet balance between the two. It has been increasingly realised that any evaluation of the place of individual in
socialism is not one of sweeping denial but one of degree. It would
be relevant to cite a prominent socialist thinker, Rohit Dave, on the
point. He maintained that to any such question 'Is society for the
individual or the individual for society, no categorical answer...need
be given in the abstract.' The question was of vital interest but it
was fundamentally related to the concept of the nature of individual
and his relation with society. In his own words :

> '...the choice among various social philosophers and systems
> is not just an academic question, but is a matter of life and
> death for many, and perhaps, threatens the very human civili-
> sation we have to probe deeper and see whether it is possible
> to find out some criterian that can help us in determining how
> much of emphasis should be placed on the individual and how
> much on society.'[27]

Thus, it has appeared to the Indian socialist on the whole that
the issue of individual and society, i.e. their respective relationship,
was basically a problem of discreet balance between the two and not
a question of absolute assertion in favour of either.

State

THE CHANGING CONCEPTS

Marx had viewed state essentially as a class organization,
constituted to protect and advance the interest of the ruling class in
society. This view of Marx was the outcome of his fundamental
belief in the Materialist Conception of History. To him the state
'was nothing more than the form of organisation which the
bourgeois necessarily adopt for internal purposes, for the mutual

---

[27] Dave, op. cit., p. 12.

guarantee of their property and interests.'[28]   A natural corollary of this conclusion was that as soon as antagonistic classes in society were eliminated, *i.e.* 'classless' society established, the state as a phenomenon in social organization was to wither away and fall out like a dry leaf of a tree.   Referring to this aspect of Marx's thought, it is often said that pressed to its logical conclusion Marxism implied anarchistic trend or statelessness.

Lenin and Stalin had accepted this fundamental proposition of Marx, but still maintained that during the transitional phase, the state would be the most vital instrument of social reconstruction of society.   Lenin observed :   'We Marxists are opposed to all and every kind of state...(yet) we need revolutionary power, we need the state.'[29]   Stalin went even further and said that 'unless the capitalist encirclement is liquidated', the state could not wither away.[30] This shifting position, from Marx to Lenin and from Lenin to Stalin indicated a realistic evaluation of the importance and necessity of state under socialism.

Under the garb of a transitional phase, the Soviet communists, however, went on to erect one of the most regemented State in the world.   In the words of J. P. :

> We have today there (Russia) a structure which is a one party dictatorship.   At the same time we have there a party which has a restricted membership, which goes periodically through purges, a party in which democracy does not seem to exist any longer ; and in this one party dictatorship we have a completely bureaucratic State, which cannot in any way be described as a worker's State, as a people's State.   Obviously for the socialist movement of the world the Russian picture of political organisation would be found wanting and unacceptable.   We would have to devise a different structure.[31]

As indicated earlier, probably, J. P. never showed, especially after 1947, any sympathy with the totalitarian trends in the Soviet State.   As the General Secretary of the Socialist Party, he observed in 1948 :

...the experience of totalitarian countries, whether Fascist or

---

[28] Alexander Gray, *The Socialist Tradition Moses to Lenin*, London, Longmans, Green and Co., 1948, p. 325.

[29] *Ibid.*, p. 469.

[30] *Ibid.*, p. 475.

[31] Narayan, *Socialism, Sarvodaya and Democracy*, p. 105.

Communist has shown that if the state is looked upon as the sole agent of social reconstruction, we get nothing but a regimented society in which the state is all powerful and popular initiative is extinct and the individual is made a cog in the vast unhappy machine.[32]

At this stage he also maintained a distinction between society and state and wanted that 'society and state both should be served in their respective domains.'[33] The need for maintaining this distinction grew stronger later.

It is true that, during the colonial period, J. P. manifested considerable appreciation of the Soviet achievements, and, he even advocated the expansion of the role of state in the spheres of economic and political activities, such as the socialisation of the key industries and the monopolisation of foreign trade by the state.[34] But that approach developed in him due to his faith in the concept of Marxian socialism. What he desired, at that stage, was that state as a machinery of exploitation must cease by coming under the control of the producing masses. However, with his growing knowledge about the authoritarian nature of the Soviet state, he gradually lost faith in the machinery of state as a centralising and all-pervasive force. In a thought-provoking 'Plea for the Reconstruction of Indian Polity', he manifested this change clearly :

The old belief that State ownership and management of the means of production, distribution, and exchange will lead to economic self-government, elimination of exploitation and equitable distribution of the products of labour, a stateless order of society, has not been confirmed by experience.[35]

Once, he realised that the 'stateless order of society' may not be realised, he cautioned to be on guard against the trend of centralisation of power in a state by all means. He desired and made an earnest plea for its substitution by a 'communal or communitarian way of life.'

STATE NOT TO WITHER AWAY

The totalitarian ways of the state greatly disappointed

[32] General Secretary's Report, *Report of the Sixth Annual Conference of the Socialist Party*, Nasik, 1948, p. 98.
[33] *Ibid.*
[34] Narayan, *Why Socialism ?*, pp. 45–47.
[35] Narayan, *Reconstruction of Indian Polity*, p. 9.

Sampurnanand. He considered the state, as it evolved in the Soviet society, to be highly authoritarian in which the citizens did not find a meaningful place. He observed :

> ...Communist writers have held with Engels that the State has not existed from all eternity and will wither away at some distant date. But I am speaking of the present, not of the past or the future...the Communist State is as all-powerful and a communist citizen is as meaningless as an individual as anything under a Hegelian dispensation.
> All significance that he possesses comes to him only in and through the State of which he is a citizen...What both Hegel and the theorist of the Communist State insist upon is the absolute power of the State. They both are of the opinion that the individual is not as a matter of birthright endowed with any inherent rights which are inviolable vis-a-vis the State.[36]

The realisation that the Soviet state was as absolutist, and the individual as secondary, as under the Hegelian concept of state, made Sampurnanand think that such a philosophy could not serve the purpose of a society, which believed in the dignity and worth of the individual. He was strongly opposed to the concept of a totalitarian state.

Yet another reason for disappointment with the Marxian theory was its hollowness on the point of the prognosis of state. Day by day state was being consolidated in the Soviet society and that proved conclusively that the withering away of the state was not at all a possibility. This probably, was an additional factor in impressing upon the socialists the untenability of the Marxian proposition with regard to state.

We have already indicated that the Indian socialists, during the colonial decades, manifested no interest or little interest in the theory of the 'withering away' of the state. All of them, particularly Deva, maintained silence about it. Their main concern thus was to emphasise the exploitative nature of imperial or capitalist state and the need to capture it as the instrument of political power. In doing so, like the Soviet communists, the Indian socialists also accepted greatly the need of the continued existence of state, almost as a perpetual necessity. During the post-Independence period, the socialists became

---

[36] Sampurnanand, *Indian Socialism*, pp. 115–17.

conscious of the danger of drifting towards a totalitarian or authoritarian state. They became equally alive to the need of maintaining state as a permanent institution in human society. Hence, they were confronted with a two-fold task ; the first was to deprecate any trend towards totalitarianism and the second was to augment those forces which could strengthen the foundation of a sound and equitable socialist state. Some of the factors that moulded their line of thinking may be briefly indicated here.

One of the greatest factors that moulded the socialist's attitude towards state in India was their bitter experience about the type of state that developed in Soviet Russia during the initial stage. All socialists, without exception, denounced the cult of purges and violence. They warned against the trend of too much centralisation, bureaucratisation and totalitarianism.

The second factor was their experience of an imperial state, against which all socialists had to fight a long-drawn battle for freedom and national independence. During the mid-thirties, J. P. regarded India, to be so much a part and parcel of the British imperial structure as to appear, even without its factory-stage-civilization, as a part of the capitalistic structure. Hence India was not free from the maladies of the capitalist system.[37] The constant tug of war between the socialistically minded freedom-fighters and the imperial rulers generated an impression that the state was only a coercive power which tried to defend its own interest as against the interests of the Indian people. This led to the lessening of respect and regard for the state as a political machinery.

The danger of totalitarian trends and the experience of the coercive nature of imperial state generated among the Indian socialists some sort of a repulsion against the state as a system of power. The socialists realised that if the state was to function as a necessary instrument of society it must be based on democratic principles and the minimum of violence. At the same time, the state was to evolve neither as a capitalist nor as a communist system.

PLURALISM AND DECENTRALISATION

Another factor that greatly affected the socialist's approach towards state was their realization of the futility of the theory of

[37] In a speech at Madras, reproduced in, File No. 36/3/34 (Poll), Home Department, Govt. of India, p. 9.

absolute national sovereignty. The experiences of two World Wars, and of the Fascist States of Europe convinced the socialists that what was at the root of the War was the notion of unlimited sovereignty.[38] Nehru recorded his sense of agony at the way the wars were waged under the high-sounding principles of nationalism, and, yet under the narrowest sense of bigotry. Elaborating the trend of pluralism in contemporary socialism, Bandyopadhyaya, observed :

> Socialism rejects the monistic theory of sovereignty or the theory of unified state sovereignty which holds that sovereignty resides in the State alone, which is thus supreme, and that individuals and social groups of all kinds must, therefore, be totally subservient to the State. Centralised State power is anathema to the modern socialists and they take, on the contrary, a pluralistic view of sovereignty.[39]

The Indian socialists viewed the theory of absolute monistic sovereignty as basically opposed to the modern concept of a socialist state. We shall see as we proceed, that this trend was particularly manifested in the post-Independence writings of J. P., Lohia and Mehta.

Close to the theme of pluralism was the socialists' realization that there must also be decentralization of power within a socialist state, both functionally as well as territorially.[40] The future of democracy was doomed if the areas of power were not fragmentised into smaller units of administration. Emphasis on democracy and parliamentary institutions were the necessary concomitants of their concept of socialist state. In this connection, it may be suggested, the two most important factors were the impact of Gandhian thought on the socialist thinking, in the post-Independence period, and the

---

[38] The British socialist theoreticians like Harold J. Laski also had been arguing that 'it would be of lasting benefit to political science if the whole concept of sovereignty were surrendered.'—H. J. Laski, *A Grammar of Politics*, London, Allen and Unwin, 1967, pp. 44–45.

[39] Bandyopadhyaya, *op. cit.*, p. 13.

[40] J. P. in the course of his lecture in the 'Pant Vyakhyan Mala' series emphasised the importance of functional as well as territorial decentralisation. He also pointed out the failures of parliamentary democracy and the need to maintain the existence of primary institutions like family and primary social units like villages. He also emphasised to keep the needs under reasonable limits. These alone could assure a better socialistic future. *Bhartiya Samajvad, Aarthik Sanyojan Aur Vikendrikarna, op. cit.*, pp. 53–99.

legacies of the British parliamentary democracy, under which India was ruled for long.

PLANNING AND SECULARISM

There were other factors also, such as the concept of planning, which required for its ultimate success, a strong state. The need for planning impressed upon the socialists the necessity of evolving a democratic state with effective power to implement its plans. Nehru was among the earliest of those socialists who was convinced that planning was essential and that planning could succeed only in and through a powerful state. Nehru realised that 'any effective planning must involve a socialization of the economic structure.'[41] After independence, the need to boost up the national wealth through industries and agriculture was greatly felt and it inclined the socialists more and more towards planning. Nehru, particularly, conceived it as the mainstay of his economic ideology. The vast scientific and technological advancement had convinced the socialists about the complex needs of modern society. Without the machinery of state, and the expansion of its role, it was not possible to meet the growing needs of society.

Likewise, the demand for a separate Muslim state in India on a non-secular basis, and the disunity it involved, shaped the socialist's vision of a secular state.

NEHRU'S THINKING ON STATE

Nehru appears to have maintained consistently that the state was a permanent institution and it has its utility at all stages of civilisation. He was alive to the need of permanent existence of state in human society. In the post-Independence phase, this belief grew stronger in him than ever before. There appears to have been no stage in his thinking, not even during his prison days, at which he ever manifested any apathetic attitude towards state or towards the governmental machinery—the police, the army and the prison.[42] He considered state to be a 'socially' functioning organism, which was not only to perform the negative functions of security and protection but also the positive functions of creating a better society for

41 B. N. Ganguli, 'Nehru and Socialism', *The Economic Weekly*, XVI (29, 30 & 31) July 1964, p. 1217.
42 M. N. Das, *op. cit.*, p. 171.

the fuller development of the individual. He however, underlined the need to strike a balance between the authority of state and the freedom of the individual. He is reported to have observed :

> ...State becomes more and more of a socially functioning organism—for the good of society or the individual, as you like. And, the more it becomes that, the more benefits it confers on the individual, the more, in a sense, the individual has obligations to that State. So the two things, the rights and obligations, march together. If the State and individual are properly integrated and organized there is no conflict. Otherwise, if one side goes ahead of the other there is a lack of balance.[43]

Nehru realised that in order to function effectively and purposively, the state has got to retain adequate authority and force at its command. To that end, even the centralisation of power within the state, on a limited scale, may not possibly be avoided. But he maintained that such a power must be used for the good of the people individually as well as collectively. The State must not act arbitrarily.

Further, Nehru maintained that the state was only a means to end and not an end in itself. The State is for the man, not the man for the state. Thus, even though he greatly emphasised the importance of state, he maintained almost an individualistic point of view so far as state's relationship with the individual was concerned. Any concept of authoritiarian or totalitarian rule was farthest from his thought.

Nehru realised that the element of violence was somewhat constantly present in the state in different forms. 'Must the State', he wondered, 'always be based on force and violence, or will the day come when this element of compulsion is reduced to a minimum and almost fades away ?'[44] He recognised that some element of violence was present in the very process of life. However, there could be little justification for the violent character of state of the type that developed in Soviet Russia, in the name of Marxism.

Nehru made no mistake in realising the coercive nature of state and, yet, he did not disapprove of the machinery of state. He knew that in practical life even a coercive state may be necessary. But coercian or violence should not be indulged in for its own sake.

[43] Quoted in, *Ibid.*, p. 169.
[44] Quoted in, *Ibid.*, p. 172.

Violence is not to be defended absolutely but could be justified in the context of the practical realities of human life. He elaborated his point of view thus :

> ...even if we assume that the worst forms of violence will be gradually removed from the State, it is impossible to ignore the fact that both government and social life necessitate some coercion. Social life necessitates some form of government, and the men so placed in authority must crub and prevent all individual or group tendencies which are inherently selfish and likely to injure society. Usually they go much further than necessary, for power corrupts and degrades.[45]

His inevitable conclusion was to strike a balance between too much of violence and the total absence of it. Nehru realised that till human beings became 'perfect' and 'a single World-State' became a possibility, violence both for internal cohesion and external defence could not be dispensed with.[46]

Another factor that impressed on Nehru the necessity of state was the need of planning in society. Planning could not be done without the state. As referred to earlier, he had evinced great interest in the method of planning as early as 1927. He had also been inspired by Roosevelt's policy of the New Deal.[47] In the post-Independence period, Nehru realised even more keenly than ever before that the functions of the state must increase in order to bring about the necessary transformation of society for a better and higher standard of life.

The Directive Principles of the State Policy, under the Indian Constitution, clearly envisaged a progressive role of the state. Therein it was laid down that it would be the obligation of the state to 'strive to promote the welfare of the people by securing and protecting, as effectively as it may, a social order in which justice, social, economic and political, shall inform all the institutions of national life.'[48] The State was expected to provide the 'adequate means of livelihood' so that 'the ownership and control of the material resources of the community are so distributed as best to

---

[45] *Ibid.*, p. 542.
[46] *Ibid.*
[47] B. N. Ganguli, *op. cit.*, p. 1217.
[48] Shriman Narayan, *Socialism in Indian Planning*, Bombay, Asia Publishing House, 1964, p. 7.

subserve the common good.'[49] Further, the state was to ensure 'that the operation of the economic system does not result in the concentration of wealth and means of production to the common detriment.'[50] It is needless to emphasise that these huge obligations could not be fulfilled unless the state was to grab many spheres of social and economic life directly under its control. Nehru realised more and more that the objectives stipulated under the Directive Principles, or in the Constitution as a whole, could not be achieved without planned development. It need also not be emphasised that the *sine qua non* of planning is the machinery of the state. Hence the need of planning also made Nehru realise greatly the necessity and importance of the state.

The large-scale industrialisation and scientific and technological advancement that Nehru had cherished from the beginning and regarded as the only panacea for India's poverty demanded the existence of a powerful state. The state-owned or state-regulated industries must have impressed upon him the necessity of enlarging the sphere of states activities.

Thus, even though Nehru approached the state negatively—as a means to an end, it appears nevertheless, that he considered the function to be positive, *i.e.* wide and comprehensive enough to regulate many spheres of life. He discarded the old concept of 'police state'[51] and stood for a 'socialist state', which alone could serve the cause of the individual in modern society. The welfare state appeared to Nehru almost as a synonym for the socialist state.

SAMPURNANAND'S APPROACH

Sampurnanand considered state a necessary and inevitable tool of the society. It appeared to him that the development of individual's personality was possible largely through the state. He observed in this connection : 'Among the many instruments which society uses to serve its purpose, the State is perhaps the most powerful.'[52] While elaborating the Marxian concept of state, he

[49] *Ibid.*
[50] *Ibid.*
[51] *Jawaharlal Nehru's Speeches*, New Delhi, Publication Division, Govt. of India, 1949–53, I, p. 124.
[52] Sampurnanand, *Indian Socialism*, p. 10.

appreciated the fact that State has always represented the interest of the dominant class in society. In his own way, he even substantiated the truth on the authority of the *Puranas*.[53] But he did not accept the concept of absolute sovereignty in any form. He considered that the state was always subjected to the end for which it existed. The state was only an instrument of society, which in its own turn has 'no interests other than those of its constituent units.'[54] He regarded even society as a means to an end; the end was the individual himself. As he put it: 'Its sole interest, as its sole duty, lies in creating conditions conducive to the free all-round development of the individual.'[55]

Although Sampurnanand did not categorically repudiate the concept of the withering away of the state as a distant possibility he made no mistake about exposing the hollowness of the concept. He described the ideal as a pious wish which may or may not be realised at some 'distant date'. Sampurnanand regarded the state as useful institution so long it does not ride roughshod over the individual. Like Nehru, he maintained that the state is not an end in itself; it has to serve a vital purpose in society and that is to work for the betterment of the individual. As such, state is a permanent institution.

NARENDRA DEVA'S APPROACH

Narendra Deva, it appears, did not give much thought on the issue of state, apart from what he observed in connection with the elaboration of the general theory of Marxism. To a great extent, Deva derived his ideas and inspirations from Marx. Like Marx, to him, also, it appeared that all the states of the past as well as the states of the present were based on the interest of the ruling class. State has been an instrument of perpetuating class-rule in society. In this connection he strongly criticised and disapproved of the capitalist state as it existed in society.

The state in the past represented the class-ideal, and the interests which dominated it. The feudal states of the past gave way to the business class state, for the interest of the business was not smoothly fulfilled under the feudal states. The business classes,

---

[53] Sampurnanand, *Samajvad*, p. 220.
[54] Sampurnanand, *Indian Socialism*, p. 10.
[55] *Ibid.*, pp. 9–10.

therefore, had to create an arrangement in which the sovereign power of the state came to be vested not in a class based on family linage but in a class based on property qualification.[56] The modern capitalist state originated and thrived under the cloak of the apparant slogan 'the government of the people, for the people and by the people.' Hence, Deva maintained that all the states in the past or in the present represented class interests and were the means of exploitation of a class by a class. He desired, however, to capture the machinery of the state so as to do away with its exploitative nature.

The capitalist state, however theoretically, did grant some political rights to the people including the right to vote. Deva even conceded that in granting such rights the capitalist state made no discrimination on the grounds of religion, property, education, profession, etc. Yet he maintained that the true freedom of the individual did not lie in these privileges. Man could become truly free only when his physical needs were not separated from his total needs as a social being.[57]

The intrinsic nature of the state, as Deva saw it, was to hold aloft its particular ideals and to recognise and award only such deeds and men who accord with it. For example, the state honours the soldiers dying on the battlefield, for they serve the interest of the state and fight for the ideal which the state beholds. But no such reward usually comes to a man who stakes his life for saving the life of another person in the usual course.[58] He also found support of this analogy in a Kroptkin anecdote, wherein a prisoner had saved a man from being burnt. Without any consideration to his good deed, however, he was penalised for his earlier offence of escaping out of the prison secretly a day earlier to the incident.[59]

Deva made no reservation in depicting the state as out and out a coercive institution based on class interest. The imperialistic nature of British state, against which he had had to fight, must also have strengthened his understanding about the coercive nature of state.

[56] Deva, *Rastriyata Aur Samajvad*, p. 435.
[57] *Ibid.*, pp. 452–53.
[58] *Ibid.*, p. 694.
[59] *Ibid.*, p. 695.

Naturally, therefore, Deva was inclined to think that in a socialist state the class interest would be eliminated and a classless society established. There would be no exploitation of any class. Only in a socialist state, he maintained, men would leave their beastly existence and live like men.[60] To what extent this was his personal faith or just an appreciation of the Marxian position is, however, not clear.

Deva's thinking about the role of state may be sought, even though indirectly, in the *Policy Statement* of the P. S. P. of which he was the main author. He deftly avoided any chapter on state in the *Policy Statement* and nowhere the question of the 'withering away' of the state was even touched. But there are positive passages in it to suggest that he envisaged a progressive role for the state in society, although in a decentralised form. The *Policy Statement* laid down that 'The State will help the tillers in solving many of the difficulties that face them today.'[61] It further laid down that 'in the decentralised socialist State the village panchayat elected on the basis of universal franchise, will be the chief organ of the State authority in the village.'[62]

The *Policy Statement* clearly envisaged an order of society in which the major task for the welfare of the people, particularly of the toiling classes, was to be the responsibility of the state. It deprecated the trend to identify the state with the government and the government with the party in power. It regretted that 'the resources of the state, the authority of the government and the influence of its official's were freely used to further essentially party purposes.'[63] This of course was an indictment of the doings of the Congress, but it also implied the need for a decentralised democracy. The extent to which the *Policy Statement* reflected Deva's views, it may be suggested that he stood fully for a decentralised democratic state in India.

J. P.'S IDEAS

J. P. appears to have held a shifting position on the nature and necessity of state as an instrument to subserve the social purpose. During the colonial period, we have seen already, he regarded the state as the most important tool of socialist transformation of society.

[60] *Ibid.*, p. 426.
[61] *Policy Statement*, 1955, p. 14.
[62] *Ibid.*
[63] *Ibid.*, p. 5.

He upheld the ideal of proletariat dictatorship also.

But, by 1946 J. P. realised the inadequacies of the belief that mere control by the state over the means of production and distribution could not serve the real purpose of the individual or the society. He now realised that instead of state-owned industries, co-operatives and community-owned industries should be organised for solving the unemployment problem of India. That might prove to be a preventive force also against the totalitarian trends in the state, particularly of the type which was reflected in the Soviet system. In 'My picture of Socialism', J. P. observed :

> I desire to prevent the State from acquiring the sole monopoly in industry and employment. The State under socialism threatens, as in Russia, far from withering away, to become an all-powerful tyrant maintaining a stranglehold over the entire body of citizens. This leads to totalitarianism of the type we witness in Russia today.[64]

The trend towards state monopoly and totalitarianism convinced J. P. that unless dependence on the state was lessened, to set a limit to its centralised power was not possible. If at all it was possible, it could be through organising 'co-operatives' and 'small industries', and establishing 'community ownership' over them. These were the logical corollaries of a decentralised concept of state without which, he maintained, it was difficult to achieve the objectives of a socialist society. This was an evidence that there was a gradual shift of emphasis in him regarding the role of state in society. He now emphasised the need to minimise the dependence on the state and to encourage the process of decentralisation of power in it. In his personal writings, as well as through the forum of his party, he began to plead the necessity of evolving social and primary institutions like the 'co-operatives' and the 'panchayats' on the grass-root level.

There was a similar drift in J. P. from the ideal of proletariat dictatorship. He was now convinced that the state in a socialist India must not be dictatorial in nature. It must be a fully democratic state. He observed :

> It is a common mistake these days to think that there must be the dictatorship of the proletariat in a socialist State. This is against the teaching of Marx. The dictatorship of the

[64] Narayan, *Socialism, Sarvodaya and Democracy*, p. 46.

proletariat has a place only in the transitional period from capitalism to socialism. And in this period too it is not inevitable in every case. Marx visualised a capitalist State, such as England, where political democracy was in full vogue and there was no large standing army, where democratic processes could be used to bring about socialism.[65]

He further clarified that Marx never meant the dictatorship of a single party ; what he meant was only the dictatorship of a class—class of workers, peasants and only middle classes.

The burden of J. P.'s thinking now was to prove that proletariat dictatorship was not an inevitable creed of socialist state. While he had emphasised the need of proletariat dictatorship in the 'thirties, he now focussed his attention towards highlighting the exceptions to that rule. On the point of the undesirability of a single party dictatorship, he became more vocal than ever before. He was certain that Marx did never visualise a one-party-dictatorship as it had developed in Russia. J. P. stood for giving a democratic state its full chance, with full democratic processes inhering in it. At this stage 'democratic socialism' became his professed goal.

An important aspect of J. P.'s thinking in the post-Independence period was that even in a socialist state absolute authority or sovereignty must not have any place. He declared that 'the State will only be an instrument in the hand of a popular socialist movement i.e. of the people organised independently of the State for a socialist way of living rather than the sourse and fountainhead of all authority and will.'[66] He criticised the concept of absolute sovereignty of the State. If at all the state would have power, its source would be the people, who would ultimately wield it.

Closely linked with the problem of totalitarianism or proletariat dictatorship was the problem of how to prevent one-party dictatorship. In fact, a dictatorial state was always manned by a dictatorial party. J. P. did not think that the solution could be had by developing the conventional ways of a multi-party system. He thought radically and conceived the idea of a state without any party. He tried to establish a logical hypothesis : 'If the State is to melt away, to wither away, the party must also wither away.'[67]

[65] Ibid., pp. 46–47.
[66] Ibid., p. 62.
[67] J. P.'s Address to the First Asian Socialist Conference, 1953, reproduced in, Ibid., p. 107.

What is important here to note is not the validity or otherwise of the suggestion but the way he reacted to the totalitarian and dictatorial trends in the state. He went to the extent of suggesting the abolition of the party-system altogether.

With J. P.'s adoption to the philosophy of Bhoodan, the trend towards minimising the importance of the state grew further in his thinking. He made a strong plea to rely more an the Janashakti (power of the people) than on Dandashakti (power of the state). And in this connection, he further elaborated his point of view thus :

> It is for this reason that the Bhoodan or Sarvodaya movement insists that if our ultimate aim is to do without the State we must here and now create those conditions in which the people will rely more and more on themselves and less and less on the State. No one can tell whether the State will ever completely disappear, but, if we accept the ideal of a non-violent democracy, we must begin today to work for it.[68]

The above observation is significant in so far as it indicated a line of thinking that was similar to the Gandhian approach. J. P. was one of the most ardent critics of Gandhian ideas during the colonial phase. But with the gradual evolution in his ideas he came to appreciate more and more the ideal of a society in which greater reliance was to be put on the individual and on self-help than on the coercive apparatus of the state. The zest with which he had once advocated the expansion of the role of the state was singularly absent now. Not sure whether the state could be fully dispensed with, he pleaded for greater individual effort with a view to achieving the ideals of a non-violent democratic social order. He emphasised that democracy requires the individual to play a creative part in it.

At this stage J. P. manifested a considerable change from what his attitude had been in the past. In his own words :

> As questioning about politics were not confined to the party system alone, fundamental questions arose in my mind as to the place and role of the state in human society, particularly in relation to the goals of social life that had fixed themselves before me. Perhaps my schooling in Marxism with its ideals of a stateless society, made these questions more pointed and

---

[68] In an article entitled 'Jeevandan', reproduced in, *Ibid.*, p. 128.

troublesome. Though I had given up the basic postulates of
Marxism . *I continued to feel strongly that human freedom
could be fully and wholly realised only in a stateless society.
I was, and am, not sure if the state would ever wither away
completely (italics ours).*[69]

It is clear from the above observation that J. P. had come to
believe now in some sort of a stateless society, but it is not the same
ideal which could be compared to the anarchistic concept of 'state-
less-ness'. If anything, it can only be suggested, that J. P. has
become indifferent towards the state today, and he now aims at a
society of 'state-without-ness'.

The culmination of this trend of thinking was reflected in his
A Plea For Reconstructions of Indian Polity and *Swaraj For The
People.* Both the booklets were the outcome of his serious thinking
on the problem of organising a social order, in a manner in which
the powers of the State were to be diffused into smaller units of
'communitarian' centres, such as the village panchayats. He felt
that in the smaller areas or units of power there will be a greater
scope for the individual to play his part without being organised in
political parties. He observed in this connection :

> 'Ancient Indian thought and tradition, social nature of man,
> social science, ethical and spiritual goals of civilization, the
> demand of democracy that the citizen should participate in
> the ordering and running of his life, the need of saving man
> from alienation from himself and from the fate of robotism,
> the requirement that the State and other institutions of society
> be reduced to a human scale, the ideal, above all, that man
> should become the centre of civilization—all these point in the
> same direction, to a communal or communitarian way of life,
> communitarian ethics and education, communitarian social,
> economic and political organization.'[70]

The most important thing that was to be done for the achievement
of a decentralised polity was to do away with the method of indirect
election and to lay the foundation of a society on the basis of the
'self-governing, self-sufficient, agro-industrial, urbo-rural, local
communities.'[71] The existing villages and townships have to be
reorganised on the pattern of a decentralised society. This would
naturally be a plural society in which the units of power would be

[69] Narayan, *From Socialism to Sarvodaya*, p. 37.
[70] Narayan, *Reconstruction of Indian Polity*, p. 63.
[71] *Ibid.*

located at the bottom, and not concentrated in a monolithic state at the top.

The relevance of socialism to such a reconstruction of society was explained by J. P. thus :

...socialist philosophy need not be opposed to the communitarian picture drawn here. But in that case, socialism will have to be less interested in institutions and more in man. The old faith that state ownership of the means of production, distribution, and exchange plus planning will bring about socialism has been falsified. In its extreme form that faith led to Stalinism. But a new faith has not been created to take the place of the old. For this the socialists will have to go to the pre-Marxian socialist idealists, the philosophical Anarchists, to Tolstoy, Ruskin and Morris : to the post-Marxian social idealists : to Gandhi and Vinoba.[72]

It may be recollected here that Indian socialism, particularly since Independence, had indeed been taking great inspiration from the pre-Marxian, as well as the post-Marxian socialist thought. J. P. tried to carry conviction on this issue by tracing back to the ideas of Chittaranjan Das and Bhagavan Das who together had produced an 'Outline Scheme of Swaraj', for India wherein they had underlined the need of the 'formation of local centres.'[73] The attempt to derive inspiration from the 'Ancient Indian thought and tradition', as outlined by Chittaranjan Das and Bhagavan Das might appear as a new phenomenon in J. P.'s thinking, but it was the logical outcome of his conviction that centralised state could never achieve the ideals of a true democracy.

What was further remarkable was that J. P. was inclined now to eulogise the ideals of the pre-Marxian idealists, philosophical anarchists, including the ideals of Tolstoy and Ruskin and of the post-Marxian idealists like Gandhi and Vinoba. From both the pre-and post-Marxian currents of thought he derived a common inspiration, i.e., to put more reliance on the individual's own creative faculties than on the coercive machinery of the state. This line of thinking inclined him more and more towards the need for evolving a decentralised social order.

The pamphlet entitled Swaraj For the People underlined a

[72] Ibid., pp. 64-65.
[73] Narayan, Reconstruction of Indian Polity, p. 72.
Also, Das, Ancient Vs Modern Socialism, pp. 135-36.

194

similar trend of thought. He pleaded therein for a devolutional society in which *Panchayati Raj* or 'the Swaraj from below' was to form the base of society. He, however, clarified that devolution of power did not necessarily mean a weak centre. It only meant that 'the centre has only as much of it as required to discharge its central functions and all the rest is exercised by the lower organs.'[74] He conceded that the state should regulate and legislate for the formation of a *Panchayati Raj*, but the 'day to day working should be outside the purview of the State Government.'[75] It is clear that what he desired was not the elimination of the state-control altogether, but only reducing it to the minimum possible level, so that the working of the communitarian areas like *Panchayati Raj* were not 'subjugated' completely by the state. It was mainly a question of balancing the local centres of power with the central power of the state. Any imputation of 'statelessness' in his concept of the reconstruction of Indian polity would be wide off the mark.

LOHIA'S APPROACH

Rammanohar Lohia appears not to have concerned himself much with the issue of the state as such. He was, however, critical, like other socialist thinkers, of a dictatorial and totalitarian party with a state, particularly of the kind that had developed in the Soviet Russia under the impact of the communist ideology. Communism, he considered, to be a doctrine of 'social ownership' and, 'a centralized state later.'[76] For, under communism, 'the morality of a stateless society is in no contradiction with the immorality of a dictatorial party and state.'

While deploring the trend in both capitalism and communism to build a civilization based on multiplication of needs and large scale mechanisation, Lohia underlined the need to adopt the Gandhian ideals of decentralisation.. He observed :

> ...if an effort is made to build Gandhiji's postulates into economic and administrative systems and work them out, it would be possible for India to help in the creation of a new civilization. This is the specific job of socialism all over the

[74] J. P. Narayan, *Swaraj For the People*, Varanasi, A. B. S. S. S. Publication, 1961, p. 5.
[75] *Ibid.*, p. 15.
[76] Lohia, *Marx, Gandhi and Socialism*, p. 323.

world and especially of socialism in India.[77]
He pleaded with conviction for creating a 'new civilization' which
could avoid its dependence on big industries, and do away with the
centralisation of administrative powers that was the natural outcome of it. Lohia preferred a small-scale industrialised civilization,
which naturally meant that heavy machine and its counterpart
'Leviathan State' should not 'deluge man, and his new socialist
civilization.'[78] Decentralisation of authority in the state was one of
the points on which he put emphasis.[79]

It is strange that having undergone political arrests many
times, Lohia still appeared to have clung to his faith in the continuance of the machinery of state, and showed, in no appreciable
way, any such anarchistic leanings in his thought and deeds, as the
anarchists generally did. He not only adopted the parliamentary
procedure for the achievement of his socialist state, but also actively
participated in the functioning of the Indian Parliament towards the
closing years of his life. He, frankly confessed that the state, constituted as it was today, necessitated some sort of inflexibility and
drastic measure and not just soft conventional or constitutional ways.
He observed :

> Socialism henceforth and in the rest of the world must be
> drastic, unconstitutional when necessary, and lay the accent
> on production. The great deeds of European socialism in the
> sphere of the welfare state must remain an inspiration and a
> model....It has to set up the investing and capital-forming
> community before it can achieve the welfare state.[80]

The fact that Lohia did not consider even a little drastic and
unconstitutional method to be incompatible with the concept of a
welfare state was itself indicative of the fact that parliamentary
system was, in no way, a check upon his unorthodox approach
towards the state and parliament.

MEHTA'S APPROACH

Asoka Mehta has been one of the strongest critics of a totali-

[77] *Ibid.*, p. 136.
[78] *Ibid.*, p. 328.
[79] In his Presidential Address to the Pachmarhi Special Convention in
1952, he laid great stress on the decentralisation of power and building up of a
Four-Pillar State.
[80] Lohia, *Marx, Gandhi and Socialism*, pp. 329–30.

tarian state and the concept of proletariat dictatorship—in the sense of the perpetuation of a one-party rule. At the same time he is an exponent of the concept of democratic state, which implies parliamentary system with the greatest amount of cooperation among the various parties. He tries to analyse the realities in Marxian approach with regard to bourgeois and proletariat states. He found many of the postulates of Marxism concerning bourgeois state as inadequate and incorrect and many generalisations about the proletariat state as unfounded. Pointing out to one of the important inadequacies, as he found it in the Marxian concept of state, he observed : '...in constructing a general theory of state, Marx and Engels disregarded power conflicts within a class' as a whole.[81] Personally he maintained that, in any concept of democratic state, there must be room for multi-parties, because 'it is possible within the same class, or a group of classes, to heave a variety of policies.'[82] He described a single-party rule within a state as 'one of the tragedies perpetrated by the Bolsheviks.'[83]

Mehta had no rigid approach to any *a priori* theory of state, and pleaded : 'Please remember that I am trying to point out to you that state is to be viewed in terms of different historical settings. As the background changes, the analysis has to change *pari pasu.*' Hence, he not only refused to attack on any theory of the state, but also urged earnestly to evolve a sociological and democratic approach towards the understanding of the state.

He did not believe in the concept of withering away of the state, for the simple reason that the existence of a state is a reality.[84]

He also maintained that planning could never be possible without the continued existence of the state. Further, he also put emphasis on decentralisation and primary institutions like panchayats, cooperatives, and trade unions, etc. Through these institutions he visualised the concept of society.

P.S.P.'S APPROACH

The party literature of the Socialist parties and the Congress also followed the line of thinking of the individual socialists on the

---

[81] Mehta, *Democratic Socialism*, p. 81.
[82] *Ibid.*, p. 71.
[83] *Ibid.*
[84] In an interview on 2nd April, 1968, at New Delhi.

issue of state. The *Policy Statement* of the P. S. P. clearly indicated its preference for a 'decentralised socialist state'.[85] It also maintained that the concept of 'Welfare State'—functioning in different parts of the world—was, to a great extent, the result of labour movement in the world.[86] Hence, it can be inferred that, if not totally to some extent at least, it contained the elements with which the *Policy Statement* manifested some sort of an affinity. But both the concepts of decentralisation and the Welfare State could have meaning only if they were conceived in the over all context of democracy, and not dictatorship or totalitarianism, or bureaucratism.[87]

CONGRESS AND WELFARE STATE

The Indian national Congress, which used the term 'Co-operative Commonwealth' at its Avadi session in 1955, adopted the 'Socialist Pattern of Society' as its chief goal. The resolution intended to cast 'National Planning' in such a way as to achieve the objectives laid down in the Constitution of the Congress and also in the Directive Principles of State Policy, formulated in the Constitution of India. The resolution declared that planning in India.

> ...should take place with a view to the establishment of Socialistic Pattern of Society where the principal means of production are under social ownership or control, production is progressively speeded up and there is equitable distribution of national wealth.[88]

In a separate resolution on the 'Economic Policy the Congress further resolved to take concrete steps towards increasing production, the standards of living and wages, according to the changing price-index of the last ten years. This implied, according to Nehru, an

---

[85] The *Policy Statement*, 1955, pp. 5–9.

[86] 'It is often maintained that the phenomenon of the Welfare State completely negatives the validity of class struggle. But it is a misreading of the social dynamics of the Welfare State. In the U. S. A., the Welfare State is largely a product of the economic crisis which started in 1929 and failed to be resolved through usual capitalistic processes. But in Europe the Welfare State is as much the product of class struggles of the organised labour. No Welfare State has ever been a free gift of the capitalist class or a product of its imaginative sympathies or moral consciousness.'—*Ibid.*, p. 30.

[87] *Ibid.*, p. 8.

[88] Sriman Narayan, *Samajvadi Dhang Ka Samaj*, New Delhi, Bhartiya Rastriya Prakashan, n. d., p. 3.

affirmation of building up a 'welfare state' with a 'socialist economy.'[89] Commenting on the above resolution, Nehru observed :

> At no stage in the history of the freedom struggle, have we been thinking of mere political freedom. We thought of the economic aspect when the content of freedom grew before us. Now the time has come when we should march forward. We want a welfare state...we cannot have a welfare state in India with all the socialism and Communism in the world unless our national income goes up...We must produce well and then divide equitably.[90]

The Congress adopted the terminology of welfare state to connot its economic concern and socialistic objectives to the extent they could be achieved. It was a positive indication that the Congress was leaning towards socialistic objectives, even though the welfare state was only 'a half-way house', and not socialism completely. Of course, in a round about way, the Congress was now being gradually drawn towards the concept of state on the patterns of Western democracies and socialistic states. It was still farther from its professed ideology of 'democratic socialism', an ideal, which it adopted much later in 1964.

SOCIALIST PARTY'S APPROACH

The Socialist Party also, having broken its ties with the P.S.P. in 1956 adopted the same constitution as that of the P. S. P. It portrayed picture of a 'Four Pillar State', the outlines of which had been drawn up earlier in the Address of Rammanohar Lohia at the Pachmarhi Special Convention of the Socialist Party in 1952. The Election Manifesto of the Party, on the eve of the Second General Elections in India, held its picture of the State as under :

1. One fourth of all governmental and plan expenditure should be through village, district and city panchayats.
2. Police should be subordinate to village, city and district panchayats or any of their agencies.
3. The post of collector should be abolished and all his functions distributed among various bodies in the district. As far as possible, the principle of election should be

---

[89] *Ibid.*

[90] P. R. Chakravarti, 'Passage to Socialism', *AICC Economic Review*, XV (14–15), Jan. 9, 1964, p. 91.

applied in administration, instead of nominations.

4. Agriculture, industry and other property, which is nationalised, should, as far as possible, be owned and administered by village, city and district panchayats.

5. Economic decentralization, corresponding to political and administrative decentralization should be brought about through maximum utilization of small machines.[91]

In the above outlines the Socialist Party tried to evolve a picture of a decentralised state which could function both in political and economic spheres. The Manifesto also indicated its preference for some sort of a welfare state which could regulate the social, economic and political life in society.

SOCIALIST'S APPROACH TOWARDS WELFARE STATE

But the socialists' concept of a welfare state should not be equated with the general use of the term. Rohit Dave, pointed out the difference clearly :

The difference would arise in the definition of the welfare of the whole community as well as in the methods whereby it should be achieved. New capitalism, for instance, would agree with old capitalism, in measuring the welfare of the community in terms of the capital accumulated. Socialism, on the other hand, would measure it in terms of the help given to the individual to overcome their biological limitations so as to widen the range of their attainable objectives. Again new capitalism would primarily depend upon the economic competition to safeguard the abiding values of equality, security and freedom, Socialism would make the state primarily responsible for the same.[92]

According to Dave, a socialist state has to undertake manifold activities in order to create a socialist society. It has to see that :

...the economic system works in a way whereby there is no great inequality of income or of wealth, that machinery does remain idle when there are men to work them merely because of the owner of the machinery does not think worth its while to run it ; that competition among various economic factors, economic organisations, economic sectors is not such as to deprive some of the fair returns on their work; that the interest of the future generations is not sacrificed in the greedy consump-

[91] 1962 Manifesto of the Socialist Party, reproduced in, Lohia, *Marx, Gandhi and Socialism*, p. 523.

[92] Rohit Dave, *op. cit.*, pp. 23–24.

200

tion of resources by the present ones; that the community has
the capacity to defend itself under modern conditions.[93]

This naturally meant that the state was to regulate the 'various social
relationships' and enlarge the 'social consciousness of the individual',
so as to realise the fundamental values of 'equality, security, and
freedom.' Thus, by welfare state, the socialists implied an all
embracing image of a state. An essential element of their vision of
state was also the decentralisation of power, implying pluralism in
political set-up.[94]

---

[93] *Ibid.*, p. 27.
[94] S. K. Dhar, 'Concept of Socialist Society is Pluralistic', *Janata,* XIX
(30–31), Independence Day 1964, p. 24.

6

THE METHODOLOGY OF SOCIALIST TRANSFORMATION OF SOCIETY

THE DETERMINING FEATURE OF SOCIALISM : ITS METHODOLOGY

It has often been said that the speciality about socialism does not lie so much in its objectives as in its methods. Gandhiji maintained that socialism was essentially a matter of technique and method. In his own words : 'Socialism was not born with the discovery of the misuse of capital by capitalists.... What is true is that when some reformers lost faith in the method of conversion, the technique of what is known as scientific socialism was born.'[1]

Not only Gandhiji, but even socialists have maintained that the methodology of transformation of society was the hard core of the socialist theory and practice. According to M. R. Dandavate, 'The methodology of social change constitutes one of the most significant aspects of socialist theory.'[2]

In India, particularly, the question of method and means have received great emphasis, ever since Gandhism was introduced in the Indian politics. Since independence, the one major factor that exercised the minds of the socialist thinkers and Socialist Parties most was the question of the method and means. Addressing the first conference of the Socialist Party of India, after Independence, its General Secretary, Jayaprakash Narayan observed :

I seek your indulgence now to bear with me in examining a

---

[1] Gandhi, *My Socialism*, p. 3.

[2] Dandavate, *op. cit.*, p. 7. Also, A. B. Shah a prominent socialist maintains that the difference between democratic socialism and Marxism was essentially in the methods they envisaged.

A. B. Shah 'Socialist Movement Must Avoid Cheap Melodrama', *Janata*, XIX (30–31), Independence Day 1964, p. 11.

problem that has deeply worried me of late. The problem is that of method or means...From times immemorial there have been politicians who have preached that there is no such thing as ethics in politics...Since the victory of Stalinist methods in Russia, it has been commonly believed that there is no room for moral values in Marxism and it is usual for a socialist who talks of such matters to be branded as a renegade or, at least, a deviationist. I should therefore, like to state before you in the clearest possible terms that I for one have come to believe that for the achievement of socialism a strict regard for means is of the highest importance.[3]

BELIEF IN CLASS-STRUGGLE

During the colonial period, when the C. S. P. was an inner group within the Congress, it had to accept the non-violent means of national struggle, and this necessarily meant a considerable modification of their stand on 'class struggle' and its inevitability for the socialistic reconstruction of society. However, their essential belief in class struggle remained unchanged. 'Such doctrines of class harmony, similar to those preached by Gandhi,' observed Hari Kishore Singh, 'were unlikely to appeal to young socialists who, under Marxist influence, had convinced themselves of the inevitability of the class struggle.'[4] Hence the Gandhian emphasis on class-harmony and the concept of trusteeship appeared to the socialists as unrealistic.

Jawaharlal Nehru explained : 'I was not afraid of raising the class issue...but I recognised that the Congress, being what it was, could not then patronise class conflict.'[5] During the colonial period J. P. believed that violent means might have to be adopted for the achievement of independence. However, 'Narayan never thought highly of the Gandhian technique of satyagraha as an effective weapon for achieving independence, and he had no faith that parliamentary democracy was likely to be any more effective. Throughout the colonial period, he was a convinced believer in the class struggle and in insurrectionary methods for achieving national as well as socialist aims.'[6]

[3] *Report of the Sixth Annual Conference of the Socialist Party*, Nasik, 1948, pp. 95–97.

[4] H. K. Singh, *op. cit.*, p. 4.

[5] Nehru, *Autobiography*, p. 232.

[6] H. K. Singh, *op. cit.*, p. 17.

To what extent the C. S. P., as a whole, was wedded to the insurrectionary method is an open question.[7]   Indeed, however willy nilly, the C. S. P. did try to conform itself, to the creed of the Congress which had been described as 'legitimate and peaceful'. The only exception was the underground activities during the Quit India Movement, which was explained by the socialist leaders as a necessary evil of compulsion and exceptional situation.

But one thing was beyond any shadow of doubt.   Whether he was Nehru and Deva or Sampurnanand or J. P., none committed himself to the Gandhian scruples of non-violence as the ultimate creed or the last article of his faith.

The attitude of the Congress socialists was clearly indicated in the Joint Statement of Deva, J. P., Prakasha, and Sampurnanand on the charges levelled against the C. S. P. by the AICC that the socialists were pleading for the 'confiscation of property' and waging of 'class-war'.   They asserted :

> The creed of the Congress is attainment of *Purna Swaraj* through legitimate and peaceful means.   There is nothing in our programme adopted at Patna, which in any sense whatever can be said to be contrary to this creed...the very fact that we are within the Congress means that we accept the principle of using peaceful and legitimate means.[8]

Earlier, in the same statement they clarified their stand on class-war :

> As regards class war, to speak of the necessity of creating a thing which is ever present is meaningless.   The question is not of creating a class-war but of deciding which side we should take in that War, the side of the oppressed or the oppressor.[9]

This was a calculated statement which wholly accepted the fact of class-war in society as a historical phenomenon.   Without accepting

[7] Rammanohar Lohia revealed that, excepting what might have been in some corner of J. P.'s mind, on the whole, we the socialists did not consider that insurrectionary and violent methods would bring independence to India.

He added, however, that his present feeling was different, and a violent revolutionary method might have achieved things better for India ; Partition could have been avoided ; some people like him might not have been alive but India would have been better and the world would have been different.   In an interview on 13.4.65 at New Delhi.

[8] Mitra, *Indian Annual Register*, Jan-June, 1934, I, 344.

[9] *Ibid.*

any responsibility for advocating class-war, they suggestively held that, unless classes were eliminated from society, the inevitability of class war, or the day-to-day class struggle, could not be avoided. Therefore the constant tug-of-war between the interests of the 'haves' and the 'have-nots' in society must be eliminated altogether through the establishment of a classless society. Whether it could be done through violent or non-violent means was immaterial at that time. On the score of 'non-violence' the socialists remained non-committal and evasive, because they were not sure that the creed of the Congress —'legitimate and peaceful'—was unfailing and certain.

ADVOCACY OF REVOLUTIONARY METHODS

The socialists appeared not to have shown 'any special love for the non-violent means, as also for liberal parliamentary ways. The C. S. P. preferred militant and revolutionary methods for national struggle and social change. The term 'revolutionary', however did not necessarily imply violence. Nehru explained it only as an expression of 'change' rather than destruction.[10] He abhorred revolution for mere destruction's sake. The C. S. P. also at its Faizpur Conference in 1936, proclaimed that 'revolutionary parliamentarianism is an integral part of the struggle' for national freedom ; and the opposition to imperialism on the parliamentary front to be effective required mass backing and 'mass action.'[11] Here also the word 'revolutionary' was tagged with parliamentarianism. Any element of violence or destruction is generally considered incompatible with the accepted ways of parliamentarianism. The word 'revolutionary' was further affixed to the expression 'mass action'—a term, in itself, but certainly it did not imply any conspiratorial method or minority manoeuvres. Hence, it is reasonable to infer that the expressions 'revolutionary' and 'mass action' did not mean violent insurrection or terroristic methods. It was strongly suggestive of the need of radical change, however, and the giving up of the slow and sluggish ways of constitutional processes. It might be recalled

---

[10] In a letter to Indira, Nehru explained : 'Nothing in the world that is alive remains unchanging. All nature changes from day to day and minute to minute, only the dead stop growing and are quiescent. Fresh water runs on, and if you stop it, it becomes stagnant. So also is it with the life of man and the life of a nation.' Nehru, *Glimpses of World History*, p. 8.

[11] *All India Congress Socialist Party*, 1937, p. 12.

here that even Engels had suggested the possibility of revolution through the parliamentary process ; hence the socialists' resolution of 'revolutionary parliamentarianism' was nothing more than to suggest the need of rapid and radical change without bloodshed and violence. Therefore, the socialists were not enthusiastic about the slow and sluggish ways of parliamentarianism. But the extent to which parliamentary method could lead to revolutionary change, it appealed to them, and they were all for giving it a full trial.

DISAPPOINTMENT WITH GANDHIAN TECHNIQUE

During the colonial period the socialists remained greatly disappointed with the Gandhian method of non-violence, and described their own method as a Marxist-Leninist one, without bringing out its full implications. They conceded to the non-violent method of national struggle for independence only as a matter of expediency or policy and not as a matter of creed or faith. Even Nehru had declared :

...for us and for the National Congress as a whole the non-violent method was not, and could not be, a religion or an unchallengeable creed or dogma. It could only be a policy and a method promising certain results, and by those results it would have to be finally judged.[12]

Significantly enough, the Presidential Speech of Narendra Deva, at the Patna gathering of the Congress socialists did not even once use the word 'non-violence', while he used the term 'revolution' and 'revolutionary' over twenty times. He observed :

We can perform the task before us only if we try to comprehend the principles and purposes of socialism and to understand the dialectical method propounded by Marx for the correct understanding of the situation and make that understanding the basis of true action. Above all, we should avoid dogmatism and sectarianism. We must take our stand on scientific socialism and steer clear of utopian socialism or social reformism. We can in no case allow ourselves to be satisfied with superficial modifications in the present-day arrangements. Nothing short of a revolutionary transformation of the existing social order can meet the needs of the situation.[13]

[12] Nehru, *Autobiography*, p. 84.
[13] N. V. Rajkumar, *Development of the Congress Constitution*, New Delhi, All India Congress Committee, 1949, pp. 18–19.

THE METHODOLOGY OF SOCIALIST TRANSFORMATION OF SOCIETY

The above observation, it may be argued, was still within the framework of non-violence, and yet, it would be equally correct to infer that it did not suggest acceptance of the non-violent creed of the Congress. For, suggestively the emphasis was on the attainment of objectives and not on the methods to be adopted. The method and means were clearly subordinated to the need of achievements of objectives. Thus, the socialists, including Nehru, did not accept the Gandhian creed of non-violence wholly. It is no wonder, therefore, that Gandhiji's proposal to replace the words 'legitimate and peaceful' by 'truthful and non-violent' in the Constitution of the Congress was not accepted by the Subjects Committee itself. A vague presumption either way was left to cover the questions of method and means for the Congressmen, and even more so, for the socialists.

NON-PARLIAMENTARY APPROACH

Since the C. S. P. was organised as a radical group within the Congress with a view to check its drift towards liberal constitutionalism, it did not cultivate strong faith in and affinity with the accepted notions of parlimentary methods. It was thus said to have 'extra-parliamentary origin.'[14] Even Nehru subscribed to the view that 'our final aim can only be a classless society...every thing that comes in the way will have to be removed, gently if possible, forcibly, if necessary.'[15] J. P. did not think that 'parliamentary democracy was likely to be any more effective.'[16] Deva criticised the revival of the old Swaraj Party mainly on the ground that it was to grow as 'an autonomous parliamentary section of the Congress' and 'become a pacca constitutional and reformist body and will develop a mentality which will run counter to the revolutionary policy of the Congress.'[17] Thus the Indian socialists generally did not grow more than just skin-deep affinity with the parliamentary methods of social reconstruction. This was evident as many of them later gave up parliamentary ways altogether including party-policies. A few of them, who continued to work through parliamentary ways, never hesitated in advocating openly the breaking of the laws and adopting

[14] Quoted in, H. K. Singh, *op. cit.*, p. 217.
[15] Nehru, *Autobiography*, pp. 551–52.
[16] H. K. Singh, *op. cit.*, p. 17.
[17] Deva, *Socialism and National Revolution*, p. 26.

extra-parliamentary ways. In this connection we might recall J. P. and Lohia—the former lost faith in the parliamentary system and the latter in sheer parliamentarianism. Lohia observed in this connection that :

> If parliamentary and constitutional methods were the only way to achieve salvation, I have no doubt in my mind that two-thirds of the world, particularly Asia, will rush to systems and creeds that believe in insurrection or violence of the dagger and the acid bulb.[18]

Even Deva considered a little violation of the laws to be inevitable even within a democratic set-up.[19] This may also be recalled that in 1937 the socialists opposed the council-entry, and in 1946 they refused to join the cabinet in the Interim Government. Consequently, they did not have much experience of the practical working of the parliamentary ways.

ADMIRATION FOR THE METHOD OF PLANNING

Another trend in the colonial period was growing appreciation of the method of planning as a necessary tool for socialist transformation of society. Within the Congress, of course, Nehru pioneered this trend. The fifteen-point programme adopted by the C. S. P. included the 'development of the economic life of the country to be planned and controlled by the State.' The socialists, including Nehru, eulogised the method of planning in Soviet Russia. Deva also observed in this regard :

> Russia is the only land without unemployment. The great merits of its planned economy are being freely recognised even by capitalists. ...Factories, land, transport and credit system have been socialised the collectivisation of farming is taking place. In place of anarchy we have planned guidance of economic development.[20]

This inspiring account reflects the socialists' approach towards the method of planning then. However, as India was not yet free, it was realised by the socialists, including Nehru as chairman of the National Planning Committee, that any effective planning could be done only in a free India.[21] It was certainly under that belief that

[18] Lohia, *Marx, Gandhi and Socialism*, p. 127.
[19] Deva, *Socialism and National Revolution*, p. 26.
[20] *Ibid.*, p. 19.
[21] Norman, *Nehru*, I, 690.

THE METHODOLOGY OF SOCIALIST TRANSFORMATION OF SOCIETY

208

after Independence all socialists generally agreed in principle that
planning was essential to boost up the retarded economic growth in
India. Although strongly critical of the Five Year Plans as formulated by the Congress government and its Planning Commission, the
socialists have emphasised its importance consistently. The election
manifestoes of the P.S.P. included planning as one of its programmes
during the last four general elections.

MILITANT METHOD OF THE EARLY 40s

Shocked by the violent and terrorist methods that the
communists had pursued both in and outside India, and equally
disappointed with the soft, liberal and compromising methods of the
Congress, the method that C. S. P. evolved was something in between
the two extremes; neither violent and 'bloody' like the former, nor
soft and compromising like the latter. But the emphasis was clearly
on the radical methods of struggle, not excluding even underground
militant methods. As Thomas A. Rusch, observes :

> In the realm of methods, it (C. S. P.) aided the Congress to
> further broaden, activise, and democratise its organization to
> reach and recruit industrial workers, peasants and Moslems,
> on the basis of a secular economic appeal. More important,
> it successfully urged the Congress to make explicit that which
> was implict in the Gandhian technique of non-violent civil
> disobedience, namely, a nation-wide, full scale, mass revolt,
> from which the leaders had shrunk in previous compaigns.
> The 'Quit-India' resolution of 1942 embodied this concept of
> using the Gandhian methods to the limits of their possibilities,
> as subsequent events proved. In this respet, then, the Party
> represented the most consistent, militant, uncompromising
> element of Indian nationalism.[22]

The reference to the 'subsequent events' obviously was to the underground militant methods pursued by the socialist leaders like J. P.,
Lohia, Patwardhan and Aruna Asaf Ali, during the course of the
1942 Revolution. They tried to justify their method and conduct in
terms of the Bombay resolution of the Congress. It was clearly
explained by J. P. in one of his letters to the Freedom Fighters :

> Congress has stated repeatedly during this war that if India
> became free, or even if a national government were set up, it
> would be prepared to resist aggression with arms. But, if we

[22] Rusch, *op. cit.*, pp. 468-69.

are prepared to fight Japan and Germany with arms, why must we refuse to fight Britain in the same manner.[23]

The organisation of the 'Azad Dasta' by J. P. was directed towards carrying revolution through insurrection, sabotage and arms. It did not appear to him and to his other socialist colleagues that it ran counter to their previous commitments and the creed of the Congress. Hence, the limit of their possibilities, referred to by Rusch, rightly indicated that under socialists' understanding of the creed of the Congress even insurrectionary methods and resort to arms were not entirely ruled out. Patwardhan and Lohia, no less Gandhians, cooperated in the underground militant technique of the struggle. It is true that Mahatma Gandhi and the Congress did not accept any responsibility for such violent deeds, yet the Congress leaders, including Nehru, 'declared their full support for what happend during this phase.'[24] Acting upon that knowledge, and especially owing to the nation-wide heroic popularity that the 'militant' methods of struggle had won for the C. S. P., the socialists generally, even during the early years of the Post-Independence phase appeared reluctant to adopt the non-violent creed with Gandhian scruples.

POST-INDEPENDENCE RETHINKING ON METHODS AND MEANS

At the Kanpur session of the Socialist Party in 1947, on the eve of Independence, the ideal of democratic socialism was firmly adopted by the Socialist Party. J. P.'s two important articles entitled 'My Picture of Socialism' and 'The Transition to Socialism', referred to earlier, emphasised the need to adopt democratic methods for socialism. Narendra Deva also observed in 1949 that 'one of the prevailing misconceptions that socialism is incompatible with democracy deserves to be removed.'[25]

While recalling the ideal of democratic socialism, J. P. addressed the partymen

Some of you openly ridicule the word 'democratic.' They say that the deep red of socialism has been rendered pink by the word democratic. But they are confusing democratic socialism

[23] Narayan, *Towards Struggle*, p. 25.
[24] H. K. Singh, *op. cit.*, p. 84.
[25] Deva, *Report of the Seventh Conference of the Socialist Party*, Patna, 1949, p. 19.

THE METHODOLOGY OF SOCIALIST TRANSFORMATION OF SOCIETY

with traditional social democracy...I am convinced that there can be no real socialism without the enlargement of our liberty and freedom, without complete democracy. I have read Marx, I have studied Lenin's writings, I was once a communist. Marx and Lenin had both said that democracy and socialism are inseparable...Democratic socialism must become, our life's mission, the philosophy of our life.[26]

With such passionate attachment with the ideal of democratic socialism, which he did not consider incompatible with Marxism, or even with Leninism, J. P. advocated the need for adopting democratic means. He strongly deprecated the trend favouring totalitarianism and dictatorship. Even more basic change in him was that while he had talked about the inadequacy and even the failure of political democracy and maintained that there could be no real democracy during the colonial period, he had now come to emphasise that there could be no real socialism without democracy. He reminded the socialists

Remember the goal I have laid down is that of democratic socialism. The method of the violent revolution and dictatorship might conceivably lead to a socialist democracy; but in the only country where it has been tried, it has led to something very different, i.e., to a bureaucratic State, in which democracy does not exist. I should like to take a lesson from history.[27]

LESSON FROM GANDHISM

J. P. deprecated dictatorship and violence that had come to stay in Russia. After the death of Gandhiji, and after witnessing the bloody riots of the post-partition period, he was further convinced of the futility of violent means for achieving the socialist objectives. With regard to this, he observed :

There were many things that Mahatma Gandhi taught us. But the greatest thing he taught us was that evil means can never lead to good ends. Some of us may have been sceptical of this truth but recent world events and events at home have convinced me that nothing but good means will enable us to reach the goal of a good society, which is socialism.[28]

The reference to Gandhian theory of end and means was a clear

[26] *Ibid.*, pp. 49–50.
[27] Narayan, *Socialism, Sarvodaya and Democracy*, p. 51.
[28] *Report of the Sixth Annual Conference of the Socialist Party*, Nasik, 1948, pp. 96–97.

indication that henceforth the Socialist Party in India, including some of its one time zealous Marxists, had come to accept the Gandhian technique of non-violent and peaceful means, and had also come to realise that the method and means were not immaterial or secondary, but as important as the end itself, or even more so !

J. P. took a particular lead in the matter and impressed upon the socialists the need to follow the Gandhian method of non-violent means. We have already indicated that ever since 1940 he had been drawing closer to Gandhiji and his ideas. With the adoption of 'Democratic Socialism' as the ideal of the Socialist Party on the eve of Independence, the Gandhian technique of non-violence came to have even more pointed relevance.

In 1950, as the Secretary of the Party, J. P. explained that the *Policy Statement* of the Socialist Party, adopted at Kanpur, had indicated the existence of two methods for social revolution—the insurrectionary or violent and the democratic or peaceful methods. He further explained that neither the first meant out-and-out violence nor the second meant out-and-out constitutionalism. For India the above *Policy Statement* considered democratic method to be the 'only right method to work for socialism.'[29] J. P. was now in no doubt that peaceful means were suitable for the attainment of socialist goals. He deplored the tendency of double thinking in some corners *i.e.*, to talk of democratic means and also to maintain that ...at the last stage violence would somehow be essential.[30] He wanted to give non-violent democratic methods the first and full trial and, only when it failed, the question of revolutionary methods could arise at all.

J. P. also explained at the same time that democratic method has to be distinguished from sheer constitutionalism. He said :

The Socialist Party is not a mere parliamentary party. As a matter of fact, the Socialist Party hardly exists in the Parliament. The party is a revolutionary party and while it may use the parliamentary methods it relies for its success mainly on its work outside parliament and among the people.[31]

He further maintained :

Socialist Party is not an election machine and it does not rely

[29] Quoted in, Narayan, *Socialism, Sarvodaya and Democracy*, p. 70.
[30] *Ibid.*, p. 74.
[31] *Ibid.*, p. 75.

THE METHODOLOGY OF SOCIALIST TRANSFORMATION OF SOCIETY

on propaganda alone. The Party organises at the same time trade unions, kisan panchayats, youth leagues. It carries on agitation and and fights for the people. It conducts local struggles, strikes and *satyagrahas*. It may have to launch even a national struggle.[32]

A significant aspect of this explanation was a reference to the teachings of the *Gita*, *i.e.* doing one's duty without any attachment with the result, as well as to B. G. Tilak's emphasis on the purity of ends and means through his commentaries on the *Gita Rahasya*.[33]

How much this trends in J. P.'s throught, with regard to the method and means, was inspired by Gandhiji cannot be over-emphasised. He frankly acknowledged it himself :

Gandhiji was a social phenomenon which socialism must understand rather than explain away. The post-Gandhi world can never go on as if there never had been a Gandhi. At every turn, on every occasion, his great voice will echo forth.[34]

The Gandhian impact on J. P., as well as on the Socialist Party, was probably the greatest factor in the evolution of the attitude of the socialists on the issue of non-violent means. Whatever little reluctance there was on the issue of accepting democratic methods. implying peaceful and non-violent means, came to be finally over-come with the marger of the K. M. P. P., led by J. B. Kripalani, with the Socialist Party in 1952.

Regarding the apprehension caused among some socialist members that the merger with the K. M. P. P. had diluted the ideology and methodology of the Socialist Party, J. P. made no secret of it that the dilution indeed was calculatedly arrived at. He, however, explained, probably more to assuage the feelings of his partymen than to express his personal conviction, that

...if we consider the practical implications of this problem we will have to agree that the issue of insurrection *vs* peaceful and democratic methods is fast becoming a purely academic issue. ...If at all the situation changes redically and beyond our expectations and violence becomes inevitable I do not think that the spokesman of the former K. M. P. P. will think in any way differently from those of the former Socialist Party.[35]

[32] *Ibid.*, pp. 75–76.
[33] *Ibid.*, p. 77.
[34] Narayan, *Socialism to Sarvodaya*, p. 1.
[35] *Ibid.* p. 18.

It was, thus, still maintained, although remotely that violent means could not be ruled out ultimately as the last resort, if ever such a need arose. A significant aspect of this turn of thinking was that, even though he eulogised the democratic, peaceful and non-violent means, it was still hedged around with the Marxian ideas and the distant possibility of resorting to the methods of insurrection. The fundamental difference between his colonial and post-colonial position in this regard was that during the colonial period J. P. generally believed in insurrectionary and violent means and yet worked under the accepted policy of the Congress—'legitimate and peaceful means'; but in the post-colonial period the position was reversed; he now came to believe in non-violent and peaceful means, but the weapon of violent struggle was not completely discarded from the political armoury of the Socialist Party.

DEVA'S LEANING TOWARDS GANDHIAN TECHNIQUE

Narendra Deva, as indicated earlier, appears to have been greatly inspired by Gandhiji and his ideas, particularly after his death. He eulogised the Gandhian method of non-violent *Satyagraha* and considered it not only a precept for personal conduct but a great weapon which could do away with those social disparities that were the cause of enmity and conflict.[36] Having pioneered the ideal of democratic socialism, he fully realised that peaceful, non-violent and democratic procedure ought to prevail over the ways of dictatorship, violence and totalitarianism. He warned that 'totalitarianism creates terror and makes man a mere cog in the state machine.'[37]

Within the framework of non-violent means, Deva justified the method of *Satyagraha*, *i.e.* civil disobedience, in a democratic society, even to the extent of violating certain rules and laws. He found support in an editorial of the *New Statesman and Nation* to justify that strike was a legitimate method for furthering labour interests.[38] He appreciatively quoted a statement from Bevan to justify that sometimes a little illegal conduct and strike were also useful in a constitutional set-up.[39] Hence, with regard to Indian labour, he

[36] Deva, *Rashtriyata aur Samajvad*, p. 734.
[37] *Report of the Seventh National Conference of the Praja Socialist Party*, 1949, p. 19.
[38] Deva, *Rashtriyata aur Samajvad*, p. 379.
[39] *Ibid.*

emphatically declared that *Satyagraha* including strike was the only means through which labour could get some relief from their sufferings. No government should try to trample over this right. He warned that excessive legislation could not solve the problems of the labour, and might even compel them to take resort to violent means.[40] This was a line of argument that Lohia developed further. We shall deal with it subsequently.

THE POLICY OF THE P. S. P.

In a statement to a London bulletin *Indian Socialist* Deva made a significant observation about the P. S. P.'s objective. It was to create a free society. He observed :

> ...free society of equals where the common people participate in the direction of the process of production and manage their own affairs. It was, therefore, opposed to the concentration of all economic and political power in the hands of the state, which leads to totalitarianism and bureaucratic administration. For the same reason it considers Western parliamentary democracy imperfect and in need of being supplemented by direct democracy.[41]

The above observation was very significant, in so far as the *Policy Statement* of the P. S. P. was drafted by Deva himself, and contained a line of direction that democratic socialism was to take under the vision of the socialists. He made it clear that the P. S. P. stood for social ownership, as against state ownership of the means of production, and also that violent means were not only unnecessary but positively harmful to the socialist cause. The workers and peasants could achieve political victory through parliamentary and direct methods—such as labour strikes and civil disobedience.

The *Policy Statement* of the P. S. P. in 1955 was, indeed, a development on the earlier *Policy Statement* of 1947. In the *Policy Statement* of 1955, Deva declared that

> Some socialists condemn rigid constitutionalism and hold that only an armed insurrection can lead to socialism. Both rigid constitutionalism and armed insurrection have to be condemned. Democratic means cannot be identified completely with constitutional parliamentary means. They do include peaceful means of resistance such as strikes and *Satyagraha*...Even in

[40] *Ibid.*, p. 382.
[41] N. Deva, 'Indian Socialism', *Janata*, X (16), May 8, 1955, p. 7.

democratic countries with strong constitutional traditions the possibility of unconstitutional counter—revolutionary activities, cannot altogether be ruled out...

It cannot, however, be maintained that democratic means which include parliamentary struggle have not in any way advanced the cause of socialism, and that violent means alone are effective to bring about socialist transformation. Terroristic action and conspiratorial violence are only infantile maladies of anarchism and frustration. They are condemned by responsible socialist leaders...

From all this it is obvious that it will not be wise on the part of Indian socialists to strive for a violent insurrection.[42]

It was thus professedly a middle course which the Party did not fight shy of in adopting during the 'forties. While individual socialists like J. P. now denounced the method of violent insurrection openly, the P. S. P., as a whole, still maintained flexibility in its attitude over the issue. It declared that peaceful parliamentary and non-violent means could be effectively used for socialist objectives, but at the same time sheer constitutionalism or parliamentarianism should be identified with the socialists' notions of democratic socialism. It conceivably implied even extra or non-parliamentary ways as well.

While conceding that Indian society had not been democratic and the Congress government had not conducted always democratically, the *Policy Statement*, nevertheless, indicated its preference for the democratic method, implying both parliamentary as well as extra-parliamentary ways. It reminded the socialists :

...the purity of means is necessary as purity of ends. Evil means can never lead to good ends. Adherence to certain human values and standards of conduct is necessary to achieve our objective.[43]

This realisation of the 'purity of means' had a Gandhian ring in both its spirit and phraseology. It was now unmistakably clear that the P. S. P. had tilted towards the Gandhian ideals. It was also an open admission that the socialists within the P. S. P. had come to realise that means and ends were inseparable.

Rammanohar Lohia maintained, even more emphatically, that the method and means were the essential determinants of Indian socialism. He strongly advocated the need for adopting the Gandhian

[42] *Policy Statement*, 1955, pp. 32–33.
[43] *Ibid.*, p. 35.

method of non-violent-*Satyagraha* as the only effective weapon for Indian socialism. He pointed out :

> Individuals unsupported by organisation and weapons are negligible in the context of modern civilization. And in the context of this modern civilization Mahatma Gandhi came along and said that even if you do not have an organization to support you, even if you do not have arms to wield, you have got something inside you which enables you to resist oppression and injustice and also to bear suffering manfully.[44]

It was because of this newness in the Gandhian method that he found a promising hope for the future of a 'new world.'

Closely related to the weapon of *Satyagraha* was the question of ends and means, Lohia fully agreed with the philosopher, John Dewey, who maintained that ends and means were convertible terms.[45] He explained that 'means are ends in the short run and the ends are means in the long run' and 'whatvever one does in the immediate goes into the total of what one achieves in the future.'[46] It was this realisation that made him also to appreciate what Gandhiji used to say for himself 'one step enough for me.'

LOHIA'S THEORY OF 'IMMEDIACY'

Lohia built upon the above realisation what has been termed as the theory of 'Immediacy', that is; the immediate results of a conduct must be in conformity, even through only partially, to what is being tried to be achieved in the distant future. He pointed out :

> One does not pay enough attention to the immediate steps that one undertakes, with the result that certain mysticism has begun to operate in collective life. When asked as to how an immediate and a particular act is related to the end in view, one is told 'wait for the next act', and when one has waited for the next and is still waiting to get an answer, one is again told, 'wait yet for the next act.' The chain of acts goes on lengthening and no single act is a justification in itself. Its justification is continually sought in the succeeding act that never occurs, and the chain goes on lengthening and in the name of truth and world peace, wickedness abounds.[47]

[44] Rammanohar Lohia, 'Gandhism and Socialism', *Mankind*, 4 (8), March, 1960, p. 43.
[45] *Ibid.*, p. 44.
[46] *Ibid.*
[47] *Ibid.*

The way many things are done in the world today without in any way considering the compatibility of the immediate action with the end in view, disappointed Lohia greatly. The present is sacrificed in the hope of some brighter future, and this, according to him; was an illusion. The present act must be in conformity with the future objectives to be achieved. He cautioned, however, that

> There is a danger that those who adopt the doctrine of immediacy may lose the end from view. That again would be as disastrous as the fallacy of not paying any attention whatever to immediacy.[48]

Therefore, Lohia did not mean sheer absorption with the present and the immediate. What was required was a discreet balance between the present and the future, between the immediate action and the future attainable goals. This was possible only when one pursues his objectives right from the present. For, he explained that

> It is not possible to achieve the victory of truth through falsehood, of health through murder, of one world through the sacrifice of national freedom, of democracy through dictatorship.[49]

He insisted upon the dictum 'as the means so the end.' He also added that immediate means must also be good, if our ultimate objective was to be good. If that could be possible, he had no doubt in this mind that the pursuit of the Gandhian method of non-violent *Satyagraha* for fair ends, together with the doctrine of immediacy, would be a vastly improved technique over the past two alternatives of parliamentary and insurrectionary methods. Repeating the similar expression as that of the *Policy Statement* he declared that both parliamentary and insurrectionary methods were incomplete, and hence unsuitable. 'The European mind', he maintained 'was unable to go beyond these two alternatives until Gandhiji came on the scene and showed that there was a third course of action.'[50]

INADEQUACY OF PARLIAMENTARY METHOD

Lohia was greatly alive to the inadequacy of the sheer parliamentary method in achieving socialist objectives. He explained thus:

I believe that parliament may not always prove to be satisfac-

[48] *Ibid.*
[49] *Ibid.*
[50] *Ibid.*

tory agency of change and I am not prepared to subscribe to the reactionary view of Engels that parliament is capable of achieving the revolution, particularly in the modern world where two-thirds of the world is so steeped in misery and poverty that parliamentary means will often be found to be inadequate.[51]

Gandhiji suggested a new and a third course of action which was, according to Lohia, an improvement on both constitutional and insurrectionary methods. He observed :

When constitutional methods have proved incapable of achieving redress, it should be open for the people to violate unjust laws and wrongs and injustices that are inflicted upon them.

To violate laws, to court imprisonment, to invite punishment by authority, even to the extent of death, is the only satisfactory way of effecting change.[52]

It would, therefore, be correct to hold that Lohia 'the rebel', that has often been spoken of in recent times, was the product of such a realisation. A little anarchistic spirit in his thought, if not as much in deeds, was clearly discernible here. Because of the belief that parliamentary or constitutional means may no longer prove to be wholly effective, he pleaded for adopting extra-parliamentary methods also.

AVERSE TO THE CREED OF VIOLENCE

However, if Lohia was disappointed with the parliamentary ways, he was equally aware of the futility of the recourse to violence and 'bullet'. He observed :

The alternative is not between parliament and insurrection, between the bullet and the ballot. ...The alternative is between *satyagraha* and the bullet. The ballot has its own place. It is supreme in its own sphere...In that sphere there is no challenge to the ballot. But with regard to injustices and oppression,...the alternative is between bullet and civil disobedience. Should our century, before it dies out, learn this lesson all the world over, that the individual as well as the masses have had placed in their hands this unique weapon of civil disobedience to defeat their tyrants, we may be ushering a new civilization.[53]

---

[51] *Ibid.*
[52] *Ibid.*
[53] Lahia, *Marx, Gandhi and Socialism*, pp. 127–28.

As a socialist he was conscious that he was pitched against injustice and tyranny in society, and as such, soft, compromising, and law-abiding methods alone could not suffice. At times the violation of laws may be necessary. He violated so many laws and was arrested for a record number of times but all these were considered necessary for achieving the socialist objectives.

PERMANENT CIVIL DISOBEDIENCE

In short, Lohia maintained that for socialism neither passive constitutionalism nor aggressive violence was the correct method, the effective method could be civil disobedience with preparedness to die for the cause. He was inclined to launch a permanent civil disobedience against tyranny and oppression of all kinds. The inspiration for this ideal came from Gandhiji again. He maintained that Gandhiji taught two things : how to love others and how to non-cooperate with dispassionate anger against injustices of all kinds. Lohia regretted that in the anxiety to learn the one, the other was forgotten. But for a true socialist, he maintained, the other lesson was more important. There should be a permanent rebellion in the human heart against all sorts of injustices. With that conviction, he led at times himself those forces of rebellion. He exhorted that civil-resister has not to calculate in terms of gain and loss and has nothing to fear. If that be the approach then the method by itself would be a success.[54]

Lohia maintained that civil disobedience was perfectly within the framework of democratic socialism, and, in a way, even of Marxism. He considered Marx to be a democrat through and through, and observed :

> Although Marx may have occasionally talked in terms of force, he did not outline the whole strategy and tactics of deciet and lies and bad conduct which Lenin did, perhaps because he had to operate in conditions of backwardness.[55]

Marx, he thought, had talked essentially in terms of England and Germany, not in terms of Russia, China and India which were then 'semi-barbarous and semi-retarded nations.'[56] The use of violence

[54] Lohia, *Civil Nafarmani* : *Siddhanta aur Amal*, Hyderabad, Samajvadi Pothi 4, 1957, pp. 7–8.
[55] Lohia, *Marx, Gandhi and Socialism*, p. 111.
[56] *Ibid.*

in the context of undeveloped nations, like Russia, was Lenin's particular stipulation as the particular need of the particular conditions. Hence, the compatibility of socialism with democracy and peaceful means could not be sweepingly questioned.

SOCIALIST PARTY'S APPROACH

It is in this background that Lohia laid down in the 'Statement of Principles' of the Socialist Party, which he founded in 1956 :

> Traditional Socialists believe that the ultimate overthrow of the existing order cannot be carried out except by force...The use or non-use of violence in the last stages of a revolution, particularly since the traditional alternatives between parliamentary and insurrectionary action have been supplemented by the third choice of civil resistance, is a matter of secondary detail.

> While a revolution may regrettably erupt into violence in its last stages, particularly when a decaying government seeks to dispense with democratic forms, participants in a revolution must definitely resolve to organize on the continuing base of peaceful methods...Organization of violence inevitably leads to concentration of power.[57]

It is interesting to note here that the eruption of violence was not ruled out by him but its responsibility was not owned by the party. The statement warned that 'no greater disaster could befall socialism than if the historical peculiarities of its career in Europe were sought to be universalized and reproduced in the other two-thirds of the world. Socialism in Europe has been gradual, constitutional, and distributive. Socialism hence-forth and in the rest of the world must be drastic, unconstitutional when necessary, and lay the accent on production.'[58] It underlined the need of somesort of a drastic, unconstitutional and direct method for achieving socialist objectives.

It was realised by the Socialist Party that 'the processes of persuasion and law-making are not always available or timely ; to them must be added the methods of class struggle.'[59] But the class struggle implied anything, other than the use the arms and violence, and its effective tool was taken to be *satyagraha* alone. The 1962 Manifesto of the Party declared that *satyagraha* was not something

[57] *Ibid.*, pp. 491–92.
[58] *Ibid.*, p. 477.
[59] *Ibid.*

to be treated as a museum piece and 'something that belonged only to the period of slavery.'[60] The party considered that *satyagraha* was a 'permanent weapon'. It declared, 'As long as man lives and injustices exist, he would fight, whether with arms or with civil disobedience. *Satyagraha* is a wonderful combination of reason and force. It is the only alternative to arms.'[61]

MEHTA'S OPPOSITION TO TOTALITARIAN WAYS

Asoka Mehta, exhibited a lofty sense of idealism by infusing an ethical appeal into socialism. He pointed out, as early as 1950, that two methods of reform and revolution broadly existed for realising socialist objectives, but failed to draw his own preference for either. Rather, he was inclined to agree with Rosa Luxemburg's view that both were complementary with each other in the long term process of historical transformation.[62]

One thing is unmistakable in Mehta's approach today : he deprecates the method of totalitarian and dictatorial ways. He has constantly emphasised the need for democratic, *i.e.* peaceful and parliamentary methods. As he derived more inspiration from what has been called 'European Social Democracy' than Marxism or Leninism, he did not and still does not believe that violence would be inevitable so long as parliamentary processes are worked through people's active cooperation.[63] He pointed out...that totalitarianism is a denial of the socialist vision,...socialism can be realised only through the acceptance of democracy.[64]

With regard to the efficacy of the parliamentary and extra-parliamentary means, Mehta pointed out that it would depend on our choice for the negative or the positive states. By negative state, he meant a class-state, *i.e.* anti-democratic state dominated by class interest ; and by positive state he meant democratic state with free 'associative life'. He maintained that under the two different types of states two different methods would be required. Under the negative state 'extra-parliamentary, even insurrectionary' method might be required. But under the positive state parliamentary method

[60] *Ibid.*, p. 518.
[61] *Ibid.*
[62] Mehta, *Democratic Socialism*, pp. 12–13.
[63] In an interview on 2nd April, 1968 at New Delhi.
[64] Mehta, *op. cit.*, p. 138.

alone could succeed.

APPRECIATION FOR THE TECHNIQUE OF SATYAGRAHA

Mehta greatly appreciated the utility of the *satyagraha* technique in so far as he underlined the need for non-violent struggle :

> The technique of 'Satyagraha meets...all difficulties and yet does not become helpless for it combines the peaceful basis of constitutional agitation with the courage, disciplines self sacrifice, and militant obduracy of war. It gives to every individual spiritual and moral sanctions in his fight for freedom and peace in a world ridden down by material considerations.[65]

Mehta has now come to realise that 'the predominant spirit of socialism has been peaceful, not violent.'[66] He reminded that :

> Socialist revolution is not achieved through coups d'etat, because they merely alternate inside the social status quo. Violent upheavals do not achieve a revolution, a transformation of life, work and culture from one level to another, sophisticated and modern. Such a process needs for its unfolding the involvement of the people. Social revolution has to be democratic not only in its aspirations but in its every day expression. That is unescapable lesson of a hundred years of socialist struggles, and of the thoughts distilled from them. That is why we call our programme Democratic Socialism.[67]

The most dominant trend in his thinking today is that he is out and out an advocate of democratic socialism. This implies broadly, two things for him ; first, the parliamentary process through full cooperation of the people as mentioned earlier, and secondly, planned economy for progress and plenty. After Nehru, he took up the task of planning in India through constitutional and parliamentary methods. When questioned about the efficacy of planning through the slow and tedious method of the parliamentary ways and reminded of its comparatively greater success in the authoritarian countries, he emphatically declared that the Soviet Russia and China have not brought heavens on the earth. What is important is to carry the people with the planning. It matters not whether plan-

---

[65] Asoka Mehta and Achyut Patwardhan, *The Communal Tringle*, Allahabad, Kitabistan, 1942, p. 179.

[66] Asoka Mehta, *The Plan Perspective and Problems*, Bombay, Bhartiya Vidhya Bhawan, 1966, p. 31.

[67] *Ibid.*, p. 32.

ning succeeds or fails; what is important is its democratic processes involving people's cooperation.[68]

One of the main contributions of Mehta in this connection is his theory of 'Political Compulsions of Backward Economy', enunciated and developed since 1953.[69] He pointed out :

> That compulsions of a backward economy tend to push towards totalitarianism or timidity. The dilemma can be resolved by (1) so broad-basing the government that it gets power to move forward, because opposition is driven to fringes, and (2) strengthening the forces of *pluralism in authority and initiative.*' (italics ours).[70]

By 'pluralism in authority' he meant that the institutional framework should be so shaped as to make the village cooperatives, union-shops and trade unions share fully in the powers and functions. He cautioned that in the absence of such an arrangement, democratic socialism or planned development might not be feasible. Thus the transformation of society or the achievement of socialistic objectives was conditioned by the existence of certain pre-requisites, and not dependent on violent or non-violent, means. He believes today in the non-violent, peaceful and democratic methods of planning for realising socialist objectives.

SOCIALIST'S APPROACH TOWARDS CLASS-STRUGGLE

The socialists, whom we have covered thus far, advocated the technique of socialist reconstruction, keeping in mind both the negative problem of doing away with class-struggle or class-antagonism in society as well as the positive goals of creating better living conditions, better society and higher production. All socialists under reference, believed in the existence of class-struggle, in the sense of class antagonism, in society even in the post-Independence period : although, nothing was suggested about the historical phenomenon of the inevitability of class-war. The *Policy Statement,* maintained that 'class conflict is a perpetual phenomenon of class society.'[71] The doing away of this class conflict still remained the goal of

[68] In an interview on 2nd April, 1968, at New Delhi.
[69] Asoka Mehta, 'Political Compulsions of Backward Economy', *Janata,* VIII (19), June 7, 1953, pp. 4–5.
[70] *Ibid.,* p. 4.
[71] The *Policy Statement,* 1955, p. 29.

THE METHODOLOGY OF SOCIALIST TRANSFORMATION OF SOCIETY

the socialists, but the task had to be carried through under the framework of non-violent civil disobedience and parliamentary as well as extra-parliamentary ways.[72]

SAMPURNANAND'S APPROACH

Like most of the socialists, Sampurnanand was greatly inspired by Gandhiji. He disapproved of the approach of the communists that 'any means that leads to a realisation of the end in view with the minimum expenditure of effort is good.'[73] In his own way, he maintained that the means to be adopted for the achievement of an objectives are very important, as every individual has his own eternal ego. It is with that ego that certain characteristics and urges grow in each individual. He pointed out that

> ...certain modes of behaviour are in accord with the nature of the Ego and certain others are not. It may be that the norms of behaviour in harmony with the nature of the Ego may not bring quick results; nevertheless, they have to be pursued.[74]

Thus, according to Sampurnanand, it was not open to us always to adopted any means: the means must be in accordance with the pre-determined norms of behaviour that the 'eternal ego' particularizes. Since it is spiritual phenomenon, it is clear that the means must also be spiritual and ethical. It need not be recalled here that this view of Sampurnanand also was the direct outcome of his philosophical and Vedantist approach.

[72] J. B. Kripalani, who had joined the socialists in 1952, however, had his serious reservation on the P.S.P.'s view with regard to class conflict or class struggle, regarded as the 'perpetual phenomenon' in society. In the context of changed situations since Marx's time, Kripalani considered class struggle to be an outmoded theory. 'In practice as long as democracy has not been repudiated and scrapped and the vote made into a nullity and the trade union and Kisan movements suppressed and a totalitarian regime of some sort established in India, there is no possibility of class war or conflict in the country.' J. B. Kripalani, Class Struggle, 2nd edn., Kashi, 1959, p. 93.
To the extent the concept of class war was only the logical or historical outcome of the principle of class struggle, he repudiated both. The idea of having non-violent class struggle appeared to him as confused thinking. He wrote : 'It does violence to the philosophy of non-violence. It is psychologically impossible to have a non-violent class struggle.' Ibid., p. 68.
[73] Sampurnanand, Indian Socialism, pp. 16–17.
[74] Ibid., p. 17.

Sampurnanand explained that Mahatma Gandhi gave priority to truth over non-violence in the code of individual conduct, and also, taught that violence did not lie in the use of weapons but in the motive which actuated it. 'A surgeon who removes a patient's limbs cannot be accused of violence even though he inflicts grave physical injury.'[75] With such an understanding about Gandhiji and his methods it appeared to him that non-violence did not mean only the absence of arms but also the will or motive not to use it. It is with reference to it that he maintained that Indian socialism must stand for the purity of means quite as much as the purity of ends.

Sampurnanand appears to have maintained that class conflict or class struggle is constantly going on in society particularly with reference to economic interests. He agreed with the *Policy Statement* of the P. S. P. which held class struggle as a 'perpetual phenomenon'. He desired equally to 'liquidate' it. But the difference was in the method ; while the P. S. P. wanted to do away with it by encouraging class struggle, Sampurnanand wanted to do so through 'cooperation' and 'organized effort'. Thus he showed his preference for the Gandhian method of trusteeship, as against the concept of class war and class conflict. With regard to *Satyagraha*, he observed that :

I have said that class cooperation should take the place of class conflict. I believe that the object every socialist has in mind will be served by appealing to man's finer and nobler instincts. But success in these directions may take time...To submit to injustice and oppression is cowardice and an insult to man's true nature. Where every other effort fails, resistance, is justified but it must be non-violent. Satyagraha, even if undertaken through an error of judgement, has a chastening effect on character. It must not be used as a camouflage for violence and coercion.[76]

The *Satyagraha* appeared to him to be a righteous method, if it was used for a just cause ; its adoption was not only justifiable but also ennobling. A relevant question that he raised in this connection was how far democratic method and planning were compatible with each other ? In an answer to it, he pointed out that :

[75] *Ibid.*
[76] *Ibid.*, p. 23.

> Planning implies a regimentation of life to some extent, and the more authoritarian the regime which sponsors and implements it, the more it is likely to be successful on a purely material plane.[77]

He pleaded that no such limitation should be imposed on our desire to accelerate the pace of planning which might 'spell the ruin of democracy.'[78]

He earnestly pleaded that Indian socialism should remain firm over its fundamental principles in which democracy ought to remain central. It appears that planning was a secondary issue with him; his primary ideal was democracy.

NEHRU'S PREFERENCE FOR NON-VIOLENT MEANS

Throughout the colonial period, as indicated already, Jawaharlal Nehru showed his preference for non-violent method but did not, at any stage, adopt a dogmatic position on the issue of method and means. Even with his knowledge about the historical perspective that 'violence has had a long career in the world' and his confession that 'I am full of violent thought', he persuaded himself to believe that 'the salvation of India and, indeed, of the world will come through non-violent non-cooperation.'[79]

So far the achievement of the political objective of independence was concerned, he had no doubt about the superiority of the non-violent means. But, probably for effecting social and economic changes in society he was not equally sure of its effectiveness. In his talks with Tibor Mende he explained thus

> I had many doubts. Of two kinds—one: whether non-violence itself would be adequate. That really applied more to the British than to the social aspect. In regard to the social aspect, the doubts really came because I was not quite sure that our own colleagues were so socially conscious.
>
> It was not about the method. The method was effective enough.[80]

With regard to social objectives, therefore, Nehru was convinced of the need for using radical and coercive method. While he did

[77] *Ibid.*, p. 36.
[78] *Ibid.*
[79] Norman, *Nehru*, I, 109.
[80] Mende, *Conversations With Nehru*, p. 19.

believe, in the post-Independence phase, in the method of legislation, he maintained, however, that mere legislative process may not lead to desired goal ; even surgical operation may be required. This could be possible only if in addition to legislation, direct approach was made to the people, and of course the parliament would be the agency to conduct such operation. Thus while Nehru fully believed in the method of the parliamentary ways, he wanted it to be supplemented through direct appeal to the people in the matters of social change. In this regard he exhibited a preference for a middle position : neither Soviet type of violent revolution nor rigid constitutionalism. Being in office and authority, probably, it was not possible for him to think in terms of *satyagraha* as he had done in the colonial period ; but, the fact that he realised the inadequacy of the legislative, *i.e.* parliamentary method, was in itself of significance. As a convinced democrat, he believed in the direct appeal to the people as the ultimate method of effecting social change in society. In a way, it was just widening the parliamentary method itself.

FIRM BELIEF IN PLANNING

The king-pin of the methodology of socialist transformation of society in the post-Independence phase was democratic planning. From the beginning, Nehru manifested strong disapproval of the dictatorial and authoritarian ways of the communists in the U.S.S.R. While, he enthusiastically upheld their method of planning, he equally strongly denounced their authoritarian regime.

Even though, he had full control over the political machinery of India continuously for seventeen long years, he did not for once waver in his fundamental belief that planning must follow democratic lines. He agreed that authoritarian regime might implement planning in less time and with greater success, yet he wanted India to follow only democratic ways. In a democratic set-up where parliament existed it was not difficult to judge as to what people desire and can tolerate. Whatever was acceptable to the parliament had got to be tolerated by the affected section of the society.

Since Nehru believed that socialism was largely an economic theory and was chiefly concerned with the problem of bestowing economic freedom and benefits upon all sections in society, he

228

believed that planning was essential for achieving socialist objectives.[81] It is regarded as his major contribution to the sphere of economic strategy under democratic socialism in India. Through planning he wanted to steer clear of the dangers of too much 'centralised statism' and the extreme retrogression towards the concept of 'village self-sufficiency.'[82]

An essential feature of Nehru's concept of planning was its complete dependence on democratic and parliamentary processes. He was convinced that planning without democracy was only as meaningless as democracy without socialism. He stressed that mere taking over the wealth of the rich people could not solve the problem : what was required was greater production along with equitable distribution. This could be possible only when socialism 'entered people's mind' ; merely through laws it could not be possible.[83] Socialism and planned development required full cooperation from the people.

Nehru denounced both big scale or small scale violence for achieving socialist objectives. He observed that :

...violence cannot possibly lead today to a solution of any major problem because violence has become much too terrible and destructive. The moral approach to this question has now been powerfully reinforced by the practical aspect....

If the society we aim at cannot be brought about by big-scale violence, will small-scale violence help ? Surely not, partly because that itself may lead to the big-scale violence and partly because it produces an atmosphere of conflict and of disruption...The basic thing, I believe, is that wrong means will not lead to right results and that is no longer merely an ethical doctrine but a practical proposition.[84]

It was a different approach with regard to violence and non-violence, than what he had indicated during the colonial period. His dislike of

[81] J. Nehru, 'The Basic Approach', *AICC Economic Review*, 10 (8/9), Aug. 15, 1958, pp. 3–6. Reproduced in, Sampurnanand, *Indian Socialism*, pp. 77–78.

[82] M. L. Dantwala, 'Economic Ideology of Jawaharlal Nehru', *The Economic Weekly*, XVI (29, 30 & 31), July 1964, p. 1209.

[83] J. Nehru, 'Socialism by Consent', *AICC Economic Review*, IX (4), June 15, 1957, p. 7.

[84] Nehru, 'Basic Approach', reproduced in Sampurnanand, *Indian Socialism*, p. 72.

the communists' methodology, its violent ways, was indicated as early as 1927, but stronger deprecation of violence, whether on big or small scale, was noticeable in the post-Independence period.

In the concluding remarks of his article 'Basic approach', Nehru reminded the approach of peaceful means, and also 'the old Vedantic ideal of the life force which is the inner base of everything that exists.'[85] His leaning towards the Vedantic philosophy was greatly marked in the post-Independence period : although, its vague appreciation was noticeable even in the 'forties.

PREFERENCE FOR PARLIAMENTARY METHODS

With his growing experience in the office, Nehru came to be further strengthened in his belief in parliamentary democracy. For its success, he pointed out, it demanded 'many virtues' such as ability, cooperation, self-discipline and restrain from the people. Parliamentary democracy, which was as much suited for a 'time of change and ferment' as for a 'continuity' with the past, appealed to Nehru greatly.[86] He explained that it 'naturally involves peaceful methods of action, peaceful acceptance of decisions taken and attempts to change through peaceful ways.'[87] His affinity with parliamentary democracy was increasingly manifested in the post-Independence period. He further maintained that parliamentary democracy was not in conflict with socialism, rather it might be in conflict with the private enterprise and the capitalistic ways, as such.[88] He believed that parliamentary methods might achieve socialist objectives, and private enterprise might diminish in such a set-up. He confuted also the idea that planning 'involves a measure of regimentation and compulsion and is opposed to democracy.'[89] He maintained on the other hand, that in a parliamentary democracy the existence of Parliament and adult franchise were by themselves a check upon the 'unrestrained forces of the market.'[90]

[85] *Ibid.*, p. 79.
[86] In a Speech in Lok Sabha, on March, 28, 1957, *Jawaharlal Nehru's Speeches, op. cit.*, III, 156.
[87] *Ibid.*, p. 158.
[88] Jawaharlal Nehru's Speeches, IV, 70.
[89] *Ibid.*, p. 124.
[90] *Ibid.*

THE METHODOLOGY OF SOCIALIST TRANSFORMATION OF SOCIETY

RELATIONSHIP BETWEEN THE END AND MEANS

With regard to the method and means Nehru maintained that there was a vital relationship between the two. He pointed out that there was some lesson to be learnt from India's peaceful revolution. While eulogising the Gandhian technique of non-violent struggle, he observed that 'we were working for results but for the moment we were satisfied with the act of doing.'[91] This indicated the impact of Gandhiji on his approach with regard to the method and means.

GANDHIAN APPROACH OF KRIPALANI

A few words may not be out of the place here with regard to J. B. Kripalani's views, who, having merged his K. M. P. P. with the Socialist Party, infused greater Gandhian bias in the ideology of the P. S. P. It is correct to suggest that the K. M. P. P.'s association with the Socialist Party strengthened further the socialists' belief in the method of non-violence. Kripalani recalled Gandhiji's dual programmes of non-violent civil disobedience and constructive work; the former for wresting independence and the latter for realising social, economic and cultural objectives. The constructive programmes of Gandhiji appeared to him as suggestive of the Gandhian concept of socialism. He greatly emphasised the need to follow both the ideals.[92]

Civil disobedience, whether by workers or by political parties, according to Kripalani, was completely a legitimate means. He confuted the approach of the Congress Party that in a free democratic society *satyagraha* or civil disobedience had no place. *Satyagraha* was not only a political means but also a socio-economic method. Since it was non-violent, it was always democratic. The only consideration he put forward was to give up fast-unto-death method, and to resort to *satyagraha* only after the permission of the party had been obtained, full propaganda made and all methods for compromise fully tried.[93]

With regard to parliamentary method, he suggested that, as the P. S. P. did not stand for destructive violence, it could work

[91] *Jawaharlal Nehru's Speeches*, II, p. 402.

[92] Kripalani, *Class Struggle*, pp. 82–83.

[93] Presidential Address of J. B. Kripalani, *Report of the First National Conference of the Praja Socialist Party*, Allahabad, 1953, pp. 15–16.

under parliamentary system; even Gandhiji had sanctioned it. He pointed out, however, that, if legislative assemblies could be done away with and the party could be made to work by remaining outside the parliament, it would have been, indeed, an interesting idea. But, probably, in the given context work through parliamentary system was rather desirable. So long as the P. S. P. would work through parliament, it should try patiently with it and study the system in its entirety.[94] He observed further :

> 'Violent upheavals may usher social and economic equality, but they are likely to do so at the expense of political liberty. ...We see this happening before our eyes under Communist dictatorship.'[95]

Therefore, for retaining both social and political liberty, avoidance of violence was necessary.

PLANNING : PARTIES' VIEW

Before we conclude a reference need be made about the method of planning as conceived by the Congress and the Socialist Parties. In all their manifestos from 1952 to 1967 the Congress and the P. S. P. emphasised the importance of planning. In 1962 the Congress described 'Public Sector' under planning as the 'important tool for a socialist transformation of our society', while the P. S. P. also described it, almost in similar phraseology, as the 'effective instrument for democratic socialism.'[96] The Socialist Party, led by Lohia, also stood for planning but not the way it was implemented by the Congress. In 1957 its manifesto proclaimed to do away with 'the glamorous modernization of unnecessary large-scale industry.'[97] Its 1962 manifesto announced the need to put greater emphasis on decentralised planning, giving more importance to the needs of 'little man.'[98]

In the manifesto of the Congress in 1957 there was no specific mention of planning, while earlier the Congress believed in the

---

[94] *Ibid.*, pp. 11-12.

[95] *Report of the Special Convention of the Praja Socialist Party*, Betul, 1953, p. 141.

[96] M. Pattabhiram (ed.), *General Election in India 1967*, Bombay, Allied Publishers, 1967, pp. 172 & 193.

[97] Lohia, *Marx, Gandhi and Socialism*, p. 496.

[98] *Ibid.*, p. 516.

THE METHODOLOGY OF SOCIALIST TRANSFORMATION OF SOCIETY

concept of 'total planning'. The P. S. P.'s manifesto stressed the need for planning but the emphasis was on 'the base and not at the apex'. The S. S. P.'s manifesto did not mention about planning specifically, but the decentralisation and economic programmes it envisaged put implicit faith in the planned development.[99] On the issue of industrialization the Congress toned itself down and, like the P. S. P. and the S. S. P., put greater emphasis on food and agriculture.

[99] Pattabhiram, *op. cit.*, p. 150.

7

THE CONCEPT OF DEMOCRATIC SOCIALISM IN INDIA

AFTER THE WORLD War II the terminology of democratic socialism that was in vogue in the British socialism was first adopted by the Socialist Party of India in 1947. From that time onward, the Socialist Party described its ideology as democratic socialism. The Indian National Congress took a long and circuitous route between 1947 and 1964 through the milestones of 'Cooperative Commonwealth', 'Socialistic Pattern of Society', 'Welfare State' and finally 'Democratic Socialism'. In 1964 the Samyukta Socialist Party also professed to have been wedded to the concept of democratic socialism. It thus appears that the experiences between 1947 to 1964 resulted in a common realisation of the goal of democratic socialism in India.

Hence, even though it might involve a few repetitive references, it would be interesting to recall its genesis in the Socialist Parties and in the Congress. This might present also as a clearer picture of what the terminology implied in essence in terms of its principles and characteristics.

THE GOAL OF MARXIAN SOCIALISM

The Congress Socialist Party, during the eight active years of the colonial period between 1934-42, had broadly adopted the Marxian ideology, and openly took its cue from the Soviet Russia and its communist ideology and programme. During the colonial period, we have seen, that 'Marxism was the most important single influence in the political thinking of the younger generation of Congressmen who were...discontented with the Gandhian techniques of struggle.'[1] Meerut and Faizpur theses, referred to earlier, 'laid the ideological foundations of the socialist movement. Marxism was the corner stone of these foundations.'[2] J. P. exhaustively dealt with the Party ideology and programme in his book *Why Socialism*? together with its Bolshevik experimentation, and Marxism was treated as the ideological base of the Party. We have already indicated these trends in the earlier chapters. The purpose in repeating this here is to emphasise that 'Marxism', not 'Democratic Socialism', was the professed ideology of the C. S. P.

However, even during the colonial period, the interpretations put on Marxism in many ways reflected the distinctive stand of the Indian socialists ; and, on some points, they fundamentally differed not only from the Soviet Communists' but also from the Indian Communists'.

We might recall that J. P. did not become a member of the Communist Party in India, because of the knowledge that the C. P. I. took dictates from Moscow, and also because of the anti-national and anti-Congress stand it often took. This might appear to be a non-ideological factor of a personal nature, but the initial repulsion generated thereafter did project itself into the ideological plane. He never failed to interpret Marxism in his own independent way.

Agreeing full well with Marxist analysis of class struggle, J. P. nevertheless took care to emphasise that socialism did not mean that *Taluqdars* or *Rajas* and *Maharajas* should be 'blown up to bits' ; it was 'something more sensible, more scientific, more civilized than all that.'[3] The main concern of socialism, according to him, was the doing away with the 'painful fact of inequalities' by abolishing private ownership of the means of production and establishing over them the ownership of the whole community. By limiting the central issue to the question of equality, he at once compressed Marxism to a clear-cut ideal. Further, whatever be his personal failings on the issue of violent means, he had conceded that the C. S. P. was bound by the Congress's creed of 'legitimate and peaceful' means. Even, as the Organising Secretary, he pinned himself down to the 'peaceful' creed of the Congress.[4]

[1] H. K. Singh, *op. cit.*, p. 13.
[2] Dandavate, *op. cit.*, p. 4.
[3] Narayan, *Socialism, Sarvodaya and Democracy*, p. 5.
[4] In a speech at Madras on 27-7-1934. File No. 36/3/34. Poll, Home Department, Government of India.

Narendra Deva also, through his interpretation of Marxism, tried to convey to the Indian socialists as well as to others that the core of Marxism was its humanism.[5] In his Presidential Address at Patna, we have seen, that he dwelt upon Marxism without any reference to Bolshevism on the Soviet Communist Party. He maintained that Marxism did not mean priority of 'matter' over 'spirit' or 'mind'—a common misconception widely prevalent. Marxism does not pretend for assured perfection. It points out that only after 'the socialist revolution is completed…man leaves the conditions of animal existence behind him and acts as a human being.'[6] On the issue of economic equality, as indicated earlier, he quoted Marx :

The real content of the proletarian demand for equality is the demand for the abolition of classes. Any demand for equality which goes beyond that of necessity passes into absurdity.[7]

It is doubtful if a Russian communist, at that point of time, would have chosen to highlight the points that Narendra Deva did in the Indian context. His interpretations were at once distinctive in the attempt to clarify the existing misconceptions of Marxism and this was indicative of the political pulse of India. He also realised that in India, irrespective of the fact that the working class was the 'vanguard' and the peasantry only 'auxiliaries', the socialist movements however must bring into its fold workers and peasants together.[8] These clarifications made the Indian socialists view Marxism with an open mind, and not rigidly in the light in which it was presented by the Soviet communists.

GENESIS OF DEMOCRATIC SOCIALISM IN THE SOCIALIST PARTY

The independent way of thinking by the Indian socialists, even during the hey-day of Marxist fervour, were suggestive of the fact that those who intended to constitute the C. S. P. were consciously alive to the need for evolving Indian socialism largely on Marxian lines, but only as a mixture diluted with the Indian conditions. It has, therefore, appeared to some of the socialist theoreticians today that 'the task of organising Democratic Socialist forces in India has been in progress for the last 30 years. During this period, the

[5] Deva, *Rastriyata Aur Samajvad*, pp. 447–48.
[6] Deva, *Socialism and National Revolution*, p. 21.
[7] *Ibid.*, p. 22.
[8] *Ibid.*, pp. 23–24.

organisational framework as well as ideological foundations of the party of Democratic Socialism changed but urge to evolve a democratic way of life and build an egalitarian society remained throughout, the guiding spirit of the Socialist movement. The organisational evolution of the party of socialism passing through the phases of Congress Socialist Party, Socialist Party, Praja Socialist Party and Samyukta Socialist Party was accompanied by corresponding evolution of socialist policies and perspective.'[9]

Indeed the Congress socialists, since the very beginning, had shown concern for the democratic principles of equality and freedom; the 'Programme' and the 'Immediate Demands' of the C. S. P. were largely indicative of it.[10] Although they did not indicate much favourable disposition towards the constitutional and parliamentary ways then, they, nevertheless, did not oppose the democratic methods. J. P. mentioned as early as 1934 that political democracy was not adequate ; there must also be 'economic democracy, economic freedom.'[11]

The attempt to read-back the genesis of democratic socialism in the past records and the ideology of the C. S. P. is strong now. As indicated earlier, in J. P.'s thinking the phase of democratic socialism appears to have begun in 1940 when he placed before Gandhiji and the Congress 'An Outline Picture of Swaraj'. Therein J. P. had elaborated a democratic and non-violent social order in which the 'people' were described as the real fountain of power and the constitution supreme. That was suggestive of the fact that socialism had come to be closely associated with democratic principles and democratic methods. The 'freedom to over throw' the established constitution through violence was clearly ruled out. The fact that J. P. had drawn this picture and as early as 1940, indicated that, even during the time Marxism was the chief goal of the Congress socialists, they were more or less one on the point of following non-violent means and democratic ways.

In his article 'My picture of Socialism', J. P. maintained that 'The State in socialist India must be a fully democratic State. There

---

[9] Dandavate, *op. cit.*, p. 3.

[10] *All India Congress Socialist Party*, 1937, pp. 7–9.

[11] In a Speech at Madras, Reproduced in File No. 36/3/34/Poll, Home Department, Government of India, p. 4.

can be no socialism without democracy.'[12] He reminded that Marx himself had visualised both 'dictatorical and democratic processes.' The latter process, Marx thought, could be effectively used in countries like England and Holland. For India also, J. P. maintained, that the proletariat dictatorship was not required ; and even in the 'transitional' phase democratic processes could be useful and adequate. J. P. further added that the 'dictatorship of the proletariat' never meant dictatorship of a single party, as has been the case in Soviet Russia. He visualised democratic socialism with 'more than one political party of the working people.'[13] It also implied 'full freedom for expression of opinion' and the right to form 'voluntary organisations for political purposes.' He also considered that the trade unions should not be the 'limbs of the State and subservient to it, but independent bodies supporting the State, and also exercising a check over the government of the day.'[14] Summing up the total picture of Swaraj, he observed :

> Thus my picture of a socialist India is the picture of an economic and political democracy. In this democracy man will neither be slave to capitalism nor to a party or the State. Man will be free. He will have to serve society which will provide him with employment and the means of livelihood, but within limits he will be free to choose his avocation and station in life. He will be free to express his opinions and there will be opportunities for him to rise to his full moral stature. There will be no great difference between man and man.[15]

The above observation clearly outlined the socialist's vision of democratic socialism. It implied economic freedom as well as political freedom. J. P., being the leading thinker in the C. S. P. and also the General Secretary of the revived Socialist Party in 1947, it need not be emphasised that more than any single individual he reflected the ideology of the Party. After its Kanpur session in 1947 'democratic socialism' was formally declared as its professed ideology.

Many factors influenced the ideological shift from Marxism to democratic socialism. An important factor was the realisation that the conditions in India were different from that of Russia or other communist and socialist countries—a fact on which the zealous

[12] Narayan, *Socialism, Sarvodaya and Democracy*, p. 46.
[13] *Ibid.*, p. 47.
[14] *Ibid.*, p. 48.
[15] *Ibid.*

socialists had not applied their minds fully earlier. The Gandhian influence and the predominately democratic faith of the Congress also had much bearing on the Socialist Party's newly found goal of democratic socialism. They realised that much of their popularity was due to their association with the Congress and Mahatma Gandhi. All these inclined the socialists to embrace the ideal of democratic socialism.

KANPUR SESSION AND IDEOLOGY OF DEMOCRATIC SOCIALISM

In 1947, more at the instance of the Congress than on their own, the Congress socialists decided to organise themselves independently of the Congress and drop the prefix 'Congress' from the name of the party. Its membership was now made upon to non-Congressmen as well. The ideology of democratic socialism was formally adopted but was continued to be explained on the basis of Marxian ideology. It emphasised that the individual, i. e. the worker, was free and the state could not deprive him of his rights and privileges 'except through due process of law.'[16] Hereafter the Socialist Party began its new phase. The old concepts of proletariat dictatorship, inevitability of violent revolution, hostility to constitutional and parliamentary methods, and even, transitional necessity of authoritarian and dictatorial rule were openly and frankly repudiated in the Indian context.[17]

Personally J. P. appears to have been driven towards the ideal of 'democratic socialism' because he had been deeply affected by the totalitarian and authoritarian trends in the Communist Party of Russia. Ever since then he has retained the goal of democratic socialism. The adoption of *Sarvodaya* has not changed his position rather strengthened him in his belief that true democracy cannot be had without reviving the primary institutions like *Grampanchayats* and cooperatives.

IMPLICATIONS OF DEMOCRATIC SOCIALISM

In his Report to the Eighth Session of the Party, J. P. outlined the basis of democratic socialism. He said that 'the roots of the Socialist Party are in the Indian soil. Indian history and background and experiences of the past sixteen years have moulded and shaped

[16] *Policy Statement*, 1947, p. 6.
[17] Narayan, *Socialism, Sarvodaya and Democracy*, pp. 46–48.

it ; as also international socialist thought...It was as a result of this process of ideological evolution that...Democratic Socialism came to be inscribed so indelibly on its banner.... For the new enthusiast, with a smattering of the obvious writings of Marx-Engels-Lenin, the issue of Democratic Socialism is likely to appear to be a fruitless repetition of an issue settled long ago. Mentally he still lives in the age when one contrasted the failures of European social democracy with the brilliant successes of Lenin. But years have rolled by since then, years of poignant and tragic history, of lost dreams and of the very God that failed.'[18]

J. P. maintained that socialism was not merely 'anti-capitalism nor statism.'[19] Nationalization of industry and collectivization of agriculture are in themselves not socialism. Important thing was that man should not be exploited and his freedom should not be overthrown. He advised those who did not accept the ideal of democratic socialism to leave the party and to attempt their revolution in a 'tea cup'.

One of the motivating forces behind this ideology was the realisation that the means must be pure, peaceful, and democratic. That is, the violent methods of the communist party must not be pursued or sympathised.[20] He also took care to emphasise that none of the conditions of China existed in India ; she had a central government, a central army, a Constituent Assembly and opposition parties with adult franchise. These democratic traditions, he maintained, could not permit the developments along the lines of China.[21] Within the term democratic socialism only five kinds of activities such as organisation, propaganda, agitation, struggle and constructive works were permissible.[22]

LOHIA'S EXPOSITION

Rammanohar Lohia also stressed that Indian socialism must develop along its own lines ; it should tilt towards neither capitalism nor communism. What was important, according to Lohia, was to realise that the fundamentals of socialism should be clarified and the

[18] Reproduced in, *ibid.*, p. 66.
[19] *Ibid.*, p. 67.
[20] *Ibid.*, p. 72.
[21] *Ibid.*, p. 73.
[22] *Ibid.*, p. 76.

'facing-both-ways' policy must be abandoned. Democracy and national freedom, together with the need for change, should constitute the goals of Indian socialism. He warned that the tensions and emptiness of modern life seem difficult to overcome, whether under capitalism or communism, as the hunger for rising standards is their mother and is common to both.[23] He also pleaded that Gandhism alone could provide the proper base for socialism in India.

Referring to the economic democracy reflected in communism and political democracy in capitalism, Lohia cautioned that the 'grafting' of the one ideal over the other—which even democratic socialism, in a way, does—was not proper.[24] Probably the type of socialism he conceived for India was not adequately expressed through the term 'democratic socialism', although he fully stood for the integration of 'economic and general aims' and described the ideal of democratic socialism as 'otherwise felicitous concept'.[25] He maintained that the true ideal of socialism could be achieved only through Gandhian method.

Somehow Lohia felt that such adjectives like 'Marxian' or 'democratic' for socialism should not be carried beyond a precise meaning in the context of the changing times. It should not become a dogma by itself. In the sense of 'decentralization' of power, he was personally all for democracy and democratic ideals.[26]

Asoka Mehta has been one of the greatest advocates, and probably one of the most consistent also, of the concept of democratic socialism in India. As the General Secretary of the Socialist Party between 1950 and 1953 he did much to popularise the concept. Mehta observed,

> Socialism as we understand and strive to develop is neither a middle way between capitalism and communism nor efforts at softening certain harsh features of the one or the other, but a distinct alternative all its own...Our socialism which has to be different in many ways, from the 'Social Democracy' of the economically developed countries of the West, has thus a distinctive and to our mind, a decisive, role to play.[27]

[23] Lohia, *Marx, Gandhi and Socialism*, p. 334.
[24] *Ibid.*, p. 321–22.
[25] *Ibid.*, p. 322.
[26] *Ibid.*, p. 479.
[27] *Report of the Special Convention of the Socialist Party*, Pachmarhi, 1952, p. 118.

He maintained, that democracy was the very 'heart of socialism'. Democracy and socialism together, and only together, constituted the ideal of democratic socialism.

Mehta further explained that the economic equality, the pluralist theory of state, the negation of totalitarian philosophy, the acceptance of the moral values of human nature and the vision of 'a society of integrated and fully responsible individuals united in liberty and free harmony' constituted the fibres of democratic socialism.[28] He denied that Scientific or Marxian socialism was the sole concept of socialism. His emphasis was on the need to develop a synthetic ideal in which the utopian and the scientific socialism, the collective and the individual, the authority and the freedom, the material needs and the spiritual values, and the economics of socialism and the politics of democracy, were to be woven as the warp and woof of its total design. It was that vision of democratic socialism which was developed by him in his book 'Democratic Socialism.'

THE DRAFT PROGRAMME OF 1953

In 1953 a 'Draft of the Minimum Programme' was prepared by J. P. which outlined the vision of democratic socialism. The Draft was of course a tentative list of important 'priorities' and, in no way, it contained a systematic picture of democratic socialism. Nevertheless, the programmes outlined therein the removal of obstacles in the way of social change, abolition of guarantees to the princes, abolition of the Second Chamber of the Indian Parliament, etc., and they clearly reflected the anxiety to attain the ideals of social and political democracy. The suggestion for decentralization of political power in the administrative sphere, promotion of the 'spirit of Swadeshi', encouragement to cooperatives and *panchayats* reflected socialists' concern for a plural and devolutional society.[29] The programmes for nationalisation of banks, insurance, coal and mines, development of state trading, redistribution of land, etc., were fully economic in content and were pointers to the economic direction that socialism, under democratic socialism, was likely to take.

P. S. P. AND DEMOCRATIC SOCIALISM

A more comprehensive elaboration of the concept of democratic

[28] Mehta, *Democratic Socialism*, p. 177.
[29] Narayan, *Socialism, Sarvodaya and Democracy*, pp. 85–87.

242

socialism was attempted in the *Policy Statement* of the P. S. P. adopted in 1955. It underlined the contents of democratic socialism in a 12–point elaboration. These were :

1. it is opposed to hierarchical conception of society ;
2. it is opposed to the control of social power, political or economic, by a single person or a privileged class in any form of despotism, dictatorship, feudalism or capitalism ;
3. it is opposed to imperialism and foreign domination in all forms and recognises entire humanity's right of democratic freedom ;
4. it favours democratisation of social relations and behaviour ;
5. it establishes the control of the working people over social, economic and political powers ;
6. it provides for self-government in all social, political and economic affairs ;
7. it evolves order on the basis of liberty, *i. e.* free participation of all concerned ;
8. it provides for democratic decentralisation of authority and responsibility ;
9. it ensures social equality and justice by securing priority to the needs and claims of full physical, mental and moral development of all ;
10. it promotes social happiness, of which individual happiness is a constituent ;
11. it regards the people as a source of authority and recognises their right to rebel in case a single person or a minority group or class attempts to seize or retain control over governmental institutions or social power ;
12. it favours the democratic organization of peace and international relations.[30]

It declared its opposition to individualistic concept of 'society' and believed that 'society' itself was an element of life. What was persistently pinpointed was the opposition to communism and the communists. It declared that the P. S. P. was 'definitely opposed to Communists' subservience to the Soviet Union and detest oscillation between democratic means and conspiratorial terrorism.'[31]

Following upon it the amended Constitution of the P. S. P. in 1955 also described its objective as 'The achievement, by peaceful

[30] *Policy Statement*, 1955, pp. 59–60.
[31] *Ibid.*, p. 61.

revolution, of a democratic socialist society free from social, political and economic exploitation.'[32]

Ever since then the above ideal came to be reiterated in the writings of the individual socialists as well as the Party's. In 1956 the General Secretary's Report to the Banglore National Conference of the party affirmed democratic socialism as the basic ideology of the party. The distinctive ideological stand of the party was claimed to be

Its emphasis on freedom and equality, its ingrained opposition to authoritarianism and bureaucratism, and its consequential insistence on decentralisation and economy, its policy of democratic transformation of society into a Socialist society based upon informed participation of the people in the processes of development, ...its living faith in the constructive capacities of our people.[33]

While enunciating the 'Positive Programme' of the P. S. P. in the light of its democratic ideals, the party resolved

...to establish political democracy on sound foundations, to promote democratic spirit and traditions, to develop democratic ways of life in all spheres and to advance political democracy to Socialist democracy.[34]

The other programmes indicated its big concern for the all-round betterment of the social conditions and the existence of democratic ideals.[35]

Since the adoption of the *Policy Statement* the line of elaboration followed strictly the similar lines and in some respects advances were made upon it. The Chairman of the P. S. P.

[32] *Constitution and Rules*, P. S. P., 1956, p. 3.
As both the *Policy Statement* and the *Constitution* adopted in 1955 remain unamended to this day, they are still the ideals of the P. S. P.

[33] *Report of the Third National Conference of the Praja Socialist Party*, Bangalore, 1956, p. 215.

[34] *Ibid.*, p. 217 ; the eleven-point positive programme included criminal justice through Judicial Magistracy ; limitations on the ordinance-making powers, revision of police code in the light of human dignity and the values of life ; the decentralisation of powers, fostering education in democratic citizenship and habits of cooperation...and social responsibility. It repudiated the evils of communalism, casteism and linguism. It assured full guarantee to the minority and other cultural entities. It pleaded for organising the 'agrarian economy at par with the industrial development.'

[35] *Ibid.*, p. 217.

THE CONCEPT OF DEMOCRATIC SOCIALISM IN INDIA

244

reiterated in 1958,

> We have increasingly realised that while the economic aspects of socialism are very important, by no means do they exhaust its entire content ; that in our preoccupation with the need for the satisfaction of basic requirements of our broad masses we should not neglect the other ideas of socialism, *viz.*, equality and *brotherhood of man*. We have never accepted the objective of enlarging the cake for its own sake unless it resulted in rehabilitating the dignity of the individual, enlargement of his creative powers and the development of his cultural and ethical faculties (emphasis ours).[36]

The 'brotherhood' of man was yet another form of indicating its bond of affinity with democratic ideals and the values of life. The 'dignity of individual' and development of cultural and ethical virtues received fresh emphasis.

DEMOCRATIC IDEALS AND THE MANIFESTOES

The Election Manifesto of the P. S. P. adopted on the eve of the General Election of 1962, sub-titled itself as the 'Shape of Things Under Real Democratic Socialism.' It emphasised 'equality, security and participation' of the people, for these were considered to be the tests of democratic socialism.[37] It declared that 'the urge for freedom expresses itself in the fight for equality.' It also declared that 'Freedom is rooted in security. Freedom gains in meaning and asserted itself only when economic and social security are assured.' Therefore 'Democratic socialism's test lies in the security it offers to the citizens.'[38] The Manifesto further underlined the need to 'invest in man' implying that for social progress proper education and efficient administration was a vital necessity.[39]

The Election Manifesto of the Socialist Party of 1957 declared its chief objective to be equality. It put great emphasis on social equality also. It declared : 'Inequality between little and big men is there in all the world, but in India this difference is killing.'[40] It also declared that Socialist Party was to work for the destruction of

[36] *Report of the Fourth National Conference of the Praja Socialist Party,* Poona, 1958, p. 113.
[37] *Election Manifesto of the P. S. P.,* 1962, p. 5.
[38] *Ibid.*
[39] *Ibid.*, p. 11.
[40] 1962 Manifesto, reproduced in, Lohia, *Marx, Gandhi and Socialism,* p. 515.

caste system. Equality, in all forms and implications, appeared to the Party as the synonym for socialism.

Thus freedom, equality, security and the importance of the individual formed the core of democratic socialism as conceived by the Socialist Parties. In the evolution of the ideal of democratic socialism, the year 1964, probably, marks a high watermark in India. This was the year which experienced a brief period of unity between the P. S. P. and the Socialist Party under the banner of Samyukta Socialist Party. In the estimation of S. M. Joshi the formation of the Samyukta Socialist Party this year, as a result of the merger of the Socialist Party and the Praja Socialist Party, opens a new perspective for the democratic socialist movement in India. It has sparked off a unifying process of various trends of democratic socialism and the merging entity assumes much greater significance than is usual in the context of the prevailing dreadful economic situation in the country.[41]

LOHIA : SOCIALISM ROOTED IN EQUALITY

S. M. Joshi maintained that the new party, the S. S. P., was a party of democratic socialism and 'wedded to democracy and socialism.' Lohia also greatly emphasised the need of equality as the basis for concept of socialism. He observed,

> Moral exhortation or pious hopes of an altruistic revolution in human nature have disfigured the examination of equality as much as the irrational, short-sighted, and narrowly-selfish abuse heaped upon it. Whether equality corresponds to human nature or not is a secondary question when primary issues are raised, such as what constitutes a high aim of life and how it is best attained.[42]

Lohia pointed out that socialism must have strong roots in Equality. Just as a family reflects the spiritual as well as material equality, likewise, on the universal scale, equality requires a surer spiritual foundation rooted in the high aims of life.[43] Equality being one of the chief pillars of democratic socialism, it reflected the central concern of democratic socialism as conceived by the S. S. P.

The ideal of democratic socialism has been understood to imply

[41] S. M. Joshi, 'A Cadre of Active Socialist Workers Imperativ *n*. XIX (30-31), Ind. Day, 1964, p. 18.

[42] *Ibid.*, p. 7.

[43] *Ibid.*

many things and involve delicate processing. Asoka Mehta, for example, made a distinction between democratic socialism in a developed and affluent society from that in a developing society. In the latter, the main task was 'of initiating and furthering the development process' which might involve 'economic, social and cultural' transformation.[44] To attempt it democratically indeed involved considerable political effort. But the doing of it was a 'historic' responsibility.[45]

MUKUT BEHARI LAL'S ENUNCIATION

In the depiction of the ideal of democratic socialism in the P. S. P. the contribution of Mukut Behari Lal, a senior and respected theoretician of the P. S. P., has been significant. Lal has maintained that the P. S. P. has presented to the people 'a democratic socialist alternative to build through peaceful democratic process a new India' free from social, economic, and political exploitation. He has professed full faith in the parliamentary institutions as the most effective organs of our democratic way of life. In one of his pamphlets entitled 'Principles of socialism' he observed that

Socialist revolution, for which democratic socialism stands, is all-comprehensive. It stands for radical transformation of all aspects of life—social, political, economic, intellectual, cultural and moral. It aims at the establishment of a socialist society free from domination and exploitation of man by man and of nation by nation, as well as at the re-orientation of life on the basic norms and values of democracy and socialism.[46]

While Lal held that socialism envisaged intimate relation between the individual and society, there should be a clear distinction between the state and society. He fully realised the importance of state and maintained that 'even in a class society the state has not been absolutely indifferent to the interests and claims of other classes.'[47] This was a significant realisation ; for, implicitly, it did not accept the Marxian proposition that a class-state was solely a means of exploitation of a class by a class. He saw some utility even

[44] Asoka Mehta, 'Economic Development Through Socialism', *Janata*, XIX (30–31), Ind. Day 1964, p. 17.
[45] *Ibid.*
[46] Mukut Behari Lal, *Principles of Socialism*, Varanasi, Tara Printing Works, 1965, p. 1.
[47] *Ibid.*, p. 3.

in a class-state.

Lal made an interesting study of the distinctive ideology of democratic socialism *vis a vis* the ideology of *Sarvodaya*. He indicated that both democratic socialism and *Sarvodaya* accepted the ideals of universal evolution and happiness in a classless society ; both insist on man's obligation to society, both regard material well-being as essential pre-condition of human welfare ; both lay stress on moral values and both stand for a world society.[48]

The respect in which they differ are that democratic socialism (as represented by the P. S. P.) believes in class struggle but *Sarvodaya* does not ; the former is opposed to 'exploitative property' and regards private ownership of the means of large-scale production as untenable, while the latter 'is not opposed to individual ownership of property including means of production of small industries.'[49] *Sarvodaya* holds that even a modern state suffers from partiality and spirit of violence, the P. S. P. also admits this lapse, but holds that 'in a class society the state is buttress of the established economic order' hence the state-machinery must be won over before effecting socialist transformation of society.[50] Democratic socialism is opposed to the concept of trusteeship, while *Sarvodaya* believes in it ; *Sarvodaya* advocates *Sampattidan* but democratic socialists are not impressed by it ; *Sarvodaya* advocates *Bhoodan* but democratic socialists do not think that it could bring out a real change of heart of the rich ; *Sarvodaya* believes in a decentralised industrial order, while democratic socialism believes in the planned socialist economy ; the former believes only in *lokniti,* not *rajniti,* the latter believes in both. The he maintained that 'in short, *Sarvodaya* and democratic socialism agree in many important matters, but differ in many others.'[51]

Developing further the concept of democratic socialism, Lal greatly emphasised that the 'socialists should beware of the horrors of dictatorship and try to build a socialist society on the foundations of democracy and secularism which are to be deemed as two most important pre-requisities of socialist reconstruction.'[52] He struck a

[48] Mukut Behari Lal, *Sarvodaya and Democratic Socialism,* Praja Socialist Publication, n. d., pp. 1–3.

[49] *Ibid.,* pp. 7–8.

[50] *Ibid.,* pp. 9–10.

[51] *Ibid.,* p. 37.

[52] Mukut Behari Lal, '*Social Prerequisites of Socialist Reconstruction,* Varanasi, Acharya Narendra Deva Samajvadi Sansthan, 1967, p. 22.

note of warning that

> Socialism can grow best in an atmosphere of secularism which requires humanity to think inductively and scientifically of socio-ethical problems. In a community torn with religious conflicts and surcharged with communal feelings and loyalties, common culture and way of life can be built only on secularism. It alone can rid India of casteism, communalism and outmoded inhibitions which are causing social tensions.[53]

Thus both secularism and social equality were greatly emphasised as the ingredients of democratic socialism.

At the same time Lal also presented a stringent criticism of the Congress brand of 'democratic socialism' as it was envisaged in its Bhuvaneshwar resolution on 'Democracy and Socialism'. He described the Five-Year Plans to have been inspired by the ideology of 'mixed economy' and not socialism.[54] He maintained that the Plans could not be accepted as documents on socialism because the 'Congress is allergic to the reality of class struggle' and public sector by itself is no socialism.[55] He maintained that the

> Congress brand of socialism is no socialism. It is not intended to substitute a socialist economy for the capitalist economy. It aims at promoting economic development through a type of mixed economy.[56]

Lal foresaw in democratic socialism the room for moral and cultural advancement of the people, because 'Socialism stands for the democratic way of life and consequently for the reorientation of the entire social life on democratic principles of liberty, equality, justice and fellowship.'[57] The socialist culture and morality had to be evolved not on personal plane through '*Tapasya*' but on social plane with universal human ideals of '*Samata*' and '*Lokahit*'.[58]

Thus democratic socialism as conceived by the Socialist Parties or the individual socialists has a distinctiveness all its own. Before we take a stock of its overall contents and characteristics we need

[53] *Ibid.*, p. 8. ; see also Bandyopadhyaya, *op. cit.*, p. 17.

[54] Mukut Behari Lal, 'Five-Year Plans Lack Socialist Orientation', *Janata*, XIX (30-31), Ind. Day, 1964, p. 37.

[55] Mukut Behari Lal, 'Democracy & Socialism—II', *Janata*, XIX (5) Feb. 23, 1964, p. 15.

[56] *Ibid.*

[57] Mukut Behari Lal, 'Democratic Socialism—Moral And Cultural', *Janata*, XXI (2), Jan. 30, 1966, p. 3.

[58] *Ibid.*, p. 4.

refer to here the Congress brand of democratic socialism.

GENESIS OF DEMOCRATIC SOCIALISM IN THE CONGRESS

Ever since the Karachi Resolution of 1931 the objectives of the Congress have been described to be 'socialistic'. An enthusiastic Congressman traced the genesis of democratic socialism to the writings of R. C. Dutta, M. G. Ranade and Dadabhai Naoroji, and even referred to a resolution of as back-dated a period as 1887.[59] We have indicated already the contributions of Jawaharlal Nehru in infusing socialist ideas in the Congress since 1927. Indeed the Congress had been passing resolutions constantly concerning the socio-economic problems of the country, and some of these had socialistic bias.

We need here emphasise only the post-Independence phase of the socialists' goal of democratic socialism in the Congress, especially, as it was reflected in the writings and speeches of Nehru and Sampurnanand who remained throughout in the Congress.

SOCIALISTIC OBJECTIVES IN THE INDIAN CONSTITUTION

One of the greatest tasks undertaken immediately after independence was the framing of the Constitution of India. As the socialists did not choose to be associated with the Constituent Assembly, it was largely the Congress-framed Constitution for the nation. Hence, it has often been suggested, and the Congress also has accepted, that the Constitution itself reflected the ideology of the Congress in this period. K. N. Katju, a senior Congress leader, maintained that the articles 39, and 41 to 48 of the Directive Principles of State Policy laid down in 'clear and emphatic language the basic principles of socialism and how to achieve the target of establishing a socialist pattern of society in India.'[60] He added also that the existence of these principles by themselves made it unnecessary for the Congress to adopt any further note or resolution on socialism.

B. R. Mishra, in a study of the economic objectives of the Constitution explained that

[59] Amarnath Vidyalankar, 'Democratic Socialism : A Constant Quest', *AICC Economic Review*, 15 (14–15), Jan. 9, 1964, p. 93.

[60] K. N. Katzu, 'Democracy And Socialism', *AICC Economic Review*, XV (14 & 15), Jan. 9, 1964, p. 73.

Equal right of work, equal pay for equal work and adequate means of livelihood, both to men and women, are guaranteed under the State Policy. The future State shall endeavour to make provision for full employment, old age pensions, sickness and disablement allowance in order that the haunting shadow of insecurity that darkens many lives may be abolished. It shall also be the duty of the State to give just and humane conditions of work and a living wage to agricultural and industrial workers to ensure a decent standard of living.

Finally, the economic system is to so operate that wealth and means of production are not concentrated in the hands of a few for the common detriment. This implies an equitable distribution of wealth and income among the masses in order that economic power, due to disparity in distribution of wealth, may cease to influence the working of the body politic of the country.[61]

As no socialistic commitments of the past such as the nationalisation of the key industries, collective farming, abolition of the intermediary classes, etc., cropped up in the wordings of the Constitution, Mishra rightly described the ideology as that of a 'Welfare State' and not socialism. Even decentralisation envisaged through the creation of panchayats was not an attempt to devolve and diffuse the powers of the centre but only to create a village-level unit of local self-government.

The concept of 'Welfare State', however, was considered by Nehru to have been directed towards the socialist objectives itself. He had before him the broad objectives of 'human welfare, human development, providing opportunity to every human being to develop to the fullest measure possible.'[62] He also conceded that the socialist approach meant 'economic approach', and, if that was so, the Directives Principles of State were probably not far off from the objectives of socialism. It was considered a mile-stone on the road to socialism.

EMPHASIS ON SOCIO-ECONOMIC DEMOCRACY

In 1946 the Congress had resolved that the *Swaraj* could not be real unless democracy extended from the political to the social and economic spheres, no opportunity was afforded to the privileged

---

[61] B. R. Mishra, *Economic Aspects of the Indian Constitution,* Bombay, Orient Longmans Ltd., May 1952, pp. 10–11.

[62] Karanjia, *op. cit.,* p. 37.

classes to exploit the bulk of the people.[63]

In another resolution in 1947 the Congress addressed itself to the 'establishment of real democracy' through 'planned central direction', 'decentralisation of political and economic growth', and 'popularly elected Panchayats', etc.[64] It was considered 'an alternative to the acquisitive economy of private capitalism and the regimentation of a Totalitarian State.'[65]

A Committee for economic programme comprising some socialist leaders, like Nehru, J. P., J. G. Ranga, Patwardhan, and a few others recommended 'A quick and progressive rise in the standard of living' and, to that end, suggested to make an effort for full employment, increasing production, equitable distribution of national wealth, and decentralised economic structure.[66] The recommendations were eventually accepted and resolved at Bombay in April 1948. An 'Agrarian Reforms Committee' of the Congress also in 1949 recommended a number of land reforms, i. e. abolition of intermediary classes, fixation of maximum holding, pilot scheme for cooperative farming, statutory village panchayats, etc.[67]

In 1950, at Nasik, the resolution on 'Economic Programme' declared that the objective of the Congress was 'the establishment of of a welfare state wherein there is economic democracy....'[68] It also indicated the need of planned economic development in the nation. Ever since then a series of economic programmes and resolutions were passed by the Congress, and the first Five Year Plan was launched with a view to achieving some of its targets. But in none of these the terminology of 'democratic socialism' or socialism was adopted. The Congress appeared to be mainly concerned with the reforms in the industrial, agrarian and other spheres.

SOCIALISTIC PATTERN OF SOCIETY AND WELFARE STATE

In 1955, for the first time, at its Avadi session, the objective of the Congress was declared to be

[63] Resolution on 'Congress Manifesto' moved by J. P. at the Congress Session, Meerut, Nov. 1946, *Congress Bulletin*, No. 1, Jan. 1, 1947, p. 18.

[64] *Indian Nation Congress*, Being Resolutions on Economic Policy and Programmes 1924–54, New Delhi, AICC Publication, 1954, p. 20.

[65] *Ibid.*, p. 21.

[66] *Ibid.*, pp. 21–23.

[67] *Ibid.*, pp. 41–51.

[68] *Ibid.*, p. 67.

...the establishment of a socialistic pattern of society, where the principal means of production are under social ownership or control, production is progressively speeded up and there is equitable distribution of the national wealth.[69]

This was to be pursued in conformity with the amended article of the Congress Constitution[70] and with the Directive Principles of State Policy, referred to above. In yet another resolution entitled 'Economic Policy', it was declared : 'The national aim is a welfare State and a socialist economy'.[71] It was also resolved that 'In view of the declared objective being a socialist pattern of society, the State will necessarily play a vital part in planning and development.'[72]

Much literature has grown since then on the professed ideology of the Congress. Many held it, as a step towards socialism, and many strongly denounced the half-hearted and tricky way of diluting the concept of socialism through the phrase 'Socialistic Pattern of Society'. It is interesting, however, to note that none claimed it as socialism pure and simple.

It was only since 1955 that Nehru began to describe his goal as socialism, in the way he had done during the thirties and forties. In a speech at Avadi, Nehru conceded that the time had 'come for us to advance on the economic and social plane. In a sense we have been doing it, but we have not been doing it adequately.'[73]

He also declared that the Second Five Year Plan 'must keep the national aims of a welfare state and a socialistic economy' before it. On the eve of the 1957 General Election he also referred to the goal of socialistic pattern of society. In 1958, for the first time, he declared that 'India's goal is Socialism' without any adjective qualifying it.[74] Following upon it, for the first time at the Nagpur Congress in January 1959 he described its objective as socialism.[75]

In 1962 Nehru declared that political democracy was incomplete without economic democracy. To that end he observed that

[69] *Congress Bulletin*, No. 1, Jan. 1955, p. 3.

[70] The amended objective was 'the well-being and advancement of the people of India and the establishment, by peaceful and legitimate means, of a socialist cooperative common-wealth.'

[71] *Ibid.*, p. 7.

[72] *Ibid.*

[73] *Jawaharlal Nehru's Speeches*, III, 16.

[74] A. N. Chakrabarti, *An Analytical Review of Democratic Socialism*, Calcutta, Thacker Spink & Co., p. 17.

[75] *Ibid.*

There are bits of socialism in the First Plan more of it in the Second Plan, and still more in the Third Plan. Essentially it is not socialism but scientific planning in order to lay the base for greater progress in future. Scientific planning enables us to increase our productions, and socialism comes in when we plan to distribute production evenly.[76]

It was a clear indication that Plans by themselves contained only the germs of socialism, and the scheme for even distribution of wealth, which is one of the central concerns of socialism, was yet to come.[77]

ADOPTION OF DEMOCRATIC SOCIALISM

At the Jaipur Session of the Congress in 1963, it was realised for the first time that 'any delay ...to incorporate socialism into the Constitution (of the Congress) might lead to disastrous frustration.'[78] Following upon it, at its 68th Session held in January 1964, the Congress adopted a resolution on 'Democracy and Socialism', wherein the goal of the Congress was described to be 'democratic socialism'. It read as

The Congress is working for a revolution in the economic and social relationships in Indian Society. The revolution is to be brought about through radical changes in the attitudes and outlook of the people as well as the institutions through which they have to function. The object is to attain an economy of abundance ..Every one should have equal opportunity and a just share in the fruits of progress. Privilege, disparities and exploitation should be eliminated. This change has to be achieved by peaceful means and with the consent of the people, while preserving and fostering the democratic methods and values as enshrined in the Constitution of India. The Congress ideology may thus be summed up as democratic socialism based on democracy, dignity of the human individual and social justice.[79]

It was a comprehensive resolution, running through nine long

[76] *Jawaharlal Nehru's Speeches,* IV, 151.

[77] Again, much has been written about the planning and Socialism in India, the recent treatise by Gyan Chand on *Socialist Transformation of Indian Economy* is a major contribution in this field. He holds the view that so far programmatic objectives of planning are concerned, there was little more to desire, but its implementation was not only inadequate but an evidence that there has been 'very little understanding of the essentials of socialism' itself.

[78] Chakrabarty, *op. cit.,* p. 26.

[79] *Congress Bulletin,* No. 12, 1 & 2, Dec. 1963, Jan. & Feb. 1964, p. 169.

254

pages, which contained twenty six paragraphs. The paragraph 25 laid down that 'Mere material prosperity alone will not make human life rich and meaningful. Therefore, along with economic development ethical and spiritual values will have to be fostered.'[80] And summing up the whole resolution the concluding lines read as

> This is the vision of society...wherein poverty, disease and ignorance shall be eliminated, wherein property and privilege in any form occupy a strictly limited place, wherein all citizens have equal opportunities and wherein ethical and spiritual values contribute to the enrichment of the individual and the Community life.[81]

L. B. Shastri, the mover of the resolution in the Subjects Committee of the Congress, had burrowed the source once again in the Karachi Resolution and in Mahatma Gandhi's Constructive Programme. The line of elaboration followed by Shastri, clearly demonstrated that the Congress did not think in terms of economic betterment alone, rather it thought in terms of ethical and spiritual values of life. Democratic socialism that the Congress had outlined had, therefore, both material as well as spiritual ends in view.

SAMPURNANAND'S PHILOSOPHICAL APPROACH :
'INDIAN SOCIALISM'

About the same time in 1961 Sampurnanand came to advocate strongly the philosophical base for Indian socialism on Vedantic lines—a theme in which he was interested since the days of his membership of the C. S. P. He had come to believe that there was 'no acceptable alternative to Democracy and Socialism.'[82] He believed in the inherent dignity of the individual and could not subject him to a totalitarian concept of state or regimented method of planning. Yet, at the same time, he believed that 'India will have to adopt the fundamental principles of Socialism and the policies which stem from them, if it is of maintain itself as an independent state in the modern world.'[83]

Thus democracy plus socialism was the important ingredient of his concept of Indian socialism. He was not satisfied with any

---

[80] *Ibid.*, p. 176.
[81] *Ibid.*
[82] Sampurnanand, *Indian Socialism*, pp. 31-36.
[83] *Ibid.*, p. 33.

terminology, and even toyed with the idea of *Sarvodaya* before pinning himself down to the terminology of 'Indian Socialism', which could only be a near expression for the ideal of democratic socialism. Both the twin pillars of democracy and socialism were ingested in his concept of 'Indian Socialism'.

Thus, by 1964, in addition to the Socialist Parties, the Indian National Congress also came to adopt the ideal of 'democratic socialism'. It is for this reason that it has been suggested earlier that the year 1964 was the high watermark in the evolution of the ideology of democratic socialism in India. Asoka Mehta has rightly described the adoption of the ideal of 'democratic socialism' as the 'Pole Star of the ideal of the nation's endeavours.'[84] The polemics behind this terminology apart, it has connoted an ideal which can be expressed as democracy plus socialism or socialism plus democracy, the priority of the first syllable depending largely on the individual's or the Party's traditional faith. The one emphasising democracy had come to emphasise socialism ; and the other emphasising socialism had come to emphasise democracy, till a common ground, at least in profession, appeared to have been laid open before them.

IDEOLOGIES EXPRESSED THROUGH THE LATEST MANIFESTOS

It would be interesting to note here the comparative ideological professions of the Socialist Parties and the Congress as presented in their Election Manifestos of 1967. Both the P. S. P. and the S. S. P. described their ideologies in more or less similar terms. The P. S. P. declared

> Equality and social justice have always remained the most dominant values of socialism and the Praja Socialist Party considers them as the sheet anchor of its policies.[85]

The S. S. P. also declared that 'Socialism means equality and prosperity.'[86] It emphasised the aspect of social equality greatly. Thus equality was depicted as the central concern of both the parties.

The Congress laid down, through its manifesto of 1967, its goal of 'a democratic socialist society'. It primary emphasis was on

---

[84] Asoka Mehta, 'Economic Development Through Socialism', *Janata*, XIX (30–31), Ind. Day, 1964, p. 15.

[85] Manifesto has been reproduced in M. Pattabhiram, *General Election in India 1967*, Bombay, Allied Publishers, p. 192.

[86] *Ibid.*, p. 199.

democracy, implying by it 'not only its central concept of political equality but also its equalitarian implications in social and economic fields.'[87]

Hence, the Congress also conceived socialism largely in terms of equality, both social and economic. But, at the same time, its primary emphasis was on democracy and the democratic way of life. Socialism and democracy became two floating ideals, one overtaking the other, in alternating turns, as they rolled on in the stream of 'Democratic Socialism'.

[87] *Ibid.*, p. 169.

SUMMING UP

WITHOUT, IN ANY way, pronouncing judgement on the controversy with regard to the congeniality or otherwise of the Indian soil for the growth of socialism in India atleast the economic conditions—the *sine qua non* of the growth of socialism—were present in a large measure in India ; and even the social conditions indicated possibilities for the growth of ideologies like socialism. The political conditions were also ripe and the four major periods of radicalization—of 1905, of 1919, of 1927 and of 1942—directly or indirectly contributed positively to the growth of socialist thought and movement in India.

It has not been suggested that the conditions were wholly conducive. There, indeed, were impediments in the way of the growth of socialism. Among these impediments were : the confrontation with Gandhiji and Gandhian ideas—including the ideas which highlighted the roots of indigenous socialism, illiteracy of the general masses, undeveloped form of factory stage civilisation, lack of knowledge about Marxism, orthodoxy and deep religiosity of the people, etc. But on the whole the apparent conditions by themselves could not be said to be totally unsuitable for the growth of socialism.

The general impression that Soviet communism or Bolshevism in Russia inspired Indian socialism much may not be accepted without some reservations. It did inspire no doubt ; what is generally not seen is the fact that many of the deeds of the Bolsheviks put the Indian socialists on their defensive almost as the men in the dock. It was a painful experience about the bad tactics and manoeuvres of the Soviet communists, as early as 1927, that made Nehru declare that he would never become a communist, even if at some stage he came to appreciate communist doctrine, Narendra Deva made a long speech at Patna on the enunciation of Marxism, without any reference to Soviet communism or Bolshevism. J. P.

did not join the C. P. I. for the reason that it took dictates from Moscow, even though he was professedly a communist in America. There were still others who, without any exception, denounced the 'purges' and the dictatorial ways of the Soviet communists. Thus the responsibility that Marxism could draw otherwise for the cause of Socialism in India was, probably, lost in some measure, because of the right or the wrong association of it with Bolshevism.

The deeds of the Indian communists were in no way less unhelpful. Their anti-nationalist stand, pro-Soviet approach, and hostility to the Congress, etc. did not permit Marxism or communism to develop ties of affinity with the people in general, barring a few in spotted industrialised centres in India. The responsibility for breaking the 'United Front' policy was largely thrust on the shoulders of the communists whose party circulars reportedly gave full evidence of the attempts at disrupting the C. S. P.[1] with J. P.'s break with them for good and with some disastrous consequences in the organisational work of the C. S. P., a chapter of socialist unity was finally closed. Much has been said about the loss the C. S. P. and the Congress socialists had to suffer, but there is little knowing how much the cause of communism in India might also have suffered from a larger point of view. The belief was strengthened in some that the communists could not be relied upon and their national loyalty was not always open and above board. But whosoever's might have been the greater loss, the fact remains that the experiment of the 'United Front' policy was a flop from the point of view of the propaganda and growth of socialist thought and movement. Considerably precious time was lost in and through the experiment and mutual recrimination right from the scratch.

There is still another factor that need to be mentioned. The birth of the C. S. P. in 1934, Gandhiji's 'retirement' from the Congress in the same year, the declaration of Marxian socialism as the professed goal of the C. S. P., and such other developments gave rise to the impression that the Gandhian era was over and the period of Marxian socialism had begun. The impression, of course, was not wholly unfounded. But again what appears generally not to have been noticed, even till a very late stage, was that the C. S. P.'s life

---

[1] M. R. Masani, *The Communist Party of India—A Short History*, London, Derek Verschoyle, 1954, pp. 69-70.

was too short and probably not more than just a five year period, between 1934 and 1938. It was only in this period that it was born and reared although not yet buried.

Even during this period it had to act under many limitations. First, Jawaharlal Nehru did not lend his full support to the party ; if anything, he discouraged the move for separation from the Congress. Against the background of that time, a socialist party, without the foremost Indian socialist, as Nehru then certainly was, was indeed, a bad augury. Secondly, even though among the founders of the C. S. P. only two were, in a way, 'Marxists'— Narendra Deva and Jayaprakash Narayan—we have also indicated that even these two were not unqualified Marxists ; yet, the total ideology of the C. S. P. somehow came to be described as 'Marxian Socialism'. From what we have indicated about the Vedantic leanings in Sampurnanand, Gandhian leanings in Rammanohar Lohia, Social Democratic leanings in Asoka Mehta, even during the time when the C. S. P. was formed, we might gather an idea about the ideological heterogeneity and compromises with which the C. S. P. started. Thirdly, the involvement of the socialists in the national movement, strictly from the point of view of the cause of socialism in India, was also, in a way, a considerable diversion although wholly desirable. It may be argued that it brought an unprecedented fanfare of popularity for the socialists during and immediately after the '42 Revolution. But probably such popularity had not much to do with the mass appreciation of socialist ideology. It was their heroic act that endeared them to the people, even as it did Subhas Bose later.

The impression about Gandhiji's retirement from the Congress was to an extent misleading, and the significance of his Constructive Programmes in which he came to engage himself was lost upon the socialists generally. Probably it was an error of judgement to underrate the significance of Gandhiji's Constructive Programmes. Even the Government then did not fail to notice the far-reaching consequences that the constructive work of Gandhiji, including the village industries programmes, might have had on the future course of the socio-political developments in India. The government set up a committee to study the motive behind Gandhiji's retirement and the implications of his Constructive Programmes. Socialists like G. D. H. Cole found *Charkha* and *Khaddar* to have great bearing on the

economic life of India and persons like Kripalani described them as
socialistic in content. Gandhiji's emphasis on decentralised industries,
eradication of untouchability, revival of village-panchayats, etc., were
a few such issues which the socialists had to make their major planks
in India. But, unfortunately, the significance of all these was
realised later, much later, when the bus was missed and Gandhiji
was no more.

If these were the unhelpful positive factors that hampered the
growth of socialism through the Congress socialists and the C. S. P.,
Nehru had not to face less difficulty in ploughing his lone furrow of
socialism in the Congress. Indeed, he had the support of the
Congress socialists but his position was delicate in the sense that he
had to carry the Congress with him as a whole—including its right-
wingers and devout Gandhians—as its President in 1936. His was
a curious job—to hammer on the right-wingers the need to adopt
socialist ideology, and at the same time, to sound a note of warning
to the socialists not to drag the country overmuch on the path of
socialism and, in no case, to drive a wedge between the right and the
left-wingers in the Congress. In the anxiety to sail on two boats, his
first 'flush of love' for socialism, to an extent, paled. The Congress
socialists having found a distinct forum like the C. S. P. gave less
importance to how the Congress fared on the score of socialism.

These were some of the basic factors that befogged the dawn of
socialism in India in the pre-Independence period, in spite of the
somewhat partially congenial times and conditions. But it would
not be correct to maintain that socialism did not appear as the most
prominent sign-post of the time. In fact, the ideology of socialism
became one of the most stirring aspirations of the time, second only
to the goal of Independence. And even those who desired to oppose
it did so not squarely, but in a round about way. Gandhiji straight-
way declared that he was a socialist, even a communist, himself, and
that he was engaged in solving the same problems which the socialists
were doing in their own way. Bhagavan Das discovered the
foundations of the 'Ancient Scientific Socialism'—socialism all the
same—in the *Varnashrama Dharma* and in the very order that had
once been eulogised under *Manusmriti*. He even conceded that
communist experiment was the only system near perfection, although
in an experimental stage yet, on the model of the perfect social-order
evisaged by the ancient mythical seer—Manu.

From what we have gathered in our analysis of the indigenous socialism and its roots in writings of the Congress theoreticians like Dadabhai, Ranade, Dutta and Gokhale as well as the reformers and thinkers like Dayananda Saraswati, Annie Besant, Bhagavan Das, Vivekananda, and Mahatma Gandhi, we can suggest, that they do not repudiate the basic ideals of modern socialism but, in a way, confirm many of those valuable ideals which are enshrined in socialism today. If anything, their teachings and ideologies only enriched its content. Unfortunately, however, the socialist thought and movement in India did not choose to take inspiration from those ideas in the pre-Independence period, as it has done since. There is no knowing as to what might have been the shape of things in terms of socialist thought and movement had the phase of synthesis between Marxism and Gandhism started during the period when Mahatma himself was alive.

The roots we have indicated of indigenous socialism do not in any way suggest that socialism is wholly what those ideals stood for. It is only to suggest that the inspirations to Indian socialism, particularly in the post-Independence period, did not flow from British socialism, Marxian socialism and Soviet communism straightforwardly ; but, it had also the imprint of the teachings of the socio-religious reformers, economists and modern liberal thinkers of India. In a way, the inspiration derived today from pre-Marxian socialists and idealists appear to be greater than that from Marxism. We have already seen that Indian socialism has derived much inspiration from the pre-Marxian ideals, and from the post-Marxian ideals of Mahatma Gandhi and Vinoba.

It may be curious, but it appears a fact today that Indian socialism, on the whole, is nearer to the pre-Marxian visionaries of socialism than to Marx or Lenin ; and yet, in a way, it is as involving in approach as the 'Twentieth Century Socialism' of Britain. Some of the ideological formulations of the Indian socialists in the post-Independence period found expression in the writings of the British socialists of the mid-fifties. Especially, the socialists objectives today are no longer conceived in terms of material needs alone. One of the major contributions of Gandhism, or in a way, of the indigenous ideas as a whole in India, has been to emphasise the need of harmonising the material and spiritual aspirations and not to compartmentalise the two basic aspirations of man. There are

SUMMING UP

many other experiences of Indian societies some of which have found coincidence of approach in British and Asian socialism of the recent years.

The Indian socialists realised more and more the need to emphasise the value of individual, his dignity and liberty, decentralization of political power, greater reliance on man than on institution, and more reliance on cooperation than on competition in life. The indigenous ideas also emphasised the need to attempt at the betterment of man's nature and not to rest contented with the improvement of external environment only. In this connection it showed a sense of distrust in too much mechanisation, industrialization, and craze for wealth. These lessons of indigenous socialism generally came to be incorporated, consciously or unconsciously, into the ideals of Indian socialism. Only on the issue of industrialization and machinery was there an exception in Nehru and a few like him who were all for rapid industrialization.

Our study of the socialistic accounts of the pioneers of socialist thought and movement in India indicates a few interesting characteristics which have had a great bearing on the moorings of Indian socialism today.

First, between 1920 and 1927 the socialist ideas perceivably percolated within the folds of trade unions and labour movements in India. None of its leaders, however, went beyond the advocacy of British ideology of socialism. A few like Wadia, Baptista and Lajpat Rai advocated strongly, from the trade union forums, the need to follow the 'hoary civilisation' and 'mighty spiritualism' of Indian traditions. They stressed the need for unity but did not advocate anything like class struggle and class war. Communism was yet, by and large, away from the labour fold, although the communistic ideas had begun to ferment in the Indian climate since the Kanpur Conspiracy Trial of the communists in 1924.

Secondly, between 1927 and 1929, largely through the utterances of Jawaharlal Nehru, somewhat Marxist or communistic ideas came to be preached through the trade unions and the Indian League Against Imperialism, and, to an extent also, through the Congress. In this period Subhas Chandra Bose gave valuable support to Nehru, although he had his reservations with regard to Marxist and communist doctrines. Like trade unionists of 1920–27, Bose also eulogised Indian culture and traditions of the past and desired some sort of a synthesis between the Western strands of socialism and the Indian culture and traditions. This trend appeared to have continued right down to 1933 when Nehru wrote his article, 'Whither India ?.' Of course in this period, rather since 1922 itself, some communist literature came to be published in India, and the C. P. I. was founded in 1924. But its impact on the whole was still feeble. In the period between 1927 and 1933 the communist ideas began to take isolated roots in some industrialised pockets of India like Kanpur, Bombay and Calcutta. The pioneers of socialist thought, Nehru, Deva, and Sampurnanand did not remain unaffected by the prevailing current of thought. Particularly, it had impact on Nehru and Deva, because it provided an ideological incentive to their urge for strong opposition to capitalism and imperialism.

Thirdly, the pioneers of socialist thought and movement, under reference, were greatly affected by the nationalist events. Nehru, Deva and Sampurnanand, who were of impressionable age in 1905, were emotionally stirred by the events like the Partition of Bengal and the Japanese victory over Russia. The way they all mentioned the events of 1905 was indicative of the strong feeling of nationalism that had goaded them.

Fourthly, the impact of Gandhiji on all the pioneers was great. Many gave up lucrative professions as Nehru, Deva and Sampurnanand did, and J. P. left his college at the call of Gandhiji in 1921. This early bond of affinity with and even admiration for Gandhiji appears to have set for all time the limit beyond which these socialists could not go, even during the 'thirties and 'forties when they did not see eye to eye with Gandhiji on some socialist issues, programmes and methods.

Fifthly, strong evidence of their repulsion against the communistic methods of violence, and ruthless suppression of opposition, is present in the biographical studies of all the pioneers. This feature is marked out in them as a common factor.

Sixthly, by training, temperament, education, and their place of studies, the Indian socialists generally were deprived of any great opportunity to develop strong bond of affinity with Marxian ideas and, far less, with communism of the Soviet type. Till the late 30's, only two socialists of repute had visited Soviet Russia—Nehru for just three to four days in 1927, and M. R. Masani twice, in 1927 and in 1935, for a brief period. Their experiences, outlined in their works *Soviet Russia* and *Soviet Sidelights* respectively were testimony to the glorious achievements of the Revolution, but they did not indicate any ideological appreciation of Soviet communism. Rather the second visit of Masani to Russia was a disillusionment that brought out the theme for his another work *Socialism Reconsidered*, which we have described as almost the first milestone on the track of reversion from Marxism in India. Nehru drifted away and away from communism, and Masani was disillusioned so much that he started championing the cause of private enterprise and organising the only professedly un-socialistic party in India today—the Swatantra Party itself.

During the 20's Nehru confessed having studied little about Marxism. It is not clear as to when and to what extent Deva studied Marx and Marxist literature, but the way he elaborated and explained Marxian Socialism was enough to indicate his keen insight into that theory. Sampurnanand, indeed, studied Marx and Marxist literature after 1922 but the reaction gradually generated in him showed his disbelief, rather than belief, in Marxian or communist theories. J. P. studied Marxist literature in the company of a Jew friend who was a communist himself. He also studied M. N. Roy's writings and other Marxist literature of the time. His seat of study was America—its libraries and communist cells—where he had been a scholar for the most part of the 20's. Lohia got in touch with Marxist literature in Germany, but not systematically. And whatever he learnt probably strengthened him more and more in his belief that Marxism was inadequate and incomplete for the Afro-Asian countries and also incompatible with the capitalistic developments of the colonial countries. Mehta, as we have seen already, did never develop any bond of affinity with Marxism, if anything, rather he became a determined opponent of communist theory and practice, especially as it prevailed in the Soviet Russia. It is for this reason that we are driven to the [conclusion that the pioneers of socialist thought and movement in India, under our special reference, manifested not much academic discipline into the theories of Marxism, barring, to an extent, Deva and J. P. Their alienation from the currents of Soviet communism, for whatever reasons, affected their zeal in advocating unqualified Marxian socialism.

Seventhly, many of the pioneers studied Marxist literature in the extraordinary environment of the prison-life. The resultant radicalisation in some of them was prominently marked out. Their great limitation was that there was not enough choice in the materials for their studies, and that was a big limitation, indeed. Another mode of their study was study during the train-journeys. It is not at all suggested that these could substantially affect the outcome of their studies, but only that the choice of material due to the secrecy of procurement and the censorship of the government must have acted as a big limitation on the scope of their studies during the 'thirties and 'forties. After the Kanpur Conspiracy Case the Government raided many houses, presses, and seats of learning to seize socialist literature. All these must have acted as a factor in affecting the sources upon which the total ideology of socialism on Marxist lines was to be based. At that stage the scope for comparative studies was very limited. The congeniality of the environment also was at least not as serene, composed and spacious as is provided in the modern libraries, or the kind that was available to Karl Marx during his 20 years' stay in the British Museum, with its key available to him even during its closed hours.

Eighthly, most of the socialists appeared to have imbibed great interest in the scriptural writings of India. Nehru, Deva, and Sampurnanand manifested not only a philosophical outlook but also a knowledge about the ancient Indian culture, philosophy and history. Even J. P. as a school boy had a fascination for the *Gita* and Lohia had a considerable study of the *Ramayana* and the *Mahabharata*. Sampurnanand developed belief in the philosophy of Vedanta and Nehru was also considerably inclined towards it, later. Narendra Deva's father had Vedantic leanings, but we are not sure of any such leaning in Deva himself, although his father's influence on him was great. Sampurnanand and Nehru, of course, indicated their preference to Vedantic approach towards the problems of man and society. The philosophy of Vedanta, it appears, had something to do with the conviction in Nehru and Sampurnanand that the individual is an end in himself and his life has a purpose, quite apart from the satisfaction of needs for which a man strives.

These and such indications among the pioneers of Indian socialism are enough to indicate that the formative influences and their education and environment had much to do with the evolution of their thought as well as the moorings of Indian socialism. No ideology is cast in the abstract and far less an ideology like socialism which was born largely as a philosophy and as a pragmatic movement for eradicating the socio-economic maladies, Naturally, the colouring to Indian socialism was provided by the time, environment, and experiences the socialists gained through the passage of time.

With regard to the fundamental issues of socialism such as materialism and spiritualism, the place of the individual, the concept of state and the methodology of achieving socialistic objectives, we have indicated two broad periods, of which the one between 1930 and 1947 is easily demarcated out from the other between 1947 and after. The currents of socialist thought which flowed in the Socialist Parties and in the Congress—the Parties to which all the pioneers of Indian socialism under our reference belonged—came to be harmonised together in the ideology of democratic socialism. In Hegelian terminology, it might be suggested, that the thesis of Marxism and the anti-thesis of Gandhism culminated in the synthesis of democratic socialism.

In the pre-Independence period the word materialism was largely used to mean economic content in socialism, and in this context, the Indian socialists also emphasised the economic aspect of socialism more and more. But during the post-Independence period there was a change, and if not a change, at least a marked shift in emphasis. This change or shift was largely due to the impact of the indigenous ideas including Gandhism and Sarvodaya on Indian socialism. Not that the economic aspect of socialist ideology was given less emphasis, but that now it was increasingly realised that unless there was a 'social' and 'spiritual' regeneration, even the socio-economic problems of life could not be solved satisfactorily—to the extent they could ever be solved. Now it was commonly realised that man has to be satisfied not only in material terms but also in terms of his ethical, cultural and spiritual needs. Socialism could avoid this factor only at its peril. Therefore, Indian socialism emphasised the need to give a blended emphasis on material and spiritual objectives of life and no more to make economic issues alone as the burden of their song.

Philosophically the socialists now came generally to believe that man was not just a biologically evolved heap of matter, or an accidental product of environment. It is not clear if the Indian socialists, had, even during the pre-Independence period, ever entertained such a view, with the exception that J. P. once called himself an 'environmentalist' and some others acquiesced in through their silence. But in the post-Independence period Nehru, Sampurnanand, J. P., Lohia and Mehta, all touched this issue and considered man, of course in a non-religious sense, in some measure or other, a spiritual and divine being. Even Deva regarded man as an ethical creature whose freedom required the expansion of his latent inner faculties. His earlier conviction in totally denying the theory of incarnation and the cycle of life and death, probably, came to be slightly shaken towards the closing years of his life, although at no stage he affirmed any faith in it. There was a general denunciation, however, of orthodox religious speculations about man and nature.

No socialist believed in the traditional and orthodox concepts of religion, and in this regard Nehru and Lohia were most vocal. But Sampurnanand was inclined to think that even religion had a purpose in life, not in the orthodox way of course, but in the intelligent way that after all everything that pulsates has a purpose in life. Hence life is not just birth, growth, and death, but also an opportunity for nobler experiences so as to prepare for the 'Moksha'. Even Nehru was inclined to accept the spiritual entity of the individual, without any reference to religion or 'Moksha' however ; and similarly, now J. P. came to believe that there is an element of 'Godliness' inside every human being. This transformation in the philosophical approach of Indian socialists was of fundamental bearing on all issues and programmes they contemplated in the post-Independence period.

The socialist approach in India towards the individual was, with a few exceptions, generally to emphasise the entity of the individual himself was considered an end in himself. In this regard, probably, there was only little change from what the position had been in the pre-Independence period.

While conceding that the prominent 'motif' of Indian culture has been the good of the individual, J. P. maintained that it implied the good of the society as a whole. In this connection he did not think that the individual was an end in himself. Deva also did not treat the individual as an end, and emphasised the importance of society and the social good.

In the post-Independence period, however, J. P. and Deva both realised the importance of the individual. J. P. had no reservation now in accepting the individual as the end in himself. Deva continued to believe in the importance of society, but, at the same time, realised the inner potentialities of man, so as to treat his freedom as only his own self-expansion. Thus, on the whole, the socialists in India now regarded the individual as an end in himself.

But that does not mean that the socialists in any way stood for an individualistic way of life and individualistic pattern of socio-economic order. If anything, the socialists were hostile to it, and advocated a cooperative and collective regulation through state and other auxiliary institutions. They were also opposed to *laissez-faire* concept of economic order and society. They also did not approve of the individual's freedom as it existed in a capitalist society.

The socialists' belief that the individual was an end in himself was probably realised in the post-Independence period because of greater philosophical rethinking on the spiritual make up of the human being. They saw now more clearly that the individual was not a heap of matter but was also, in some measure, a part of the 'divine essence'. This naturally entitled him, in the visions of the Indian socialists, to a dignity, status and purpose, all his own.

They realised that the individual was both his own end and means ; particularly, Lohia underlined the need for emphasising equally the individual and the environment. The socialists, on the whole, emphasised the need to evolve a discreet synthesis of the two and repudiated any undue inclination towards either.

In this respect, it appears, whether consciously or otherwise, the socialists in a way imbibed the same spirit as flowed from the indigenous ideas. They found this ideal of synthesis between the individual and society as one of the characteristics of Indian traditions, philosophy and the ancient social-order.

As the individual was the end of the socialists, the state, most certainly, was a means to an end and no more. This position appears to have been brought home to the Indian socialists more and more in the post-Independence period.

In the pre-Independence period, the socialists like J. P. emphasised the importance of state, without the 'power' of which a social order could never be transformed in the socialist mould. In this respect the socialists followed the same line of argument that Lenin had advanced for the necessity of the continuance of state throughout the transitional phase. But even during the pre-Independence period, the socialists generally kept silent about the prognosis of the state and showed no inclination to involve themselves in the debate on the issue of the possibility of its 'withering away'.

In the post-Independence phase of evaluation the socialists generally adopted two lines of approach. The one was to emphasise the continual necessity of broadening the functions of state and the other, to hammer out the diffusion of power and the need to maintain the democratic, decentralized and pluralistic nature of state. A third line of thinking, very mildly palpable, was in the present-day thinking of J. P.—in a way reminiscent of the lurking trend of statelessness in the Gandhian thought—which indicated some sort of 'state-without-ness' and not the anarchic concept of 'statelessness'—in the sense of depending more on man than on institutions, more on 'local centres' than on the monolithic political structure of state.

It may be suggested that the experience of the coercive nature of capitalist and imperialist state was also a great factor in impressing upon the socialists that state was not a wholly desirable phenomenon in all forms. It is good when socialistic and democratic, but bad when capitalistic and dominated by class-interest.

The reaction against the totalitarian ways of the Soviet state was also a great factor in inducing the Indian socialists towards advocating strongly for a democratic concept of state. The impact of Gandhian ideas and the indigenous ideas was particularly great on the need of decentralisation and pluralism in state. Some socialists like J. P. and Lohia made persistent references to Gandhian ideas, and J. P. especially drew inspiration from the ideas of Bhagavan Das and others. Once again on this issue the trend coincided with the indigenous current that flowed parallel to the Marxian ideas in India. In the post-Independence period, it was not an unconscious development, for the socialists often referred to India's past and the Gandhian and indigenous ideas and derived their inspiration from them.

On the plea for pluralistic order of state, the impact of reaction against the totalitarian ways of Soviet state was greatly noticeable. There were other factors also at work, such as, the Gandhian emphasis on the diffusion of power, the realisation that persistent wars had something to do with the unlimited notion of national sovereignty, and also, the appreciation that the manifold needs of

SUMMING UP

life cannot be served by a single dictational state. These realisation made Indian socialists conceive a pluralistic state.

The experience of the religious havoc that brought about the Partition of India and communal disturbances—the demon of which appeared or appears again and again—impressed upon the socialists the need of a secular state as well.

The greatest distinctiveness of Indian socialism was in the realm of method or technique it evolved for attaining socialist objectives. It deprecated the method of violence, which it had not done as categorically in the pre-Independence period as it has done now. And at the same time it deprecated the method of rigid constitutionalism and sluggish ways of parliamentary system. It now suggested, on Gandhian model, the technique of *satyagraha*, *i. e.*, civil resistance. This could be used negatively to ward off any evil, as well as positively to attain conditions of equitable living. Within bounds of the technique of *satyagraha* all traditional methods, such as parliamentary ways, the method of planning and the evolutionary methods were eulogised and given full trial in the post-Independence period.

There were three noticeable trends among the socialists due to the differences in the sources of their experience. Because of his big office and authority, Nehru emphasised more on the use of parliamentary methods; being in a desparate minority in the Indian Parliament, Lohia emphasised drastic and extra-constitutional ways, including 'bundhs' and 'gheraos', for achieving socialist objectives ; being disappointed with the party-politics and trends of totalitarianism in both the Soviet and capitalists states, J. P. pleaded for direct-democratic method through 'panchayati raj' and 'communitarian ways' of life. But on no single trend, indicated above, there was any unanimity of approach among the socialists, and these presented a discordant note the finale of which was never reached, nor is in sight today.

Except these, however, there, appeared some unmistakable trends on which there was almost a near unanimity. First, violent revolution was repudiated by all socialists now ; secondly, democratic method was advocated by all ; thirdly, the method of planning— barring the Congress's way or technique, was advocated by all with the only exception of Sampurnanand who expressed doubt if planning could ever succeed to any appreciable extent without authoritarian rule ; fourthly, there was unanimity on giving preference to democratic methods whatever be the degree of success of planning under it.

In the post-Independence period, the issue of class-war was relegated to the past although not buried, but the existence of class conflict was accepted by almost all socialists. The elimination of class-conflict, through *satyagraha* and legislative means, and the method of appeal to the people, was generally advocated by all. Only Nehru now appeared to have some reservation on the method of *satyagraha* and its compatibility with parliamentary democracy. On the issue of class war also his emphasis now shifted more on the need of harmony and peace then harping on the old tune of class war ; although, he still believed in the antagonistic class interests.

There was now a complete unanimity on the point that method or means was not a secondary matter but as important as the end itself, if not more. Mehta's insistence that planning might fail but authoritarianism must not be resorted to, may bear our point here. There was a recognition now that there must be ethics even in politics, and on this the Gandhian impact was writ large. To some, like Lohia, the means and ends were considered to be 'convertible' terms.

By 1964 all socialists had come to realise that neither on socialism nor on democracy there should be any exclusive emphasis. The ideal now professed was of democratic socialism, which meant nothing more to the Indian socialists than an emphasis on democracy with socialism or socialism with democracy. And in this meaning, there have been attempts to trace the genesis of democratic socialism in India almost since the early 30's, if not earlier, by both the Congress and the Socialist Parties. It has appeared, therefore, that the ideal of democratic socialism was the *summum bonum* of the nation's efforts towards its pursuit of the ideals of socialism.

Democratic socialism was conceived not in terms of a theoretical dogma, but in the form of a pragmatic ideal with a comprehensive programme, both by the Socialist Parties and the Congress. The pioneers of Indian socialism individually also presented a number of drafts and outlines with a view to realising the ideals of democratic socialism.

Ideologically, what democratic socialism implied was the goal of equality, in all its possible implications. It involved the elimination of classes, freedom of the individual and decentralisation and pluralism in power. It also meant negation of dictatorship, authoritarianism and bureaucratism.

One may wonder as to that makes India trailing behind in the socialistic transformation of its social order even in comparison with many younger nations on the march towards socialistic goals. The answer lies in the disunity of the socialist forces, in the half-hearted application, in the gap between theory and practice, and in the round about way of approaching socialism on the part of the overwhelmingly dominant Congress Party, the other parties having had little opportunity of showing their mettle. If Indian socialism leaves little to desire in terms of nobler objectives of life, on the pragmatic side it has brought some people to the brink of losing faith in socialism and dismissing it as easily as 'the pot of gold at the foot of the rainbow.' May be there is time yet to mend, if earnest attempts are made to translate some of its formulations into concrete ideals.

SPELL OF PROMISES

Post-1969 period in Indian political life has witnessed rapid changes. This period has been marked with a greater sense of realisation, within the Congress, that until the past socialistic pledges were implemented the future of the Party is doomed. However, the lingering hope that 'may be there is time yet to mend if earnest attempts are made to translate some of its formulations into concrete ideals' found queer coincidence of approach in the efforts of Indira Gandhi to bring the Congress back to the expectations of the people.[1] She realised that the Congress had lost over 100 seats within a period of just ten years between 1957 and 1967 at the Centre, let alone its loss of absolute majority in almost half the State legislatures of India. Her ten-point economic policy, 'jotted down as stray thoughts' started a turning point in the history of the Congress as also of the nation. The points raised were not new ; it was almost a restatement of the ten-point programme adopted by the AICC in New Delhi in June 1966.[2] It was only a reminder to the Congress that

[1] By Congress after its split in 1969, we have implied only the Congress led by Indira Gandhi not because the congress O departed from its past ideology, but because it was, like other opposition parties, not in effective position to implement it.

[2] June 1966, Ten-point programme included :
- (i) Social Control of banking institutions.
- (ii) Nationalisation of general insurance.
- (iii) Commodity-wise state trading in imports and exports.
- (iv) State trading in food grains.
- (v) Expansion of cooperatives.
- (vi) Regulating growth of monopolies.
- (vii) Provision of minimum needs to the community.
- (viii) Problem of unearned increments in urban land values.
- (ix) Rural work programmes, land reforms.
- (x) Termination of privileges of ex-rulers.

the time has come to restate our economic policy and set the direction in which we have to move to achieve our social goals. This has become all the more necessary in view of doubts that have been raised with regard to our intentions and our willingness to take the hard and difficult steps which are necessary.

Mrs Gandhi's note on economic policy gives an idea as to the extent the Congress was prepared to go along its socialistic commitments. Apart from the ten-point programmes suggested by her,[3] she also pleaded to include the programmes of imposing ceilings on incomes and holdings of urban properties, nationalization of private and commercial banks, nationalization of the import of raw materials, and finding reliable way of employment opportunities in both rural and urban areas. More than anything else, it underlined a concealed determination for implementing the programmes, which alone made it an unprecedented event in the history of the Congress, as also of the nation. Indeed, doubts were expressed then, and are expressed even now, if her pledges of implementation were genuine.

[3] Mrs. Gandhi's ten-point programme :
  (i) Impose ceiling on unproductive expenditure and conspicuous consumption of corporate bodies ;
  (ii) Nationalised financial institutions should introduce a change in credit worthiness criteria in their lending policies so as to encourage professional and competent persons ;
  (iii) Special efforts should be made to finance new entrepreneures in less developed regions and a special fund should be provided for provision of assistance to backward regions ;
  (iv) Expeditious appointment of Monopolies Commission manned by person of integrity ;
  (v) Public-sector projects should be given more autonomy and manned by young competent persons committed to the project ;
  (vi) Special effort should be made to build up a cadre of public sector projects ;
  (vii) The consumer industries should be reserved wherever possible for development in the cooperative and small-scale sector and entry of big business should be banned in the manufacture of these products ;
  (viii) Special efforts should be made to encourage new talent to provide avenues of employment to the young and educated ;
  (ix) Foreign capital should not be allowed to enter fields in which local technical know how is available ;
  (x) Heavy penalties should be imposed on those who indulge in restrictive trade practices.

but the fact remains that she was able to carry the country with her under the spell of her promises.

Even the vehement critics of Indira Gandhi today cannot deny that some advance has been made in terms of the implementation of the commitments of the Congress, such as land reforms and land ceiling laws, abolition of the privy purses, nationalization of the banks, wholesale trade in food grains, restoration to the Parliament of its right to unfettered amendment, including the fundamental rights, and allocation of considerable fund for the development of weaker and under-previleged sections of society. The series of amendments 24th, 25th, 26th as also the fact that out of 31 amendments in the Constitution no less than ten were initiated by her within a period of 6 years, reflect the speed with which she is determined to move. It is probably this anxiety that prompted her to break one of the most sanctified conventions concerning the appointment of the Chief Justice of India, by the convenient principle of seniority. It is a signal that the day is not far off that the radical changes to which the Congress and other socialist parties in India are committed might have to reject the present Constitution in toto, and work out a fresh constitution, making it a more effective instrument of socialistic transformation of society, or, at least, to make the amending procedure itself as simple as in Great Britain.

In recent years a greater sense of expectancy has overtaken the youth, the down-trodden and the nation as a whole. Ideologically the period, under reference, reflects a greater and meaningful sense of emphasis on socialism today and lesser emphasis on democracy than what was generally traceable under our conclusions earlier. The conventional methods of democracy have undergone a very subtle change. Democracy is defined more in terms of socialistic contents, than it had been done hitherto. Reminding the Congressmen of their new tasks, Indira Gandhi observed :

> The aim of the Congress still is to bring about far-reaching social and economic changes amounting to a social revolution... It is wedded to democratic socialism that is why it has always to keep its goal of socialism in view and maintain the democratic process within itself.[4]

Further, in a democratic set up the Press is generally accepted as the watchdog of people's liberty and freedom of expression. It is also

---

[4] Trevor Drieberg, *Indira Gandhi*, p. 217.

the medium of the expression of public opinion. But Mrs. Gandhi has recently pointed out a more delimited role for the Press in the present Indian context. She has maintained that it was not the business of the newspapers to advise the government, its function was confined to carrying the news, about what the government does, to the people. That was an indirect way of warning the big financial magnates not to use the newspaper media for their class interest. This trend, it may be pointed out, was somewhat unthinkable during the Nehru-era of Indian politics. Thus, the two most potent instruments of parliamentary democracy in India—the Judiciary and the Press have been, to an extent, weakened in the recent years.

Another important change, with regard to the degree of emphasis conceivable today, is noticeable in greater emphasis on society and social objectives than on individual and his customary rights. It is to the 'social objectives' that the Congress feels more firmly committed today ; and, suddenly, the directive principles of state's governance, originally without legalistic teeth, have come to develop more biting potentialities. The framers of the Constitution had given the fundamental rights an unprecedented character, known anywhere under parliamentary system, by declaring its inviolability and arming the Judiciary with the powers of issuing writs and decreeing laws passed against it as null and void. The whole strain of the Congress, and its socialist allies, today have just been in the reverse direction. In letters, still a rigid Constitution is subjected to such sweeping amendments that even the most flexible constitutions can hardly be made to keep pace with it. The parliamentary supremacy today, with the socialistic commitments of its majority party—the Congress, is made to assert over many conventional traditions of Indian political life.

The burden of arguments in the recent cases concerning the amendability of the fundamental rights, the majority decision of the Supreme Court, striking down its own judgement in the Golaknath case, and up-holding the parliamentary competence in effecting amendments, and above all the declaration of the Prime Minister that radical changes, leading almost to social revolution, must be effected if the nation is to advance towards socialism—all these developments go to establish the dominance of social objectives over individual's rights Not that the individual's right are denied now, or social objectives were undermined earlier, but that the greater emphasis on social objectives has positively pushed the individual to the corner, who had thus far almost always been the central concern of the socialists in India. Indian socialism had been perpherical to the individual, for the first time, the wind of change is blowing him off.

OTHER PARTIES

The reference above to the deeds of the Congress alone, is not in any way to suggest that it alone represented the socialist ideology in India, although, barring a short phase of coalition governments in a few states, it alone was in a position to implement its socialist ideology. The phase of coalition government, with its typical handicaps, queer mixtures of leftist and rightist parties, and, above all, the politics of defection, make the whole story of other socialist parties, such as, the S. S. P. and the P. S. P., almost inconsequential. The S. S. P. during the Nehru era of Indian politics was suffering from anti-Nehru phobia, just as, during the recent phase, it has been suffering from anti-Indira phobia. Anti-Congressism continued to hover over the Party, and its Sonepur convention witnessed one of its stormiest sessions, ignoring even the warning of S. M. Joshi, that :

> The Congress split and the break-up of its corrupt monopoly rule offers a unique opportunity to committed socialists like us, and if we waste it over petty internecine quarrels, history will not forgive us.[5]

The story of P. S. P. is even more bleak. It exists on sufferance.

The role of the C. P. I., probably under the impact of international events and due to the closer relation between India and Soviet Russia, had been more positive. The valuable support it gave to the Congress, after the split, in the Lok Sabha, probably lent to the Congress, a much needed assurance, to adopt radical lines. Even the C. P. I. (M) stood by the Congress. The ideological as well as tactical rapproachement between the Congress and the CPI is thus a new phenomenon of the recent years; this has helped in radicalising the socialistic climate in the country generally.

It is still too early to predict the future of socialism in India. For the present, the once casually formulated ideology and half-heartedly adopted resolutions have come to acquire a more serious

[5] 'S. S. P. : Checkmate at Sonepur', *Mainstream*, VIII (20), Jan. 17, 1970, p. 6.

concern for all, both the protagonists and opponents of socialism in India. The proposed objectives of the Fifth Five Year Plan and the progressive taxation policies proclaimed and proposed, are matters today of greater concern for the capitalists, businessmen, landlords and high salaried men, than these were in the past. The haves and the upper strata of the Indian society have come to feel its strains and stresses. That is probably a pointer towards the goal.

Yet, what is, probably, being overlooked is a less prepared nation, and even more so, a less scrupulous public character, than what might be necessary for undertaking the massive task of socialistic transformation of Indian society, especially in the context of what it had traditionally been, all these ages. The history is yet to prove if speedy transformation of a society to socialism can be effected through democratic planning, a venture that Indian socialists have undertaken. The hurdles are great ; let the socialists prove that their determination is greater.

THE MEERUT THESIS

The Congress Socialist Party grew out of the experiences of the last two national struggles. It was formed at the end of the last civil disobedience movement by such Congressmen as came to believe that a new orientation of the national movement had become necessary—a redefinition of its objectives and revision of its methods. The initiative in this direction could be taken only by those who had a theoretical grasp of the forces of our present society. These naturally were those Congressmen who had come under the influence of and accepted Marxian Socialism. It was natural therefore, that the organization that sprang up to meet the needs of the situation took the description 'Socialist'. The word 'Congress' prefixed to 'Socialist' only signified the organic relationship—past, present and future—of the organization with the national movement.

The socialist forces that were already in existence in the country were completely out of touch with the Congress and had no influence on the national movement. Therefore, there did not take place, as otherwise there would have, a fusion of the emergency Congress Socialist Party with the groups previously existing. Given the adoption of correct and sensible tactics by all the parties concerned, there is every likelihood of such a fusion taking place at a later stage.

PARTY'S TASK

The immediate task before us is to develop the national movement into a real anti-imperialist movement—a movement aiming at freedom from the foreign power and the native system of exploitation. For this it is necessary to wean the anti-imperialist elements in the Congress away from its present bourgeois leadership and to bring them under the leadership of revolutionary socialism. This task can be accomplished only if there is within the Congress an organized body of Marxian Socialists. In other words, our Party alone can, in the present conditions, perform this task. The strengthening and classification of anti-imperialist forces in the Congress depends largely on the strength and activity of our Party. For fulfilling the Party's task it will also be necessary to co-ordinate all the other anti-imperialist forces in the country.

WORK WITHIN THE CONGRESS

Consistent with its task, the Party should take only an anti-imperialists stand on Congress platforms. We should not in this connection make the mistake of placing a full socialist programme before the Congress. An anti-imperialist programme should be evolved for this purpose suiting the needs of workers, peasants and the lower middle classes.

It being the task of the Party to bring the anti-imperialist elements under its ideological influence, it is necessary for us to be as tactful as possible. We should on no account alienate these elements by intolerance and impatience. The Congress constructive programme should not be obstructed or interfered with. It should however be scientifically criticized and exposed.

In Congress elections, we should not show keenness to 'capture' committees and offices nor should we form alliance with politically undesirable groups for the purpose.

PARTY'S PROGRAMME

This does not mean that the Party should not carry on socialist propaganda from its own platform. It must continue to do so and do it more systematically and rigorously.

It follows that the Party's own programme must be a Marxist one, otherwise Party will fail to fulfil its task and leadership. Marxism alone can guide the anti-imperialist forces to their ultimate destiny. Party members must therefore fully understand the technique of revolution, the theory and practice of the class struggle, the nature of the state and the processes leading to the socialist society.*

.* Stetement on nature, task and programme of the C.S.P. adopted at its Meerut Session on 20 Jan. 1936.

THE FAIZPUR THESIS

The present thesis is an extension of the Meerut Thesis adopted by the conference of the Party at its last session. While it reiterates the earlier thesis it seeks to incorporate the experiences of the last year and to take into account the development of the anti-imperialist movement that has taken place in the intervening period.

THE UNITED FRONT AGAINST IMPERIALISM

The chief task facing us and all other anti-imperialists is the creation of a powerful national Front against Imperialism. This is not a task that has to be begun anew. The struggle against imperialism is on and has been on for many years past. It has now to be widened, integrated and raised to a higher stage of intensity.

While the working class and the peasantry has led in the past and is leading today important militant struggles against Imperialism, the main organized expression of the anti-imperialist movement has been the Indian National Congress. But as is evident it has not yet become an adequately consistent and effective anti-imperialist force. It does not yet embrace the broadest possible sector of the masses whether organized or unorganized, and still stands aloof from their day to day struggle for the satisfaction of their pressing immediate needs.

It is the task of all anti-imperialists in the country to bring together and unite all anti-imperialist sectors and to build up a mighty front against Imperialism, made up of the broadest possible sector of the masses. It is clear that in our attempt to do so, it is the Congress that we must take as the basis and starting point, and we must attempt to make it an all-embracing united front against Imperialism. The Congress has already succeeded to a large extent in uniting wide forces of the Indian people for the national struggle and remains today the principal existing mass organization of diverse elements seeking national liberation. It is for us now to find means to assist and extend that unity to a still wider front. This task though being a single whole, can be divided, for the purpose of elucidation into three main parts : our work within the Congress, our work among the masses outside the Congress ; the task of integrating the anti-imperialist struggle outside and inside the Congress and consolidating the leadership of the anti-imperialist and left forces.

This Thesis is mainly concerned with the elaboration of the triple task.

OUR WORK WITHIN THE CONGRESS

The Congress is organized at present on the basis of individual membership. Its members come mainly from the peasantry and middle class. Most of these members do not take any active part in the anti-imperialist movement and simply meet once a year to elect their delegates and representatives. The Congress Committees do not have any day to day programme of work. They have usually no contacts with the organization of peasants and workers and do not take any appreciable part in their day to day struggles. The only contact they could have had with the masses, apart from the fact that it was not calculated to develop mass struggle, was through the 'constructive programme'. But this programme too is not in the hands of the Congress Committees but autonomous associations like the A. I. S. A., A. I. V. I. A. etc. The form of open struggle— disobedience of specific laws—that the Congress has so far used does not give the masses wide scope for participation. It is not infact a form of mass struggle which can develop only out of the day to day struggle against exploitation and oppression.

The reason for this is that while the Congress is a mass organization, its leadership is predominantly bourgeois. This leadership is unable within the framework of its conceptions and interests to develop the struggle of the masses to a higher level. But it should be kept in view that the Congress leadership is no longer undivided. Recently a conscious Left has been forming within the Congress and this development is reflecting itself in the leadership also, in which a sharp division is taking place. But as yet Left is largely ineffective and effective leadership is in the hands of the Right. This should not be understood to mean that the class composition of the right is itself bourgeois. A part of it is undoubtedly so. On the whole it is petty-bourgeois but it is under the dominance of bourgeois interests and bound by the limitations of the Indian bourgeoisie.

This analysis of the character of the Congress defines our task within it. In the words of Meerut Thesis it is to 'wean the anti-imperialist elements in the Congress away from its present bourgeoise leadership and to bring them under the influence of Revolutionary Socialism.' The present thesis must further elucidate this.

The Meerut Thesis conceives of the task in too narrow a manner. Our task within the Congress is not only to wean away the anti-imperialist elements from bourgeoise leadership but also to develop and broaden the Congress itself as to transform it into a powerful anti-imperialist front. The problem is not only the one of the change of leadership. It requires a complete reorganization of the Congress from the bottom upwards. As it has already been pointed out this cannot be done by confining our activities to Congress alone. Here, however, let us see what we have to do within the Congress. Taking the organizational aspect, first, we must work for the democratization of its constitution so as to give more initiative to the primary members and committees and should endeavour to enlarge the membership and extend the organizations of the Congress further and make them active and alive. We should further try to bring the masses into the Congress by securing their representation in the committees of the latter. Till this is done we should build up a close link between such organizations and committees for the purpose of work.

OUR ALTERNATIVE PROGRAMME

As for the programme of the Congress, we should so shape it that it comes actively to develop the struggle of the masses taking their immediate demands as a basis. The formation of peasants' and workers' unions and active support to the struggle conducted by them should be kept in the fore-front of this programme. In all other possible ways also, working on the principles laid down above, we should endeavour to provide Congress Committees with a programme of day to day work among the masses.

We should try to rally the rank and file of the Congress workers around this alternative programme. The political backwardness of the rank and file is due to their lack of contact with the economic struggle of the masses. Propaganda alone will not radicalize them. They must be drawn into the peasants and labour movements so that they may realize that our programme is a more dynamic one and will raise the anti-imperialist struggle to a higher pitch.

The Meerut Thesis declared that we have to bring the anti-imperialist movement under the leadership of Revolutionary Socialism. It is necessary to further elucidate this. The anti-imperialist struggle in India is multi-class struggle of the peasantry and the working and middle classes. The working class in India though organizationally weak and politically not sufficiently conscious of its role, is nonetheless potentially the most revolutionary class. The struggle of the Indian masses for freedom will not reach its objective unless the working class is the vanguard of that struggle. Therefore, it is our task as Socialists to see that it assumes its historic role in the national movement. The leadership of Revolutionary Socialism can mean nothing else.

OUR WORK OUTSIDE THE CONGRESS

The anti-imperialist struggle cannot be separated from the day to day struggle of the masses. The development of the latter is the basis for a successful fight against Imperialism. Therefore, our foremost task outside the Congress is to develop Independent organizations of the peasants and workers and of other exploited sections of the people.

Besides these class organizations we should also attempt to organize the youth of the country so as to mobilize the most active elements of the lower middle class.

We should not be content with the formation of these separate organizations. We should try to harness them in the anti-imperialist front. These organizations while functioning independently and carrying on their own programme should be linked up with the Congress Committees and there should be joint action as often as possible. This should ultimately lead us, as already pointed out, to the masses mobilized in these organizations entering the Congress through collective representation. Thus will the Congress become a wide national front against imperialism. This transformation is bound to change the entire structure and leadership of the Congress which will be composed of the strongly welded alliance of the various anti-imperialist classes, organized and unorganized consolidation of Socialist forces.

In the conditions of India, the conscious leadership of the anti-imperialist movement falls on the Socialist forces. These forces are unfortunately still divided. The Party from the beginning has stood for unity in the socialist ranks.

It is of the utmost importance that in the Congress in the mass movement outside, in all spheres of anti-imperialist activity a united lead is given. If Socialists speak with a divided voice there will be utter confusion and it will only retard the national struggle.

Till such unity is arrived at, the minimum that is necessary is agreement on the immediate tasks and lines of action. On the basis of this agreement the various Socialist groups should work together till the time we are in a position to form a united Party.

Apart from unity of agreement among Socialist ranks, it is necessary that the forces of the Left are also consolidated and an understanding developed within its leadership. The Party should continue its efforts in this direction.

ORGANIZATION OF THE PARTY

Our Party has generally grown in the last year. In certain provinces there has been a setback and the growth has not been uniform everywhere. While there are parties with a membership of hundreds, certain other parties, also quite active have not enlarged their organization beyond a few score of members. It is obvious that the line of development and the scope of organization have not clearly been laid down. Without prejudice to the Marxist basis of our Party, it is necessary to enlarge the membership of the Party so as to include a wider section of Congress workers and conscious elements active in the labour, peasant and other movements.*

---

* Adopted at the 3rd Annual Conference of the C. S. P. on Dec. 23 and 24, 1937.

THE FAIZPUR THESIS

BIBLIOGRAPHY

Primary Sources

BOOKS :

Bharatiya Samajvad, Aarthik Sanyojan aur Vikendrikaran, being a collection of lectures in the 'Pant Vyakhyan-Mala' series by Sampurnanand, Shriman Narayan and Jayaprakash Narayan, Uttar Pradesh, Publication Division, 1960.

Das, Bhagavan, *The Science of Social Organization*, 3 Vols., Banaras, Aananda Publishing House, 1948.

Das, Bhagavan, *Ancient Versus Modern 'Scientific Socialism'*, Adyar, Madras, Theosophical Publishing House, 1934.

Das, Bhagavan, *The Laws of Manu*, Adyar, Madras, The Theosophist Office, 1910.

Deva, Narendra, *Socialism and the National Revolution* (edited by Yusuf Meherally), Bombay, Padma Publications Ltd., 1946.

Deva, Narendra, *Rashtriyata aur Samajvad*, Banaras, Gyan Mandal Ltd., 2006.

Gandhi, M. K., *An Autobiography*, Ahmedabad, Navajivan Publishing House, 1959.

Gandhi, M. K., *Ashram Observances in Action*, Ahmedabad, Navajivan, 1959.

Gandhi, M. K., *Economic and Industrial Life and Relations*, 3 Vols., (edited by V. B. Kher) Ahmedabad, Navajivan, 1959.

Gandhi, M. K., *Hind Swaraj*, Ahmedabad, Navajivan, 1958.

Gandhi, M. K., *My Non-Violence*, Ahmedabad, Navajivan, 1960.

Gandhi, M. K., *Sarvodaya*, Ahmedabad, Navajivan, 1958.

Gandhi, M. K., *Speeches and Writings*, Madras, G. A. Natesan & Co., 1922.

Gandhi, M. K., *Socialism of My Conception*, Bombay, Bhartiya Vidya Bhavan, 1966.

Gandhi, M. K., *Towards Non-Violent Socialism*, Ahmedabad, Navajivan, 1957.

Lohia, Rammanohar, *Fragment of a World Mind*, Calcutta, n. d.

Lohia, Rammanohar, *Marx, Gandhi and Socialism*, Hyderabad, Navahind Prakashan, 1963.

Lohia, Rammanohar, *The Caste System*, Hyderabad, Navahind, 1964.

Lohia, Rammanohar, *Rs. 25,000 A Day*, Hyderabad, Navahind, 1963.

Lohia, Rammanohar, *Wheel of History*, Hyderabad, Navahind, 1963.

Lohia, Rammanohar, *Will to Power*, Hyderabad, Navahind, 1956.

Masani, M. R., *Socialism Reconsidered*, Bombay, Padma Publications, 1944.

Mehta, Asoka, *Democratic Socialism*, Bombay, Bharatiya Vidya Bhavan, 1959.

Mehta, Asoka, *Inside Lok Sabha*, Madras, Socialist Book Centre, 1955.

Mehta, Asoka, *Socialism and Peasantry*, Bombay, A Praja Socialist Publication, 1953.

Mehta, Asoka, *Studies in Asian Socialism*, Bombay, Bharatiya Vidya Bhavan, 1959.

Mehta, Asoka, *1857 : The Great Rebellion*, Bombay, Hind Kitabs Ltd., 1946.

Mehta, Asoka, *The Plan : Perspective and Problems*, Bombay, Bhartiya Vidya Bhavan, 1966.

Narayan, Jayaprakash, *A Picture of Sarvodaya Social Order*, Tanjore, Sarvodaya Prachuralaya, 1961.

Narayan, Jayaprakash, *Cultural Variation*, an unpublished Thesis, presented for the Degree of M. A. to the Ohio State University, 1929.

Narayan, Jayaprakash, *Inside Lahore Fort*, Madras, Socialist Book Centre, 1959.

Narayan, Jayaprakash, *Socialism to Sarvodaya*, Mylapore, Socialist Book Centre, 1956.

Narayan, Jayaprakash, *Socialism, Sarvodaya and Democracy* (edited by Bimla Prasad), Bombay, Asia Publishing House, 1964.

Narayan, Jayaprakash, *Towards New Society*, New Delhi, The Office for Asian Affairs, 1958.

Narayan, Jayaprakash, *Towards Struggle* (edited by Yusuf Maherally), Bombay, Padma Publications, 1946.

Narayan, Jayaprakash, *Why Socialism ?*, Banaras, The All India Congress Socialist Party, 1936.

Nehru, Jawaharlal, *An Autobiography*, Bombay, Allied Publishers, 1962.

Nehru, Jawaharlal, *The Discovery of India*, London, Meridian Books, 1960.

Nehru, Jawaharlal, *Eighteen Months in India*, Allahabad, Kitabistan, 1938.

Nehru, Jawaharlal, *Freedom from Fear*, New Delhi, Gandhi Smarak Nidhi, 1960.

Nehru, Jawaharlal, *India's Freedom*, London, George Allen & Unwin, 1936.

Nehru, Jawaharlal, *Glimpses of World History*, London, Lindsay Drummond Ltd., 1930.

Nehru, Jawaharlal, *Soviet Russia*, Allahabad, Law Journal Press, 1928.

Nehru, Jawaharlal, *The Unity of India*, London, Limington Drammond, 1948.

Nehru, Jawaharlal, *Nehru on Socialism*, Perspective Publications, 1964.

Nehru, Jawaharlal, *A Bunch of Old Letters*, Bombay, Asia Publishing House, 1960.

Nehru, Jawaharlal, *Jawaharlal Nehru's Speeches*, 4 Vols., New Delhi, Publication Division, Government of India, 1949–64.

Nehru, Jawaharlal, *Speeches of Jawaharlal Nehru in America*, New Delhi, National Book Stall.

Norman, Dorothy (ed.), *Nehru*, 2 Vols., Bombay, Asia Publishing House, 1965.

Sampurnanand, *Indian Socialism*, Bombay, Asia Publishing House, 1961.

Sampurnanand, *Memories and Reflections*, Bombay, Asia Publishing House, 1962.

Sampurnanand, *Random Thoughts*, Uttar Pradesh Information Department, 1960.

Sampurnanand, *Samajvad*, Calcutta, Bhartiya Gayanpith, 1964.

Sampurnanand, *Samidha*, Uttar Pradesh Prakashan Shakha, n. d.

Sampurnanand, *Sfut Vichar*, Uttar Pradesh Suchana Vibhag, Dec. 1959.

Sampurnanand, *The Individual and the State*, Allahabad, Kitab Mahal, 1957.

Vivekananda, *Caste, Culture and Socialism*, Almora, Advaita Ashrama, 1947.

BOOKLETS AND PAMPHLETS :

Gandhi, M. K., *Congress and its Future*, Ahmedabad, Navajivan, 1960.

Gandhi, M. K., *Panchayat Raj*, Ahmedabad, Navajivan, 1959.

Gandhi, M. K., *My Socialism*, Ahmedabad, Navajivan 1959.

Gandhi M. K., *Trusteeship*, Ahmedabad, Navajivan, 1960.

Gandhi, M. K., *Voluntary Poverty*, Ahmedabad, Navajivan, 1961.

Lal, Mukut Behari, *Blue Prints of a Socialist Programme*, Varanasi, Tara Printing Works, 1965.

Lal, Mukut Behari, *Congress Brand of Socialism—A Critical Review*, Varanasi, Tara Printing Works, 1964.

Lal, Mukut Behari, *Principles of Socialism*, Varanasi, Tara Printing Works, 1965.

Lal, Mukut Behari, *Sarvodaya and Democratic Socialism*, Varanasi, Praja Socialist Publication, n. d.

Lal, Mukut Behari, *Social Prerequisites of Social Reconstruction*, Varanasi, Tara Printing Works, 1967.

Lal, Mukut Behari, *Towards Democratic Socialism*, Varanasi, Tara Printing Works, n. d.

Lohia, Rammanohar, *Dharam Per Ek Drishti*, Hyderabad, Navahind, n. d.

Lohia, Rammanohar, *Civil Nafarmani : Siddhanta aur Amal*, Hyderabad, Navahind, 1957.

Lohia, Rammanohar, *Socialist Unity*, Hyderabad, Navahind.

Mehta, Asoka, *Foreign Policy*, Bombay, Socialist Party, n. d.

Mehta, Asoka, *India in a Changing World*, New Delhi, Praja Socialist Party, n. d.

Mehta, Asoka, *Need to Reshape the Plan*, Bombay, National House, n. d.

Mehta, Asoka, *Politics of Planned Economy*, Hyderabad, Chetna Prakashan, 1953.

Mehta, Asoka, *Straws in the Wind*, Bombay Socialist Party, n. d.

Mehta, Asoka, *The Economic Revolution of Our Time*, Chandigarh, Punjab University Publication, 1966.

Mehta, Asoka, *You and the Vote*, Bombay, Socialist Party, n. d.

Narayan, Jayaprakash, *A Plea for Reconstruction of Indian Polity*, Kashi, Akhil Bharat Sarve Seva Sangh Prakashan, 1955.

Narayan, Jayaprakash, *Democratic Socialism*, Bombay, Socialist Party, n. d.

Narayan, Jayaprakash, *From Socialism to Sarvodaya*, Kashi, A. B. S. S. S. Prakashan, 1959.

Narayan, Jayaprakash, *Ideological Problems of Socialism*, Rangoon, Asian Socialist Conference, 1953.

Narayan, Jayaprakash, *Political Trends*, Bombay, The Socialist Party, 1951.

Narayan, Jayaprakash, *Sarvodaya Answer to Chinese Aggression*, Tanjore, Sarvodaya Prachuralaya, 1963.

Narayan, Jayaprakash, *Swaraj for the People*, Varanasi, A.B.S.S.S. Prakashan, 1961.

Narayan, Jayaprakash, *The Challenges after Nehru*, Tanjore, Sarvodaya Prachuralaya, 1964.

Narayan, Jayaprakash, *The Dual Revolution*, Tanjore, Sarvodaya Prachuralaya, 1957.

Narayan, Jayaprakash, *The Evolution Towards Sarvodaya*, Tanjore, Sarvodaya Prachuralaya, 1957.

Narayan, Jayaprakash, *To All-Fighters for Freedom*, Calcutta, Azad Hind Kitab, 1946.

Nehru, Jawaharlal, *Whither India ?*, Allahabad, Kitabistan, 1937.

Sampurnanand, *A Tentative Socialist Programme for India*, Banaras, enclosed in File No. 41/1/34/Poll, Government of India, Home Deptt. 1934.

Sampurnanand, *Indian Intellectual*, Uttar Pradesh Publications Bureau, n. d.

Sampurnanand, *Samajvad*, Uttar Pradesh Publications Bureau, n. d.

Sampurnanand, *The Trials of Our Democracy*, Uttar Pradesh Publications Bureau, 1957.

REPORTS, DOCUMENTS AND GOVERNMENT FILES :

All India Congress Socialist Party, Bombay, Containing the Constitution and Programme, Resolutions of the Third Conference of the Party, Theses and Report of the General Secretary, 1937.

The Policy Statement, Socialist Party, Kanpur, 1947.

Report of the Fifth Annual Conference of the Socialist Party, Kanpur, 1947.

Report of the Sixth Annual Conference of the Socialist Party, Nasik, 1948.

Report of the Seventh Annual Conference of the Socialist Party, Patna, 1949.

Report of the Eight National Conference of the Socialist Party,
    Madras, 1950.
Report of the Special Convention of the Socialist Party, Pachmarhi,
    1952.
Report of the Special Convention of the Praja Socialist Party, Betual,
    1953.
Report of the First National Conference of the Praja Socialist Party,
    Allahabad, 1953.
Report of the Second National Conference of the Praja Socialist,
    Party, Gaya, 1955.
Report of the Third National Conference of the Praja Socialist Party,
    Bengalore, 1956.
Report of the Fourth National Conference of the Praja Socialist
    Party, Poona, 1958.
Report of the Fifth National Conference of the Praja Socialist Party,
    Bombay, 1959.
Report of the Sixth National Conference of the Praja Socialist Party,
    Bhopal, 1963.
Report of the Seventh National Conference of the Praja Socialist
    Party, Ramgarh, 1964.
Report of the Eighth National Conference of the Praja Socialist Party,
    Varanasi, 1965.
Report of the Ninth National Conference of the Praja Socialist Party,
    Kanpur, 1967–68.

PSP Pamphlets :

Constitution and Rules, 1955.
Policy Statement, Gaya, 1955.
Election Manifesto, 1961.
Praja Socialist Party, a brief introduction, 1956.
Public Sector in Perspective.
We Build for Socialism, 1951.
Praja Socialist Party, Pratham Varshik Adhiveshan, Allahabad,
    1953.
J. B. Kripalani, *Main Problems : How to Solve Them,* 1958.
The Merger Annulled.
Socialist Unity, 1963.
Facts Relating to Lohia's Attempt at Disrupting the P. S. P., 1955.
Discussion Papers, containing two articles 'Some Thoughts on the

Third Plan' by Asoka Mehta, and 'Tasks Before the Party' by Rohit Dave, 1959.

Praja Socialist Party : *Dvitiya Rashtriya Sammelan*, Adhyakshiya Bhasan, Gaya, 1955.

Chairman's Address, Seventh National Conference, Ramgarh, 1964.

General Secretary's Report, Seventh National Conference, Ramgarh, 1964.

Foreword to the Defence of Nationalism, Democracy & Socialism (The message of the 9th National Conference of the P. S. P.)

SSP Publications :

Statement of Principles of the Socialist Party, Hyderabad, 1956.

Election Manifesto, 1957.

Election Manifesto, 1962.

Statement of Principles, Programme and Political Line, (adopted at the 2nd National Conference) Kota, 1966.

Karyawahi Wa Prastav, Gaya, 1968.

Adhyakshiya Bhasan, Tritiya Rashtriya Sammelan, Gaya, 1968.

General Secretary's Report, Third National Conference, Gaya, 1968.

Election Manifesto, 1967.

AICC Publications :

Report of the Twenty-first Session of Indian National Congress, Banaras, 1905.

Report of the Twenty-second Session of Indian National Congress, Calcutta, 1906.

Report of the Thirty-second Session of Indian National Congress, Calcutta, 1917.

Report of the Thirty-eighth Session of Indian National Congress, Cacanada, 1923.

Report of the Thirty-nineth Session of the Indian National Congress, Belgaon, 1924.

Report of the Fortieth Session of Indian National Congress, Kanpur, 1925.

Report of the Forty-first Session of the Indian National Congress, Gauhati, 1926.

Report of the Forty-fourth Annual Session of the Indian National Congress, Lahore, 1929.

Indian National Congress, Resolutions, 1925.

Indian National Congress, Resolutions, 1927.
Indian National Congress, Resolutions, 1928.
Indian National Congress, Resolutions, 1929.
Indian National Congress, Resoultions, 1931.
Indian National Congress, Resolutions, Delhi, 1932.
Indian National Congress, Resolutions, Calcutta, 1933.
Indian National Congress, Resolutions, Bombay, 1934.
Indian National Congress, Resolutions, Lucknow, 1936.
Indian Nattonal Congress, Resolutions, Faizpur, 1936.
Indian National Congress, Resolutions, Haripura, 1938.
Congress Ideology.
Constitution of the Indian National Congress, adopted at
    Bhubaneshwar, 1964.
Presidential Address, Indian National Congress Sixty-eighth Session,
    Bhubaneshwar, 1964.
Election Manifesto, 1962.
Indian National Congress, Nov. 1934–March 1936, Report of the
    General Secretary.

INTUC Pamphlets :

Indian National Trade Union Congress : *Constitution, Bhartiya
    Rashtriya Majdoor Congress*, Tisra Varshik Adhiveshan,
    Adhyakshiya Bhashan, 1950.
Indian National Trade Union Congress, Presidential Address at the
    Fifteenth Session.
Indian National Trade Union Congress, Resolutions, Fifteenth
    Session, Hyderabad, 1964.
Labour Policies and Programmes in the Fourth-Five Year Plan.

Files of the Government of India :

File No. 3/XI/34/Poll, Home Dept. (Political).
File No. 3/16/34/Poll, Home Dept. (Political).
File No. 7/13/34/Poll, Home Dept. (Political).
File No. 33/6/34/Poll, Home Dept. (Political).
File No. 36/3/34/Poll, Home Dept. (Political).
File No. 41/1/34/Poll, Home Dept. (Political).

Primary Journals :
The old files of the *Congress Socialist*, the official weekly organ of the

C. S. P. published from Bombay, between 1936 and 1939.

The files of the *Janata*, the official weekly organ of the P. S. P.
published from Bombay since 1946.

The Congress Bulletin, a monthly organ of the AICC published from
New Delhi surveyed between 1956–64.

The AICC Economic Review, the weekly organ of the Congress,
Published from New Delhi surveyed since 1956.

The old files of the *Mankind*, edited by Rammanohar Lohia,
published from Hyderabad between 1957–62. It has again been
revived from New Delhi. A Hindi version also appears as
Jana.

The New Socialist, published monthly since 1958 under the editorship
of N. G. Goray.

Secondary Sources

BOOKS :

Ahmad, Ilyas, *Trends in Socialistic Thought and Movement*,
Allahabad, The Indian Press 1937.

Benipuri, R., *Jayaprakash*, Muzaffarpur, Benipuri Prakashan, 1967.

Bhargava, G. S., *Leaders of the Left*, Bombay, Meherally Book Club,
1951.

Bhave, Vinoba, *Bhoodan-Yajna*, Ahmedabad, Navajivan, 1953.

Bhoodan as seen by the West, Tanjore, Sarvodaya Prachuralaya,
1961.

Bose, S. C., *The Indian Struggle*, Bombay, Asia Publishing House,
1964.

Brecher, Michael, *Nehru—A Political Biography*, London, Oxford
University Press, 1959.

Brown, D. Mackenzie, *The Nationalist Movement : Indian Political
Thought from Ranade to Bhave*, Bombay, Jaico 1961.

Brown, D. Mackenzie, *The White Umbralla : Indian Political
Thought from Manu to Gandhi*, Bombay, Jaico 1964.

Chandra, Jag Pravesh, *India's Socialistic Pattern of Society*, New
Delhi, Metropolitan Book Company Private Ltd., 1956.

Chowdhury, B. K., *Marxism and the Indian Ideal*, Calcutta, Thacker
Spink & Co. 1941.

Congress Presidential Addresses, 1911–1934 Madras, G. A. Natesan
& Co., 1934.

Das, M. N., *The Political Philosophy of Jawaharlal Nehru*, London, George Allen & Unwin, 1961.

Desai, V. L., (Trans.) *The Diary of Mahadev Desai*, Vol. I, Ahmedabad, Navajivan, 1953.

Gyan Chand, *Socialist Transformation of Indian Economy*, Bombay, Allied Publishers, 1965.

Gadre, Kamala, *Indian Way to Socialism*, New Delhi, Vir Publishing House, 1966.

Gandhi, Prabhudas, *My Childhood with Gandhiji*, Ahmedabad, Navajivan, 1957.

Gregg, Richard, B., *Which Way Lies Hope ?*, Ahmedabad, Navajivan, 1957.

Jha, M. N., *Modern Indian Political Thought*, Meerut, Meenakshi Prakashan, 1974.

Karanjia, R. K., *The Mind of Mr. Nehru*, London, George Allen & Unwin, 1961.

Karunakaran, K. P. (ed.), *Modern Indian Political Tradition*, New Delhi, Allied Publishers, 1962.

Karunakaran, K. P., *Religion and Political Awakening in India*, Meerut, Meenakshi Prakashan, 1971.

Kelkar, Indumati, *Lohia : Siddhanta aur Karma*, Hyderabad, Navahind, 1963.

Kellock, James, *Mahadev Govind Ranade*, Calcutta, Association Press, 1926.

Kripalani, J. B., *Class Struggle*, Kashi, A. B. S. S. S. Prakashan, 1959.

Kripalani, J. B., *Gandhian Thought*, New Delhi, Gandhi Smarak Nidhi, 1961.

Krishnamurti, Y. G., *Jawaharlal Nehru*, Bombay, The Popular Book Depot, 1945.

Kumarappa, Bharatan, *Capitalism, Socialism or Villagism ?*, Varanasi, S. S. S. Prakashan, 1965.

Lala, Lajpat Rai, *India's Will to Freedom*, Madras, Ganesh & Co., 1921.

Lala Lajpat Rai, *The Political Future of India*, New York, B. W. Huebsch, 1919.

Majumdar, Biman Bihari (ed.), *Gandhian Concept of State*, Calcutta, M. C. Sarkar & Sons, 1957.

Masani, M. R., *The Communist Party of India*, London, Derek Verschoyle, 1954.

Mashruwala, K. G., *Gandhi and Marx*, Ahmedabad, Navajivan, 1960.
Mehta, Asoka and Patwardhan, A., *Communal Triangle*, Allahabad, Kitabistan, 1942.
Mende, Tibor, *Conversation With Nehru*, Bombay, Wilco Publishing House, 1958.
Mitra, N. N., (ed.), *Indian Annual Register*, an Annual Digest of Public affairs of India, published in 2 six-monthly volumes between 1919 and 1947 from Calcutta.
Mookerjee, G. K., *History of Indian National Congress*, Meerut, Meenakshi Prakashan, 1974.
Namboodripad, E. M. S., *Economics and Politics of India's Socialistic Pattern*, New Delhi, Peoples Publishing House, 1966.
Narain, Brij, *Indian Socialism*, Lahore, Punjab Socialist Party, 1937.
Narayan, Shriman, *Socialism in Indian Planning*, Bombay, Asia Publishing House, 1964.
Narayan, Shriman, *Towards a Socialist Economy*, New Delhi, Indian National Congress, 1956.
Naoroji, Dadabhai, *Poverty and Un-British Rule in India*, London, Swan Sonnenschien & Co., 1901.
Overstreet, G. D. & Windmillar, M., *Communism in India*, Bombay, The Perennial Press, 1960.
Pant, D., *Socialism, Its Embryonic Development in India*, Lahore, 1919.
Patel, H. M., *A Socialistic Pattern*, New Delhi, Publication Division.
Prakasa, Sri, *Bharat Ratna Dr. Bhagawan Das*, Meerut, Meenakshi Prakashan, 1971.
Prasad, Narmadeshwar, *Change-Strategy in a Developing Society : India*, Meerut, Meenakshi Prakashan, 1969.
Prasad, Rajendra, *Legacy of Gandhiji*, Agra, Shivalal, 1962.
Ranade, M. G., *Essays on Indian Economics*, Madras, G. A. Natesan & Co., 1906.
Roy, M. N., *The Future of Indian Politics*, London, R. Bishop, 1926.
Roy, M. N., *Gandhism : Nationalism : Socialism*, Calcutta, Bengal Radical Club, 1940.
Roy, M. N., *India in Transition*, Geneva, Edition de la Librairie, J. B. Target, 1922.
Roy, M. N., *Materialism*, Dehradun, Renaissance Publication, 1940.

Rusch, Thomas A., *Role of Congress Socialist Party in the Indian National Congress, 1931–42*, an unpublished dissertation submitted to the University of Chicago, 1955–56.

Sarcar, Bibek Brata, *Socialist Movement in India from 1919 to 1947*, an unpublished dissertation submitted to the University of Delhi, 1962.

Seth, R. L., *Tagore on Socialism and Russia*, Lahore, Tagore Memorial Publications, n. d.

Sharad, Onkar, *Lohia*, Allahabad, Ranjana Prakashan, 1967.

Sheean, Vincent, *Nehru : The Years of Power*, London, Victor Gollancz Ltd., 1960.

Sinha, L. P., *The Left-Wing in India*, Muzaffarpur, New Publishers, 1965.

Singh, Hari Kishore, *A History of the Praja Socialist Party*, Narendra Prakashan, 1959.

Sitarammayya, B., *Gandhi and Gandhism*, 2 Vols., Allahabad, Kitabistan, 1942.

Sitarammayya, B., *The History of the Indian National Congress*, Allahabad, AICC, 1935.

Tagore, Saumyendra Nath, *Congress Socialism*, Calcutta, Ganavari Publishing House, 1946.

Verma, V. P., *Hindu Political Thought and Its Metaphysical Foundations*, Banaras, Motilal Banarsidas, n. d.

Verma V. P., *Modern Indian Political Thought*, Agra, 1961.

Verma V. P., *The Political Philosophy of Mahatma Gandhi*, Agra, Lakshmi Narain Agarwal, 1959.

The Complete Works of Swami Vivekananda, 8 Vols., Almora, Advaita Ashrama, 1948.

Wm Theodore De Bary & Others, *Sources of Indian Tradition*, London, Oxford University Press, 1958.

Zakaria, Rafiq (ed.), *The Study of Nehru*, A Times of India Publication, 1960.

INDEX